Denominationalism
Illustrated and Explained

DENOMINATIONALISM
Illustrated and Explained

RUSSELL E. RICHEY

CASCADE *Books* • Eugene, Oregon

DENOMINATIONALISM ILLUSTRATED AND EXPLAINED

Copyright © 2013 Russell E. Richey. All rights reserved. Except for brief quotations in critical publications or reviews, no part of this book may be reproduced in any manner without prior written permission from the publisher. Write: Permissions, Wipf and Stock Publishers, 199 W. 8th Ave., Suite 3, Eugene, OR 97401.

Cascade Books
An Imprint of Wipf and Stock Publishers
199 W. 8th Ave., Suite 3
Eugene, OR 97401

www.wipfandstock.com

ISBN 13: 978-1-61097-297-0

Cataloguing-in-Publication data:

Richey, Russell E.

    Denominationalism illustrated and explained / Russell E. Richey.

    xvi + 294 pp. ; 23 cm. Includes bibliographical references.

    ISBN 13: 978-1-61097-297-0

    1. Christian sects—United States. 2. United States—Church history. 3. United States—Religion. 4. Methodist Church—United States—History. 5. Dissenters, religious—United States. I. Title.

BR516.5 R55 2013

Manufactured in the USA

For
William and Elizabeth

Contents

Preface ix

Acknowledgments and Permissions xiii

Abbreviations xvi

Introduction: "Denominations and Denominationalism: Past, Present, and Future"   1

PART ONE: The British and Dissenting Origins of American Denominationalism

1   "Catholic" Protestantism and American Denominationalism   13

2   Toleration, Denominationalism, and Eighteenth-Century Dissent   34

3   Baptist Denominationalism in Eighteenth-Century Dissent   52

4   Denominations, British Radicalism, and the Changing Rationale of Dissent   63

5   Enlightenment Denominations in Transition: Did the English Presbyterians Become Unitarian?   77

6   From Puritanism to Unitarianism in England: A Study in Candour   98

Contents

PART TWO: Perspectives on Denominationalism

7   The Denomination as Institution   119

8   American Denominationalism: A Historical Overview   153

PART THREE: Case Studies in American Denominationalism

9   The Social Sources of Denominationalism: Methodism   179

10   History as a Bearer of Denominational Identity: Methodism as a Case Study   198

11   Culture Wars and Denominational Loyalties: The Methodist Version   223

12   Denominationalism in "Reformed" Perspective   237

PART FOUR: Denominationalism as Enacted Ecclesiology

13   Denominationalism: A Theological Problem?   261

Bibliography   281

Preface

TO THE TOPICS OF denomination and denominationalism I have returned again and again over the course of an academic career. Raised in a Methodist home and schooled in the South with Baptists and Methodists, I found myself rooming with a Jew from Brooklyn in college and the next year added an Episcopalian roommate. Seminary at Union in New York exposed me, really for the first time, to something of the wide variety of Christian belief and practice and to the different feel of working and worshipping among Presbyterians. My very first graduate seminar at Princeton University viewed the topic of denominationalism from several angles. And my last submission to my doctoral committee—John Wilson, Horton Davies, Donald Mathews, and Paul Ramsey—was a dissertation exploring the emergence of a denomination—the Unitarians—out of the intellectual ferment of Enlightenment England. I devoted my first sabbatical to the topic of American denominationalism, to reading widely on the history of various denominations, and to shopping for theory in terms of which to understand this very familiar form of American religiosity. The edited volume from that research, *Denominationalism*, has earned me quite a number of invitations to revisit the phenomena/on. And as I draft this, a soon-to-be published reappraisal will appear in *The Cambridge History of Religions in America*.

Gravitation into Methodist studies came naturally while teaching in United Methodist theological schools, having immediate access to phenomenal denominational libraries, and wanting and needing to think critically about my own church and its history. Still, the first efforts in that direction came from being invited by Henry Bowden to undertake a Methodist volume in his Denominations in America series.[1] In consequence of moving into Methodist studies from consideration of denominationalism, much of my scholarship on American Methodism, both books and

---

1. Kirby et al., *The Methodists*.

articles, in one way or another, considers the nature, self-understanding, institutional patterns and development of that denomination as a denomination. And in the next-to-last of the essays listed below, I respond as a student of American Methodism to a general question posed to scholars versed in the history of various religious bodies, does your church consider itself a denomination? It turns out that none of the churches essayed, mine included, likes to be termed a denomination.

This will be the third of my books with *denominationalism* in the title and the second one to appear with Wipf and Stock Publishers. Both *Denominationalism* (Wipf & Stock, 2010) and *Reimagining Denominationalism*, coauthored and coedited with R. Bruce Mullin (2010) bring together various authors' perspectives on the topic. This volume permits me to pull together insights and understandings of my own that have heretofore been scattered in journals and books. It did make sense to limit myself to essays that hung well together. So I have omitted some pertinent articles on Methodism and other essays as well that treat denominationalism more generally. Also pertinent to the topic but therefore not included are

"Denominationalism." In *Dictionary of the Ecumenical Movement*, edited by Nicholas Lossky et al., 265–66. Grand Rapids: Eerdmans & WCC, 1991.

"Organizing for Missions: A Methodist Case Study." In *The Foreign Missionary Enterprise at Home: Explorations in North American Cultural History*, edited by Daniel H. Bays and Grant Wacker, 75–89. Tuscaloosa: University of Alabama Press, 2003.

"Methodism as New Creation: An Historical-Theological Enquiry." In *Wesleyan Perspectives on the New Creation*, edited by M. Douglas Meeks, 73–92. Nashville: Kingswood, 2004.

"Methodism as Machine." In *Church, Identity, and Change: Theology and Denominational Structures in Unsettled Times*, edited by David A. Roozen and James Nieman, 523–33. Grand Rapids: Eerdmans, 2005.

"Understandings of Ecclesiology in United Methodism." In *Orthodox and Wesleyan Ecclesiology*, edited by S. T. Kimbrough Jr., 149–71. Crestwood, NY: St. Vladimir's Seminary Press, 2007); contributed to the UMC-ECUSA dialogue and posted at http://www.ecusa.anglican .org/documents/richey.pdf; translated by Michael Nausner and published as "Die praktizierte Ekklesiologie des Methodismus." In *Kirchliches Leben in methodistischer Tradition: Perspektiven aus drei*

Preface

Kontinenten, edited by Michael Nausner, 21–55. Göttingen: Ruprecht, 2010.

"The United Methodist Church at 40: Where Have We Come From?" *Methodist Review: A Journal of Wesleyan and Methodist Studies* 1 (2009) 27–56.

"District Superintendency: A Reconsideration." In *Doctrine in Experience: A Methodist Theology of Church and Ministry*. Nashville: Kingswood Books, 2009.

"Connection and Connectionalism." In *Oxford Handbook of Methodist Studies*, edited by James E. Kirby and William J. Abraham, 211–28. Oxford: Oxford University Press, 2009.

"Denominations." In *The Blackwell Companion to Religion in America*, edited by Philip Goff, 90–104. Oxford: Wiley-Blackwell, 2010.

"United Methodism: Its Identity as Denomination." In *Denomination: Assessing An Ecclesiological Category*, edited by Paul Collins and Barry Ensign-George, 67–85. London: T. & T. Clark, 2011.

"Religious Organization in the New Nation." In *The Cambridge History of Religions in America*. 3 vols. Stephen Stein, general editor. Forthcoming.

The essays and chapters included in this volume and the journals or publishers from which permissions came to republish in updated and edited form can be found under Acknowledgments and Permission. Since the journals and publications can be accessed in major libraries and in some cases online, I thought it made sense to retain only the footnotes needed to identify quotations or other explicit references. That economy also conforms to Wipf and Stock Publishers' guidelines, which stipulate a very lean apparatus. And in accord with those guidelines except immediately above, this volume makes footnote references in short form and provides details for books and articles in the bibliography.

As the books on denominationalism, the articles listed above, and those describing the chapters and produced below in the appendix should indicate, I have essayed the topic sufficiently often to have become identified as one of the few historians who thinks it worth serious attention. Indeed, when Bruce Mullin and I developed a Lilly Endowment–funded conference (the origin of our book), we framed the call as "The Scholarly Writing of Denominational History: An Oxymoron?" Partly because of Lilly's interest and largesse, the topic may be less tabooed now than a

Preface

couple decades ago. Individual denominations do now receive scholarly attention as does the larger phenomenon of denominationalism.[2] Still, I guess I continue to receive invitations to write on the topic because I showed more consistent attention to it than others. So it made sense to propose to Wipf and Stock Publishers to gather insights, arguments, and interpretations, to update them, and to produce something of a unified perspective on the topic.

I should note that what follows is a historian's view, reading, and rendering on denominationalism. Two of the chapters, "Denominationalism: A Theological Problem?" and "The Denomination as Institution," highlight the fact that the topic draws attention from several different academic disciplines. However, and unfortunately, those working from the distinct protocols of their respective fields find little incentive for and value in drawing on the findings from the other disciplines. This volume attempts at several points to attend to perspectives from the other fields but a truly interdisciplinary synthetic rendering will need to come later.

Attentive readers should find both a logic and a chronological ordering to the chapters but also some overlap and repetition. The latter derives from the fact that the chapters began as essays each needing to stand on its own. In revising I considered paring out that overlap but realized that the relative self-sufficiency of chapters would allow individuals to move first to topics of most immediate interest. Students of American religion or of Methodism might, for instance, want to focus on those chapters—parts 2–4 or part 3 respectively. Those readers should, I think, still find the introduction and first chapter helpful.

Russell E. Richey
Dean Emeritus of Candler School of Theology and
William R. Cannon Distinguished Professor of Church History Emeritus
Emory University

---

2. Collins and Ensign-George, *Denomination*; Harper, *American Denominational History*.

Acknowledgments and Permissions

THE CHAPTERS IN THIS volume, *Denominationalism Illustrated and Explained*, appeared in earlier form in essays written over much of my career. This topic has been one to which I have returned, often on invitation. The journals and publishers in whose works these items appeared have generously granted me the right to edit, alter, and update them for use here. I therefore express by appreciation to them for that permission.

Introduction: "Denominations and Denominationalism: Past, Present & Future."

> Originally published as "Denominations and Denominationalism: Past, Present & Future." *Word & World* 25 (Winter 2005) 15–22. Copyright © *Word & World* and used with permission.

Part 1: The British and Dissenting Origins of American Denominationalism

"'Catholic' Protestantism and American Denominationalism."
> Originally published as "'Catholic' Protestantism and American Denominationalism." *Journal of Ecumenical Studies* 16/2 (Spring 1979) 213–31. Copyright © 1979 *Journal of Ecumenical Studies* and used with permission.

"Toleration, Denominationalism and Eighteenth-Century Dissent."
> Originally published as "Effects of Toleration on Eighteenth-Century Dissent," *The Journal of Religious History* 8 (Dec. 1975) 350–63. Copyrighted © 1975 *The Journal of Religious History* and used with permission.

"Baptist Denominationalism in Eighteenth-Century Dissent."

Acknowledgments and Permissions

> Originally published as "English Baptists and 18th Century Dissent." *Foundations* 16/4 (Oct.–Dec. 1973) 347–54. Reprinted with permission of the American Baptist Historical Society, Atlanta, Georgia.

"Denominations, British Radicalism and the Changing Rationale of Dissent."
> Originally published as "The Origins of British Radicalism: The Changing Rationale of Dissent." *Eighteenth-Century Studies* 7/2 (Winter 1973–74) 179–92. Copyright © the American Society for Eighteenth-Century Studies and reprinted with permission.

"Enlightenment Denominations in Transition: Did the English Presbyterians Become Unitarian?"
> Originally published as "Did the English Presbyterians Become Unitarian?" *Church History* 42/1 (March 1973) 58–72. Copyright © the American Society of Church History and reprinted with permission of the Society and Cambridge University Press.

"From Puritanism to Unitarianism in England: A Study in Candour."
> Originally published as "From Puritanism to Unitarianism in England: A Study in Candour." *Journal of the American Academy of Religion* 41/3 (Sept. 1973) 371–85. Copyright © the *Journal of the American Academy of Religion* and used with permission of the AAR and Oxford University Press.

Part 2: Perspectives on Denominationalism

"The Denomination as Institution."
> Originally published as "Institutional Forms of Religion." In *Encyclopedia of the American Religious Experience*, edited by Charles H. Lippy and Peter W. Williams, 1:31–50. 3 vols. New York: Scribner, 1988. Copyright © 1989 Gale, a part of Cengage Learning, Inc. Reproduced by permission.www.cengage.com/permissions/.

"American Denominationalism: An Historical Overview."
> Originally published as "Denominationalism." In *The Encyclopedia of Religion in America*, edited by Charles H. Lippy and Peter W. Williams. Washington, DC: CQ Press, 2010. Published electronically as "Denominationalism." CQ Press Electronic Library, Encyclopedia of Religion in America, encyra_541.1. Published with and copyrighted

Acknowledgments and Permissions

© by CQ Press, A Division of SAGE Publications, and reprinted with permission.

Part 3: Case Studies in American Denominationalism

"The Social Sources of Denominationalism: Methodism."
Originally published as "The Social Sources of Denominationalism: Methodism." *Methodist History* 15 (April 1977) 167–85. Copyright © by the General Commission on Archives and History and used with permission.

"Culture Wars and Denominational Loyalties: The Methodist Version."
Originally published as "Culture Wars and Denominational Loyalties: A Methodist Case Study." *Quarterly Review: A Journal of Theological Resources for Ministry* 18 (Spring 1998) 3–17. Copyright © 1998 by the General Board of Higher Education and Ministry, The United Methodist Church. Used by permission.

"History as a Bearer of Denominational Identity: Methodism as a Case Study."
Originally published as "History as a Bearer of Denominational Identity: Methodism as a Case Study." In *Beyond Establishment: Protestant Identity in a Post-Protestant Age*, edited by Jackson Carroll and Wade Clark Roof, 270–95. Louisville: Westminster John Knox, 1993. Copyright © Westminster John Knox Press and used with permission.

"Denominationalism in 'Reformed' Perspective."
Originally published as "Denominationalism in Perspective." *Journal of Presbyterian History* 79 (Fall 2001) 199–214. "Special Centennial Issue: Denominational History, Today." Copyright © the Presbyterian Historical Society and used with permission.

Part IV: Denominationalism as Enacted Ecclesiology

"Denominationalism: A Theological Problem?"
Originally published as "Denominationalism: A Theological Mandate." *The Drew Gateway* 47/2 & 3 (1976–77) 93–106. Reprinted with permission of the Drew University Library.

Abbreviations

AME American Methodist Episcopal
AMEZ American Methodist Episcoapl Zion
CME Christian Methodist Episcopal
Discipline of the [name of church] (year), pages.
MEC Methodist Episcopal Church
MECS Methodist Episcopal Church, South
MC The Methodist Church
UMC The United Methodist Church
MPC Methodist Protestant Church
EA Evangelical Association
UB United Brethren
UHST *Transactions of the Unitarian Historical Society*

Introduction

Denominations and Denominationalism

Past, Present, and Future

EVIDENCE FOR THE DECLINE of American denominationalism, particularly mainstream denominationalism, virtually throws itself in our faces. The evidential litany might include the following:
- the growing religious pluralism of North America;
- the decline over the last half-century in the salience, prestige, power, and vitality of Protestant denominational leadership;
- the slippage in mainline membership and corresponding growth, vigor, visibility and political prowess of conservative, evangelical, and fundamentalist bodies;
- patterns of congregational independence, including loosening of or removal of denominational identity, particularly in signage, and the related marginal loyalty of members;
- the emergence of megachurches, some with resources comparable to small denominations, including some with the capacity to meet needs heretofore supplied by denominations (training, literature, expertise);

Denominationalism Illustrated and Explained

- the coalition of such megacongregations or parachurch organizations into quasi-denominations;
- the growth within mainline denominations of caucuses and their alignment into broad progressive or conservative camps, often with connections to similar camps in other denominations or with religious action entities like the Institute of Religion and Democracy;
- widespread suspicion of, indeed hostility towards, the centers and symbols of denominational identity—the regional and national headquarters;
- migration of individuals and families through various religious identities, sometimes out of classic Christianity altogether;
- proclamations in the light of the above of the end of denominationalism.

Denominationalism looks doomed.[1] It may be. However, viewing the sweep of American history, what impresses this longtime observer is how much denominations and denominationalism have changed, how resilient they have proved, how significant these structures of religious belonging have been in providing order and direction to American society, and how such enduring purposes find ever new structural and institutional expression.

The long-standing, enduring nature and changing character of denominationalism—central arguments of this volume—are illustrated by the definition adopted for the phenomenon and by the insistence that individual denominations and the collectivity (denominationalism) unfold in distinctive phases or stages. Since we will return several times to these two emphases, they merit brief introduction here. First, the definition, then the stages.

A Definition[2]

Denominationalism presents the denomination as a *voluntaristic ecclesial body*. The denomination is *voluntary* and therefore presupposes a condition of legal or de facto toleration and religious freedom, an environment within which it is possible, in fact, willingly to join or not join, and space

---

1. On that judgment, see Newman and Halvorson's *Atlas of American Religion: The Denominational Era, 1776–1990*.

2. This section is drawn from and therefore repeated in the chapter "Denominationalism in 'Reformed' Perspective."

to exist (alongside or outside any religious establishment if such persists). Typically, the denomination exists in a situation of religious pluralism, a pluralism of denominations.

It is *ecclesial*, a movement or body understanding itself to be a legitimate and self-sufficient, proper church (or religious movement.) It is *a voluntary* church, a body that concedes the authenticity of other churches even as it claims its own. It need not, however, concede that authenticity indiscriminately, it need not and typically did not regard all other denominations as orthodox.

And it is an ecclesial *body or form*, an organized religious movement, with intentions for and the capacity of self-perpetuation, with a sense of itself as located within time and with awareness of its relation to the longer Christian tradition. It knows itself as denominated, as named, as recognized and recognizable, as having boundaries, as possessing adherents, as having a history.

In these several regards, the denomination differentiates itself from reform impulses that may take similar structural form but construe themselves as belonging within a religion; from the church, which does not regard itself as voluntary or as sharing societal space with other legitimate religious bodies; from the sect, which, though also voluntary, does not locate itself easily in time or recognize boundaries or tolerate other bodies or concede their authenticity.

The denomination, then, is an ecclesial creature of modernity, a social form emerging with and closely akin to the political party, the free press, and free enterprise. With these other institutions, the denominations and related expressions of voluntary religion produced and have sustained the democratic state. Like these other institutions, the individual denomination fits within, contributes to, and borrows from a larger organizational ecology. We term that organizational ecology *denominationalism*. As individual papers and magazines compose the free press, individual businesses compose free enterprise, individual parties make up representative democracy, so individual denominations compose denominationalism. And these four creatures of modernity have tended to evolve together and to influence one another. Indeed, that the denomination has resembled the corporation for the last century should not be surprising. It has resembled the current business form of the day, and also the current form of the political party and of the press.

Denominationalism Illustrated and Explained

STAGES AND CYCLES

To grasp something of the long history of and changes in American denominations and the collective pattern (denominationalism), we are helped if we recognize distinctive stages in their evolution. It is important to introduce this set of stages or schema here briefly as I draw on it regularly, with differing nuances, to explain the evolution of specific denominations (including my own) as well as the overall pattern (denominationalism). Several comments about the schema and its functions are in order. First, a given denomination (or cluster of denominations, and we illustrate with Lutherans in this introduction) does differ significantly over time and functions with distinct stages or styles of denominational governance and cohesion. Second, in a given period or stage different denominations often resemble one another at least in features dynamic for that time frame. Third, each stage evidences significant cultural adaptation. Fourth, denominations and denominationalism shift gradually from strategies of expansiveness to efforts at consolidation. Fifth, certain stages, particularly the more expansive, open the denominational system to new partners—new denominations whose energy, creativity, success, and aggressiveness negotiate their admission to the system of denominationalism.

The latter perspective points to an important reality of denominationalism, namely, that it has never been inclusive of the religious impulses in North American society, that there have always been institutional outsiders, and that sometimes denominationalism has defined itself against those marginalized, occasionally violently. And this observation points also to a sixth perspective, highly important and presupposed but not developed here, namely, that in its cultural adaptiveness as well as in its very nature, denominationalism invites theological-ethical assessment, as H. Richard Niebuhr provided so eloquently in *The Social Sources of Denominationalism* (1929) and in *Christ and Culture* (1951).

The following stages of denominational formation work imperfectly with respect to any particular denomination but help us discern broad movements and rough chronological stages: plantation, ethnic voluntarism, purposive missionary association, confessional order, corporate organization, postdenominational confessionalism. Neither my denomination, Methodism, nor the Lutheranism used for illustrative purposes here, tracks this entire pattern. Both arrived or arrived in significant numbers after preconditions had been set in American society and some of the first phase had run its course. But these movements as American religions

Introduction: Denominations and Denominationalism

generally have a way of replicating earlier phases and catching up with the dominant trends.

Reformed churches—Congregationalists and Presbyterians—better illustrate all the stages, as we will indicate in parts 2 and 3. Of particular significance was the way in which the dynamic phase of Reformed or Calvinist plantation in North American reflected from the start the two impulses that would give American religion its cyclical character. Puritanism put a premium on conversion, heart religion, communions of the regenerate—patterns that would contribute to and later be known as pietism. Puritanism also prized confessions, law, order, pure doctrine—patterns already known as orthodoxy. Puritanism brought that combination of expansiveness and consolidation to bear on the social and political order and did so with the confidence of being an elect "nation," with millennial urgency, and with supple covenantal cultural theories. Later plantations, arriving after colonial governments were in place, typically lacked the Puritan opportunity to imprint their principles so fully on the social and political order and not infrequently found themselves having to come to terms with the Puritan success in so doing.

Later plantations, including the German Lutherans—which filled the American landscape with religious difference, groped their way towards being voluntaristic ecclesial bodies, and made genuine denominationalism possible—found themselves struggling to make their communities religiously vibrant with expansive strategies (that were or looked pietist) but also to find resources for order (orthodoxy). This second stage, which I term ethnic voluntarism and would be associated with the labors of Henry Melchior Muhlenberg, we often label the First Great Awakening, a period in which religious, cultural, and linguistic vitalities produced communities of Baptists, Moravians, Presbyterians, and Lutherans (German Lutherans in particular). Much of this organization came from the ground up as neighbors formed congregations and congregations reached out to one another and across the Atlantic for resources for legitimacy, order, stability, leadership, purpose, community. Church structure was extremely modest and focused on internal problem solving.

In the third stage, awkwardly labeled purposive missionary association, upstart Baptists, Methodists, and Presbyterians set the evangelical pace, racing to bring new peoples into their communions across the expanse of the new nation. The revivalism of this stage, though stylistically of a piece with what preceded and followed it, invited religious communities to open their doors to those outside the cultural-linguistic family.

Denominationalism Illustrated and Explained

Dramatically symbolizing this missionary inclusivism, denominations began concerted efforts to convert Africans, slave and free, and less coordinated efforts to embrace Native Americans. Religious bodies redefined themselves as American, some immediately doing so after national independence, others more gradually. And they saw their purposes in relation to social and cultural challenges of nation building, some having long struggles in so doing over language and culture, epitomized perhaps in the agendas and career of Samuel Schmucker. To carry out such missionary purposes, denominations began colleges, founded papers and magazines, structured themselves for expansion.

The fourth, confessional order, stage roughly coincided with the middle of the nineteenth century and had much to do with slavery, sectional crisis, civil war, and reconstruction. During this period denominations responded to the turmoil in American society by seeking churchly order. Often drawing on the deep wells of their distinctive traditions, sometimes enjoying the stimuli of trans-Atlantic conversation, occasionally reacting to the confessional energies of new immigrant populations, denominations sought to put their ecclesial houses in order. Such efforts produced discord, even division. When schism occurred, each new denomination found confessional, theological, liturgical, or ecclesial purpose in its separate identity. This stage might be seen in relation to the work of the two Krauths, Charles Philip and Charles Porterfield. And their agendas, mirrored in complex ways by the Americanizers, typified much of Protestantism.

The fifth and sixth stages are trickier to date but not to epitomize. The fifth, which I term corporate organization, derives its agendas from the socioeconomic-cultural-political-military expansionism that swept the United States and Europe in the late nineteenth and early twentieth centuries. The U.S. participation, modest in the arena of colonial empire in comparison with the British and French, loomed increasingly large religiously and economically. Corporate organization and professionalization proved as apt in the religious sphere as in the economic at achieving the efficiency, resourcing, communication, rationalization and mobilization requisite for world and national missionary enterprise. So denominations reconstituted themselves, adding corporate, board and agency structures, to care for virtually their entire work, reserving to the traditional or confessional polity matters having to do with doctrine and clerical orders.

The sixth stage, in the midst of which we seem now to find ourselves mired, might also be characterized in relation to the late twentieth- century critiques of centralized power and bureaucracy that drew energies from the left's agonies over race and war and the right's over taxes and social policy. The litany of denominational woes with which I began should indicate something of the institutional transformations that we now experience and which seem to me to represent another effort at collective consolidation. At the same time that the mainline denominations struggle to find the internal order, purpose, and unity that will staunch losses, reclaim loyalty and reenergize program, some of the leadership of evangelical denominations (clearly excepting Southern Baptists) seems to be opening itself towards the mainline and a broadened Christian witness to the society and the world. We seem to be, I think, in yet another period of denominational transformation.

SUMMARY AND POSTSCRIPT

Looked at over the sweep of American history, then, what we now sometimes proclaim to be denominational death throes may instead be those of birth but to new religious personhood that may differ markedly from what we now know. We have, indeed, gone through periods of expansionism and consolidation before, and those impulses mix and interpenetrate in curious and complex fashion. We have indeed seen distinctive denominational patterns, even identities, in these separate periods. One way of putting that is to say that a Lutheran today would be more at home in a Methodist or Presbyterian congregation than in a Lutheran congregation of an earlier period.

Each of the stages or periods has evidenced social-cultural adaptation sometimes more constructive, sometimes more derivative. Looking backwards and perhaps not too closely, one may conclude with Richard Niebuhr that "the denominations represent the accommodation of religion to the caste system. They are emblems, therefore, of the victory of the world over the church, of the secularization of Christianity, of the church's sanction of that divisiveness which the church's gospel condemns."[3] Niebuhr is certainly on target in identifying the way in which the denominations conform to social realities and, as we have also noted, to the agendas of American society as a whole. We could, in fact, say more about American denominational collusion in cultural imperialism than was obvious to Niebuhr when he wrote. And yet, having conceded that, one cannot but also be impressed with the contributions that denominations

---

3. Niebuhr, *Social Sources of Denominationalism*, 21, 25.

make to social order and social reconstruction, the prophetic roles that they play, and their capacities for self-critique and self-renewal.

One current dimension of this self-probing and clearly a contested and difficult one, points to our fourth early generalization, namely, the openness in certain stages of the denominational system to new partners, to new denominations whose energy, creativity, success, and aggressiveness negotiate their admission to the system of denominationalism. I have noted that one such boundary being currently tested is that between the evangelical and the mainline denominations. Another is between Christian denominations and Jewish, Muslim, Hindu, Buddhist, Sikh, and other religious communities. What are Christians to make of the growing religious pluralism of North America?

We have noted that denominationalism as a system, that is the collectivity of denominations, functions with an unstated but crudely operative ecclesiology. One could argue, though space has not permitted it here, that the denominational system, the system of denominationalism, has closely approximated the limits of American tolerance. Denominationalism and the experiment of American religious freedom have interacted in complex ways and have never been inclusive of the range of religious impulses in North American society.

There have always been institutional outsiders. Sometimes these outsiders do not adhere to the canons of denominationalism and religious freedom. They do not organize and structure themselves as voluntaristic ecclesial bodies. Sometimes their outsider status derives more from their rejection by existing denominations. Sometimes denominationalism has defined itself against those marginalized, occasionally violently, frequently so doing with the blessing of those in political power. The early denominational system functioned with paradigms drawn from Puritanism and treated Methodists, Baptists, and Disciples as outsiders. The evangelical system of the nineteenth century virtually defined itself against Rome. Racism and anti-Semitism persisted well into the ecumenism of the twentieth century.

The question before religious and political leadership today is, who participates in the American experiment? Whose chaplains will be recognized? Which groups will administer faith-based programs? Who belongs? For the civil realm, the question is one of the Constitution, law, public policy. For the religious community, the question is one of ecclesiology. Conservatives recognize that reality. Those of us, like myself, who belong in the progressive camp should not duck the ecclesiological challenge.

Introduction: Denominations and Denominationalism

Who we are as Christians, where the church is, what inheres in its mission in the world—such questions have much to do with whom we take to be our neighbor. Denominationalism, conjointly with the courts and the First Amendment, has identified the neighbor. The issues that denominations and denominationalism now face have import for the U.S. and the world.

PART ONE

The British and Dissenting Origins of American Denominationalism

1

"Catholic" Protestantism and American Denominationalism

AMERICAN DENOMINATIONS TEND AND have tended to understand themselves in confessional terms, and commentators on denominationalism in honoring such confessional ecclesiologies have accented their diversity and distinctivenesses—the distinguishing and divisive character of denominations. A significant counterpoint has been sounded by a few denominational leaders who envision/ed the separate denominations as part of a larger whole and believe/d the denominations to be united in a common task. This purposive and unitive quality of denominations was examined long ago by Winthrop Hudson, who argued that such an understanding constitutes a theology of denominationalism.[1] Hudson traced this ecclesiology back to English Puritanism, particularly to the party known as Independency or Congregationalism. This chapter posits an additional source for such views in the succession of irenic, "catholic" Protestants who from the Reformation on labored for Christian unity. Those whose impact on American denominationalism seems most pronounced were British—the Latitudinarians, Cambridge Platonists, Scottish Moderates, and Dissenters such as Richard Baxter, Daniel Neal, Philip Doddridge, and Isaac Watts. Also contributing were the latter's American counterparts—Cotton Mather, Jonathan Dickinson, and Samuel Davies. These "catholic" Christians mediated to nineteenth-century denominationalism a view of the church as united in fundamentals and

---

1. Hudson, "Denominationalism."

PART ONE: The British and Dissenting Origins

by charity even if divided by doctrine, practice, and government. "Catholic" Protestantism, an early form of ecumenism and apparent alternative to denominationalism, thus ironically provided an important dimension to the ethos or self-understanding of the religious pluralism we term denominationalism.

Introduction: An Essay in the Transmission of Ideas

American denominations, the late William Clebsch suggested, have been traducers of their traditions. As the twofold sense of *traduce* implies, they have transmitted and preserved (traduced) aspects of the traditions from which they sprang. In that very act of conservation, migrants to the new world—uprooted from the European communities and religious connections that had given their life meaning—utilized these communal traditions for new purposes, in a new land, and under new conditions of religious pluralism, freedom, and voluntarism. So the traditions were betrayed (traduced).[2] Clebsch's term calls attention to an ambiguity in the life of this nation of immigrants. Many of the transmitted folkways, customs, beliefs, institutions, and ideas of those who peopled this land assumed different significances here than they had in the homeland. The New England town, Puritanism, food and family practices, class and caste notions, the Commonwealthman or Republican ideology, the variety of religious movements, and aspects of African culture provide various instances or case studies of cultural imports transformed in transmission. Treasuring the life-sustaining and dynamic in their heritages, Americans fossilized it. But out of the preserved and often defining forms new dynamisms emerged. Thinking themselves pioneers, Americans have been traditional. Thinking themselves traditional, Americans have been pioneers. Culture as artifact, the American use and abuse of its cultural legacies, in part, produced what Michael Kammen terms the biformities, ambiguities, and paradoxes of American civilization.[3]

In this chapter we are concerned to extend Clebsch's insight only modestly. The traduction that he noted with respect to particular traditions also governed the transmission of ideas productive of that overall pattern of voluntaristic organization called denominationalism. As in particular denominations so in denominationalism as a whole, ideas elaborated in one context gained and lost significance when employed in

2. Clebsch, "American Churches."
3. Kammen, *People of Paradox*.

another context. Undiscussed but assumed here but mentioned in the Introduction and developed more fully in part 2 of this book is the fact that much of what is termed denominationalism derives from adjustments to the new context of religious freedom, pluralism, and voluntarism. Under examination here are certain clusters of ideas that became eventually part of the theology of denominationalism. Specifically, we examine the manner in which ideas generated in seventeenth-century England to permit dissent under an established church (diversity under unity) came to be used to explain the pluralism of churches in American nineteenth-century denominationalism (unity amid diversity).

The Theme

Comprehension and indulgence (or the principles of catholicity and toleration) were two prominent options (not necessarily exclusive options) for resolving the religious conflicts of seventeenth-century England. The Restoration and the Toleration Act compromised both principles—catholicity by settling the English church in a limited uniformity, toleration by establishing a limited indulgence. But the principles themselves survived and were transmitted as ideals—as the ideals of catholicity and toleration. Both continued to elicit much discussion, well through the eighteenth century. These two ideals, not just toleration but both catholicity and toleration, became the intellectual underpinnings of the nineteenth-century American resolution of the problem of dissent and consent—denominationalism. Though seldom adequately discussed by the nineteenth-century church leaders, these two ideals made denominationalism a viable form of the Christian church.

The thesis can be more provocatively put in this fashion: The Puritans and evangelicals who advocated indulgence and sought toleration were not the sole architects of the denominational theory of the church. Of great importance also was the intellectual contribution of Latitudinarians and Rationalists, who advocated catholicity and sought comprehension. It has been generally accepted that a coalition of Evangelicals and Rationalists won the fight for religious freedom and disestablishment—the political preconditions for denominationalism. The argument here is that the theory of denominationalism also had twin sources.

PART ONE: The British and Dissenting Origins

The Irony of Denominationalism: Division but Unity

There is a curious irony to denominationalism and to the history of many denominations. Denominationalism has become a synonym for division, schism, even ethical failure, a scandal to the church, as H. Richard Niebuhr observed.[4] Never has Christianity been so fragmented. On the other hand, despite the diversity there are unitive features to denominations and denominationalism. Many denominations by origin and at points along the way proclaimed themselves committed to Christian unity. Champions perhaps of such a unitive visions were the Restoration or Christian movements of the nineteenth century, the most prominent of which were the Disciples of Christ—movements dedicated to the overthrow of denominations and to the unification of all Christians upon Scripture alone. The irony of founding what would become denominations with loud proclamations of the end of denominations is in actuality the folly of denominationalism itself. Quite a few other movements began their pilgrimage in dedication to catholic and unitive ideals. Similarly, John Wesley committed the Methodists, a movement to spread scriptural holiness over the land, to a catholic posture. In assuming the name of catholic Christian, Wesley indicated the character of the unity to be sought:

> I dare not, therefore presume to impose my mode of worship on any other. I believe it is truly primitive and apostolical. But my belief is no rule for another. I ask not, therefore, of him with whom I would unite in love, "Are you of my church, of my congregation? Do you receive the same form of church government and allow the same church officers with me? Do you join the same form of prayer wherein I worship God?" I inquire not, "Do you receive the Supper of the Lord in the same posture and manner that I do, nor whether, in the administration of baptism, you agree with me in admitting sureties for the baptized, in the manner of administering it, or the age of those to whom it should be administered?" Nay, I ask not of you (as clear as I am in my own mind) whether you allow baptism and the Lord's Supper at all. Let all those things stand by—we will talk of them, if need be, at a more convenient season. My only question at present is this, "Is thine heart right, as my heart is with thy heart?"[5]

So also, Wesley's erstwhile colleague, George Whitefield, preached a unity of hearts transcending the division in Christendom. Whitefield's

---

4. Niebuhr, *Social Sources*.
5. Wesley, Sermon 39, "Catholic Spirit," *Works*, 2:86–87.

catholic sentiments phrased in relation to the parties of denominations bear repetition:

> "Father Abraham, whom have you in heaven? Any Episcopalians?" "No." "Any Presbyterians?" "No." "Have you any Independents or Seceders?" "No." "Have you any Methodists?" "No, no, no!!!" "Whom have you there?" "We don't know those names here. All who are here are Christians—believers in Christ—men who have overcome by the blood of the Lamb and the work of his testimony." "Oh, is this the case? Then God help us, God help us all, to forget party names, and to become Christians in deed and in truth."[6]

A third prophet spread the gospel of Christian unity among the Germans in England and the colonies. Count Zinzendorf, heir to the Pietist quest for unity, transformed the Moravians for a time into a vehicle for catholic zeal. Lutherans and the Reformed as well briefly explored unity, until Henry M. Muhlenberg rescued the Lutherans, and Michael Schlatter saved the Reformed.

More important than the catholic dimension to the movements themselves (which gives the history of the denominations no small touch of irony) was the catholicity which the labors of Wesley, Whitefield, Zinzendorf, and others made constitutive of evangelism and of the denominationism that developed therefrom. Both the First Great Awakening and its parties, and the great and minor revivals of the nineteenth century proved to be, at least in some respect, catholic enterprises, understood in relation to the millennium and undertaken cooperatively. To be sure, the end did not come, and the revivals eventually played out into reinvigorated denominations. And the revivals of both eighteenth and nineteenth century divided religious movements even as they motivated some cooperation across religious lines. But the unitive fever of the revivals never totally dissipated. Rather, it transformed itself into an understanding of the church which we call denominationalism. The separate evangelical denominations—though apparently competitive, even warring—came to be seen as one body, sharing the same great work, possessed of the same form, driven by one vision. The revivalist/evangelical mission of redeeming America became a common and inclusive task. And that uniting and unitive task made the several denominations into one body, by intention, if not law, a

---

6. Sweet, *Story*, 205–6.

PART ONE: The British and Dissenting Origins

new establishment. So recognized participant observers Robert Baird in the 1840s and Philip Schaff a decade later.[7]

Baird, for instance, attested to the essential unity of the evangelical denominations by positing a basic division in American society between the evangelical and nonevangelical denominations and by treating the former within a common framework. He took the recurrent revivals and millennial hopes to be expressive of this unity. This ideational and purposive unification, to be sure, existed despite and struggled against the great institutional and theological diversity of nineteenth-century America. But at various points and others than Baird and Schaff labored for unity among and proclaimed the oneness of the several evangelical denominations. Variously named (a Christian America, Redeemer Nation, Protestant empire, Christianized civil religion), the great voluntary empire of organized revivals; denominational expansion; and Bible, mission, and reform societies institutionalized an evangelical catholicism (despite its domination by Congregationalists and Presbyterians).

Unity despite Diversity: Theoretical Underpinnings

What underlay this unitive dimension to denominationalism? The answer, suggested Winthrop Hudson, is that this unity derives from a theology or theory of denominationalism.[8] Hudson stated his theory in an article, now a classic, "Denominationalism as a Basis for Ecumenicity: A Seventeenth-Century Conception," and worked into general histories of American religion, notably *American Protestantism* and *Religion in America*, the latter of which went through many editions, the most recent one coauthored with John Corrigan. Others, including Sydney E. Ahlstrom, have appropriated Hudson's theory as Ahlstrom did in *A Religious History of the American People*. Underlying denominationalism, argued Hudson, was an ecclesiology, a theory of the church, expressed in the meaning of the word *denomination* itself. The denomination presumed Christian unity and was used by evangelicals to denote a group within the body of Christians.

> Denominationalism is the opposite of sectarianism. The word "denomination" implies that the group referred to is but one member of a larger group, called or denominated by a particular name. The basic contention of the denominational theory of the church is that the true church is not to be identified in any

7. Baird, *Religion in America*; Schaff, *America*.
8. Hudson, "Denominationalism."

exclusive sense with any particular ecclesiastical institution. The outward forms of worship and organization are at best differing attempts to give visible expression to the life of the church in the life of the world. No denomination claims that all other churches are false churches. No denomination claims that all members of society should be incorporated within its own membership. No denomination claims that the whole of society and the state should submit to its ecclesiastical regulations. Yet all denominations recognize their responsibility for the whole of society and they expect to cooperate in freedom and mutual respect with other denominations in discharging that responsibility.[9]

This theory of the church, Hudson acknowledged, was implicit in the Reformation, but its "real architects" were the seventeenth-century Independents and more particularly the Dissenting Brethren in the Westminster Assembly. Committed to modeling the church after the primitive pattern and yet recognizing that further light was always to be gained on that primitive pattern, opposed in principle to a national establishment but firm in the belief that God's purposes transcend and even make use of divisions among Christians, the Independents searched for unity amid diversity. They found unity in several discoveries:

> First, diversity among Christians would always exist and love and peace could only be established on liberty of conscience.
>
> Second, despite the diversity a unity can exist, a unity of affections if not of opinions, a unity of the heart if not of the mind, a unity of ends if not of means.
>
> And third, a mere separation is not schism, "the true nature of schism is . . . an uncharitable, unjust, rash, violent breaking from union with the church or members of it."[10]

The Independents, then, conceived of the church as a purposive reality spiritually united in love and in respect for conscience, even though diverse in forms, professions, and practices. This Independent conception of the church, Hudson insisted, was mediated and generalized to become the denominational theory of the church.

Several questions might be raised of Hudson's thesis. It might be asked first whether denominationalism is indeed a theory of the church or, rather, a variant of voluntarism into which churches found themselves

---

9. Hudson, "Denominationalism," 32.

10. Ibid., 44–45. Hudson quotes from Jeremiah Burroughes, *Irenicum* (London, 1646).

PART ONE: The British and Dissenting Origins

propelled in adjustment to pluralism and disestablishment. Some, for instance, argue that denominationalism was a pragmatically derived form of the church whose theory or ecclesiology was developed after the fact. It might be asked, second, whether the Independents' understanding was capable of the generalization and widespread appropriation that Hudson suggests. It was, after all, an understanding of the church that served as a rationale for Congregationalism. It was conceived so as to give space to individual congregations and to provide warrant for the congregational theory of the church in defense against the threat of a Presbyterian establishment. And insofar as it engaged Puritan eschatology, such a theory of the church presumed something of a sprint, a short race in which Christians might run side-by-side towards to the goal of a coming eschaton.[11] How did these elements of Independent ecclesiology and eschatology work themselves into a form appropriate for general consumption? That suggests a third question: what were the agencies of transmission? Through whom did these ideas of English Independents become acceptable to all denominations and society generally? And finally it should be asked whether the Independents were the sole architects of the theory of the church that might be termed *denominational*.

Two Theories of the Church

These questions deserve to be addressed directly, but that enterprise is far beyond the scope of this chapter. For the present we shall assume that there was no single blueprint for denominationalism, that it was a form of the church gradually erected with materials present in Western societies, but that among these materials were clusters of ideas appropriate for a theory of the church, and that Hudson's statement of this theory will serve. Here we hypothesize that two clusters of ideas, actually quite similar and frequently intermixed, underlie and inform the denominational theory. The Independents were not the sole architects of denominational theory but shared with other religious groups responsibility for originating and developing these clusters.[12] The ideas around the principles of toleration and catholicity were so widely shared and so common to English and American religious literature of the late seventeenth and eighteenth centuries and so important for their political payoff that it is understandable

---

11. Wilson, *Pulpit in Parliament*.
12. Jordan, *Religious Toleration*.

that their part in laying foundations for a theory of the church might be overlooked.

The two principles are familiar to students of seventeenth-century England. They represent two of the prominent options for structuring the seventeenth-century church and church-state relations. The one, toleration, moved from conscience, voluntarism, and diversity toward spiritual, affectionate unity and toleration. This, closely intertwined with that elaborated by Hudson, we designate, for sake of brevity, as the principle of toleration. It became the Nonconformist ideal. The other, catholicity, the Anglican, the Elizabethan, ideal sought to interpret unity so as to permit diversity. Toleration and catholicity were ideals, tendencies. They were by no means mutually exclusive. Indeed, tolerance had advocates in every religious party. And in the judgment of some authorities it was the moderate or "catholic" Anglicans, those who espoused "a moderate, comprehensive, liberal national Church," those "who stood in the tradition of Whitgift, Hooker, and Jewel, who were among the most principled defenders of religious freedom and toleration."[13]

Actually, defenders of both views could be found in the various religious parties. This was quite natural since the two ideals shared an Erasmian quality: an openness, a tolerant posture that was a common English inheritance.[14] They shared the goal of freedom. Toleration sought openness by legitimizing pluralism and discovering some unity amid the plurality. Catholicity found freedom in a broadly conceived unity and was willing to entertain dissent within that unity and even without.

Both the idealistic character of the principles and their distinctiveness can be seen in relation to the Presbyterians who, especially after the Restoration, vacillated between the two. With interlocutors they explored two options, both in relief from the persecutions of the Clarendon Code. The first was for unification with the Anglicans in a comprehension, which would involve some compromises on both sides concerning the nature of the church, ordination, ceremonies, and the like. Efforts in this direction were furthered through conversations that went on between the Presbyterians Richard Baxter, William Bates, and Thomas Manton and, on the Anglican side, between Drs. Hezekiah Burton, John Tillotson (later Archbishop of Canterbury), and Edward Stillingfleet (later Bishop), Bishops John Wilkins and Edward Reynolds, Lord Keeper Bridgeman, and Lord Chief Justice Hales. From such discussions emerged plans for a

---

13. Jordan, *Religious Toleration*, 2:143.
14. George, *English Reformation*; Trinterud, *Elizabethan Puritanism*.

PART ONE: The British and Dissenting Origins

comprehension for the Presbyterians and an indulgence for the Independents, Baptists, and Quakers. At the same time the Presbyterians explored the second option—of renouncing the aspirations toward uniformity, establishment, and comprehension and casting their lot with the Independents in some indulgence. Conversations with John Owen developed that alternative. The choice turned out to be made for the Presbyterians rather than by them. After rejecting the ideal of settlement of the church being advanced by James II, England settled on indulgence, on toleration, but the possibility of a comprehension was retained to the last. In 1689, when the Toleration Act was introduced in Parliament it was accompanied by a bill for comprehension. Had the latter bill passed, one contemporary estimated, as many as two-thirds of the Dissenters might have come into the Church of England.[15] The latter bill failed and, as Norman Sykes once phrased it, "indulgence had triumphed over comprehension."[16]

Failure of the scheme for comprehension assured the persistence of the tradition of toleration. The Independent position outlined by Hudson and held also by members of the New Model Army, Cromwell, and the sects was to enjoy a fitful life until it came to inform the traditions of Dissent in Old England and New. And William McLoughlin's two-volume *New England Dissent* aids Hudson's cause in making clearer how that tradition worked itself into American religious life.[17]

The Catholic Principle

But what were the essentials of the catholic principle, and how, if at all, did it become a part of American religious history? The catholic position has been obscured perhaps because its adherents have borne other labels that rendered suspect their ideas and made invisible their contribution to orthodoxy and evangelicalism. The catholic tradition included irenic spirits, advocates of Christian (Protestant) unity, the churchly heirs of Erasmus and, important laity. The Italian Protestant Jacobus Acontius, the Lutherans' George Calixtus (1586–1656) and Rupert Meldenius (pseudonym perhaps of Peter Meiderlin), the Reformed Pietist David Pareus (1548–1622), the Moravian bishop John Amos Comenius (1592–1670),

---

15. Calamy, *Abridgement*, 655.
16. Sykes, "Ecumenical Movements," 123–67, 184.
17. Robbins, *Eighteenth-Century Commonwealthman*; Barlow, *Citizenship and Conscience*; Addison, *Religious Equality*; McLoughlin, *New England Dissent*: Stokes, *Church and State*.

peripatetic John Dury (1595–1680), and especially the Dutch Arminians, the Latitudinarians, and certain moderate Nonconformists ought to be numbered among the tradition's contributors.

By the catholic principle adherents offered a vision of the church's nature that united Protestantism, its national and confessional divisions notwithstanding.[18] In England the catholic principle restated and revised Elizabethan policy toward a comprehensive Protestant body. Archbishop James Ussher perhaps best summarized it in *A Briefe Declaration of the Universalitie of the Church of Christ*. Ussher insisted that the "unitie of the faith . . . such as every true Christian attaineth unto . . . must consist but of few propositions." Christians did and would differ in doctrine and practice, but there were certain fundamental principles in which all [non-Roman Catholic] true Christians concurred. It followed "that the unity of the faith, generally requisite for the incorporating of Christians into that blessed societie, is not to be extended beyond those common principles." W. K. Jordan commented: "The view of the Church which Ussher and Abbot had advanced represents considerable progress towards toleration when compared with that of the Elizabethan apologists, and it differs radically from that held so tenaciously by the Anglo-Catholic group. All men in England who profess the name of Christ and who adhere to the fundamentals of religion are Christian members of the Catholic Church. No religious group can pre-empt that title to itself."[19]

This affirmation that there are but a few fundamental articles of faith and that unity can and does exist upon them had been from the sixteenth century a cardinal unitive ploy. It had become also "a clear and conscious distinction in English Protestantism."[20] The catholic Christians dedicated themselves to this principle and self-consciously moderated between warring Protestants, in seventeenth-century England between Puritans and Laudians. Among such irenic spirits, William Chillingworth and the Latitudinarians proved most consistent and forthright in their catholic Christianity. Though it is dangerous to typify the catholic Christians (private judgment was a virtue and a reality among them), the Latitudinarians and particularly William Chillingworth will serve to illustrate the catholic posture as the Dissenting Brethren did for toleration and Professor Hudson.

18. McNeill, *Unitive Protestantism*, 259ff.; McNeill and Nichols, *Ecumenical Testimony*; Rouse and Neill, *Ecumenical Movement*.

19. Quotations from George, *English Reformation*, 377, from *A Briefe Declaration* (1631), 23; Jordan, *Religious Toleration*, 2:145.

20. George, *English Reformation*, 377–78. Sykes, "Ecumenical Movements," 123. Rouse and Neill, *Ecumenical Movement*.

PART ONE: The British and Dissenting Origins

Chillingworth's *Religion of Protestants, A Safe Way to Salvation* (1638)—a work of Protestant apologetics against the Jesuit Edward Knott (Matthew Wilson), long to be revered as a defense of Protestantism—most persuasively stated the case for Protestant catholicism. Chillingworth, with the Latitudinarians generally, stood in the tradition of Renaissance humanism, in England with Erasmus.[21]

Irenic of spirit, confident in reason, yet aware that in religion reason would be productive of only tentative truths, Chillingworth expected diversity and controversy and sought truth, unity, and authority in the church through rational discussion. In the absence of reasons to the contrary, Chillingworth sought that truth, unity, and authority in the English church. There was, therefore, a bias toward the status quo. But Chillingworth, having once capitulated to Rome and now reconverted, would not proclaim for his tradition what he denied to his opponent's: "To make any church an infallible guide in fundamentals, would be to make it infallible in all things which she proposes and requires to be believed. This . . . we deny both to your and all other churches of any one denomination, as the Greek, the Roman, the Abyssince; that is, indeed, we deny it simply to any church; for no church can possibly be fit to be a guide, but only a church of some certain denomination."[22] Chillingworth did believe there were fundamentals, and he did believe that they were constitutive of the church at any one and all time.

> When we say that there shall be a church always, somewhere or other, unerring in fundamentals, our meaning is but this, that there shall be always a church to the very being whereof it is repugnant that it should err in fundamentals; for if it should do so, it would want the very essence of a church, and therefore cease to be a church. But we never annexed this privilege to any one church of any one denomination, as the Greek or the Roman church.[23]

Chillingworth's ecclesiology proclaimed for the seventeenth-century rationalist a recasting of the Reformation insistence that the Word creates the church. For Chillingworth it was the Word, but in its written and delivered form, as Scripture, that constituted the church. Refusing on his own to define the fundamentals (and thus play the role of infallible guide that he denied to Rome), Chillingworth affirmed that "those truths will be

---

21. Orr, *Chillingworth*, 37.
22. Chillingworth, *Works*, 144.
23. Ibid., 211.

fundamental, which are evidently delivered in scripture, and commanded to be preached to all men."[24] It was those fundamental truths of scripture that defined the true church and assured salvation. "Good men and lovers of truth on all sides may be saved" who are united on scripture even though they differ on "the obscure and controverted questions of religion."[25] The disputes among Protestants Chillingworth understood to be of this character.

Consequently, Chillingworth willingly conceded considerable latitude in belief and recognized the individual's right to think for her- or himself. Religious individualism was consistent with his very Protestant conception of religious authority, truth, and unity:

> Propose me anything out of this book, and require whether I believe it or not, and seem it never so incomprehensible to human reason, I will subscribe it with hand and heart, as knowing no demonstration can be stronger than this-God hath said so, therefore it is true. In other things I will take no man's liberty of judgment from him; neither shall any man take mine from me. I will think no man the worse man, nor the worse christian, I will love no man the less, for differing in opinion from me. And what measure I mete to others, I expect from them again. I am fully assured that God does not, and therefore that men ought not, to require any more of any man than this—to believe the scripture to be God's word, to endeavor to find the true sense of it, and to live according to it.[26]

Scripture as the essential religious authority, the Christian life as quest for its true sense, and a moral life in obedience to its dictates and unity (Protestant) upon scriptural fundamentals: this Latitudinarian contribution was to hold sway over Protestantism. The sway was not limited to those who shared Chillingworth's "rational" Christianity. Rather there was widespread appeal to Chillingworth's oft-repeated statement of the religion of Protestants:

> By the religion of protestants, I do not understand the doctrine of Luther, or Calvin, or Melanchthon; nor the confession of Augusta, or Geneva; nor the catechism of Heidelberg, nor the articles of the church of England, no, nor the harmony of protestant confessions; but that wherein they all agree, and which they

24. Ibid., 19.
25. Ibid., 18.
26. Ibid., 465.

PART ONE: The British and Dissenting Origins

> all subscribe with a greater harmony, as a perfect rule of their faith and actions; that is, the Bible. The Bible, I say, the Bible only, is the religion of protestants! Whatsoever else they believe besides it, and the plain, irrefragable, indubitable consequences of it, well may they hold it as a matter of opinion; but as a matter of faith and religion, neither can they with coherence to their own grounds believe it themselves, nor require the belief of it of others, without most high and most schismatical presumption. I, for my part, after a long, and (as I verily believe and hope) impartial search of the true way to eternal happiness, do profess plainly, that I cannot find any rest for the sole of my foot but upon this rock only.[27]

The elements of Chillingworth's thought to which we have drawn attention comprise some of the essentials of catholic Christianity. Sharing variants of Protestant catholicism were the Latitudinarians, those whom W. K. Jordan designated the English Moderates and the Lay Thinkers, the Cambridge Platonists in their own ways, Jeremy Taylor, certain Puritans including Oliver Cromwell, and the Scottish Moderates. Catholicism was widely espoused, as the Georges recognize in deeming it an element of "the Protestant mind." This catholicism might better be designated an orientation, an attitude, than a mind. It was an orientation to the problem of unity and diversity, consent and dissent. For Chillingworth, presuming as he did the unity of the church—a unity of charity and a unity of fundamentals not disrupted by differences in opinion, practice, and form—catholicity served as an Anglican apologetic. Chillingworth's posture was still distant from the assent institutionalized and organized dissent and a policy of full-fledged toleration. However, within a comprehensive church he expected deviation and therefore repudiated a coercively enforced uniformity.

Transmission of "Catholic" Christianity

The "catholic" ideal continued to draw adherents long after the plans for comprehension failed. Taken over from Chillingworth by such Dissenters as Richard Baxter, Cotton Mather, Philip Doddridge, Isaac Watts, and the Americans Jonathan Dickinson and Samuel Davies, catholicity became an apologetic for trans-Atlantic Protestant evangelical unity. It belongs, strangely, to the life of both liberalism and evangelicalism. Not so strangely its place within liberalism has made its role in evangelicalism from the

---

27. Ibid., 464–65.

seventeenth century to the present less readily appreciated. The catholic Christians, especially those that kept their place among the orthodox, were generally thought, as was Doddridge, trimmers and double dealers.[28] The passion of a Baxter or a Mather for uniting the separate parties in Christendom made him seem less than fully committed to his own party. His openness to truths in other parties and to new truths made him ever suspect of heresy. The suspicion which greeted the "broad and catholick" party of eighteenth-century Boston and Harvard—Presidents John Leverett and Edward Holyoke, tutor William Brattle, Professor Edward Wigglesworth of Harvard, the Brattle Street Church, significant elements of the merchant community—was typical. Historians have added a later imprimatur to the contemporary suspicion by presenting this Catholicism as a stage toward "supernatural rationalism," "the great ecumenical theology of its age,"[29] or at best to the moribund Old Light stance of the catholic Christian Ezra Stiles, President of Yale.

Clearly, catholic Christianity does belong to the Old Light, liberal, and Unitarian traditions. One feature of catholic Christianity was a passion for liberty, often conceived as liberty of mind and an individualistic understanding of truth as private judgment. Catholic Christianity was consequently always verging on heresy (witness the charges levied at Isaac Watts) and always tending toward liberalism. However, liberalism spelled the end to catholic Christianity, since it seemed invariably to break the bond of agreement on fundamentals of doctrine. A second feature of catholic Christianity, important in its survival and orientation toward orthodoxy and evangelicalism was just its passion for unity frequently conceived in terms of fundamentals. More basic than the word *fundamentals* or any attempts at their enumeration was the perception of an agreement on the essentials in Christianity transcending party differences. Chillingworth's refusal to state a list of fundamentals and his insistence that "the Bible only, is the religion of Protestants" represented one option. Richard Baxter could agree:

> Two things have set the church on fire, and have been the plagues of it for above a thousand years. First enlarging our creed, and making more fundamentals than God ever made. Second composing, (and so imposing), our creeds and confessions in our own words and phrases. When men have learnt more manners and humility than to accuse God's language as

---

28. Orton's Memoirs in Doddridge, *Works*, 1:152.
29. Wright, *Liberal Christians*, 20; Wright, *Unitarianism*; Wilbur, *Unitarianism*.

> too general and obscure (as if they could mend it), and have more dread of God and compassion on themselves than to make those fundamentals or certainties which God never made so; and when they reduce their confessions first to their due extent, and second to Scripture phrase (that dissenters may not scruple subscribing) then I think, and never till then, shall the church have peace about doctrines. It seems to me no heinous Socinian notion which Chillingworth is blamed for, namely, let all men believe the Scripture, and that only, and endeavour to believe it in the true sense, (and promise this) and require no more of others, and they shall find this not only a better, but the only means to suppress heresy and restore unity.[30]

At another point Baxter contented himself with the Creed, the Lord's Prayer, and the Decalogue as "our Essentials or Fundamentals."[31] Cotton Mather, on the other hand, conceived of his Maxims of Piety or Godliness as effecting that unity among Christians preparatory for the coming end. He counseled candidates for the ministry: "in these Maxims of Godliness, [variously enumerated] which are all without Controversy, you behold all Controversies of Religion, as coming to an Amicable and a Comfortable Period."[32] Mather continued:

> And let the Table of the Lord have no Rails about it, that shall hinder a Godly Independent, and Presbyterian, and Episcopalian, and Anti-pedobaptist, and Lutheran, from sitting down together there . . . A Church that shall banish the Children of God from His Holy Table, and shall exclude from its Communion those that shall be Saved, meerly for such Things as are Consistent with the Maxims of Piety, does not exhibit The Kingdom of God, unto the World, as a Church ought to do. Churches that will keep up Instruments of Separation, which will keep out those that have the Evident Marks and Claims of them that are One with Christ upon them, are in Reality but Combinations of Men, who under Pretence of Religion, are pursuing some carnal Interests . . .
>
> I hope, I have said enough to disengage you from all Schismatical Combinations, and Intimate the Catholic Spirit, which I would have to be exercised, in the whole Progress of your Ministry.[33]

30. Baxter, *Saint's Everlasting Rest*, Preface to Part II.
31. Nuttall, *Richard Baxter and Philip Doddridge*, 7.
32. Mather, *Manuductio*, 119 (italics not retained).
33. Mather, *Manuductio*, 127–28 (italics not retained). Middlekauff, *The Mathers*, esp. 209ff.,

Mather's efforts to effect this unity in various schemes—the Happy Union in England, the trans-Atlantic United Brethren—did not prove successful, but by stamping catholic Christianity with millennial and evangelical marks, he provided it a more lively future.

Of similar importance to Baxter and Mather as a trans-Atlantic counselor of unity and, with them, influential through his many works of practical piety was Philip Doddridge. Doddridge's spirit was evidenced in a sermon delivered to a gathering of Northamptonshire ministers:

> The lowest understanding, the meanest education, the most contemptible abilities, may suffice to give hard names, and to pronounce severe censures. A harsh anathema may be learnt by heart, and furiously repeated by one that could scarce read it, and, as was in truth the case in some ancient councils, may be signed by those that cannot write their names. But true Catholicism of temper is a more liberal thing, it proceeds from more enlarged views, it argues a superior greatness of mind, and a riper knowledge of men and things. And the man who is blessed with such advantages should be so much the more solicitous, that he does not on any provocation add the weight of his example to so bad a curse as that of uncharitableness always is. He owes it to God and to the world, that such an influence be employed to the happy purposes of healing the wounds of the christian church, and of conciliating the affections of good and worthy men towards each other, till their united counsels can regulate its disorders, and restore it to a form more worthy of itself.[34]

Doddridge's advice touches on a third feature of catholic Christianity. The means to unity was the very sum of Pauline Christianity—love, or as it was most frequently stated, charity. This spiritual unity catholic Christians preached. By this they responded to the dogmatic warfare that had too frequently characterized Protestant Orthodoxy. This lesson Daniel Neal grounded in the history of New England and thereby made available to Americans in search of religious self-understanding. In *The History of New England* he declared himself "on the side of liberty and an enemy to oppression in all its forms and colours" and took "the liberty to censure such a conduct in all parties of Christians, wherever" he found it. Similarly in *The History of the Puritans* he pled, "And may Protestants of all persuasions

---

34. Doddridge, "Christian Candour and Unanimity," in *Works*, 3:277. Nuttall, *Philip Doddridge*: Nuttall, "Philip Doddridge"; Nuttall, *Richard Baxter and Philip Doddridge*; Gordon, *Philip Doddridge*.

improve in the knowledge and love of the truth, and in sentiments of Christian charity and forbearance towards each other, that being at peace among themselves, they may with greater success bend their united forces against the common enemy of Christianity![35]

Those who, with Neal, acknowledged themselves "catholic Christians" were a small but influential elite. Baxter called himself "a Christian," "a meer Christian," "a Catholick Christian," and wrote profusely in its behalf. His titles convey his commitment: *Christian Concord*, *Catholick Unity*, *Universal Concord*, *The Cure of Church Divisions*, *The True and Only Way of Concord*, and *Catholick Communion Defended*. Many of the English Dissenters in the first half of the eighteenth century would, with Edmund Calamy in A Defence of Moderate Nonconformity, interpret Nonconformity in terms of "Truth, Liberty, and Catholick Christianity."[36] But more important than the label was the counsel. That was and remained a property of Protestantism and functioned to make endurable the divisions, the factions, the denominations that arose.

Though few in number, the catholic Christians exercised a large role in the formation of American religion. These irenic figures were important in their own right, and their views were therefore influential. Baxter's shadow was a long one. Also catholic Christianity was absorbed into the trans-Atlantic culture of Dissent whose impact was so profound precisely in America's formative Revolutionary period. As the various interpreters of the Commonwealthman tradition have shown. Within that tradition, catholic Christianity reigned dominantly. Through that tradition it was transmitted to America as part and parcel of the Revolutionary ideology. Finally, catholic Christianity, as popular Latitudinarianism, so suffused the eighteenth-century English culture that it was absorbed and transmitted by evangelists whose religious worldview was on other scores quite the obverse of catholic Christianity.[37]

---

35. Neal, *History of New England*, preface, iii–iv; Neal, *History of the Puritans*, 1: preface, xii.

36. Calamy, *Defence*, 1, preface; *The Occasional Papers*, 1, Advertisement to first Paper.

37. Robbins, *Eighteenth-Century Commonwealthman*; Wood, *Creation of the American Republic*; Bailyn, *Ideological Origins*; Wood, *Empire of Liberty*.

APPROPRIATION

So-called catholic Christianity provided a conception of consent and dissent that amalgamated readily with the tradition of toleration (or what might be more happily termed voluntarism) analyzed by Winthrop Hudson. But catholic Christianity played a distinct role in legitimizing denominationalism. The tradition of toleration or voluntarism witnessed most strongly to the inviolability of conscience and the will and thus to dissent. It made separate congregations and denominations viable as the effective responses to the Christian gospel. Its conception of affectionate unity served the cause of revival, as when Jonathan Edwards pled for a concert of prayer and a union of wills consenting to being in general.

Catholic Christianity presented a conception of the church that would serve Protestant groups when the fires of revival, the passion for the millennium, and the affectionate unity derived therefrom were chilled. It was an understanding of the church that in witnessing first and foremost to the existing unity—to consent—proved most appropriate to the process of institutionalization and of individualization that followed the revivals. Catholicity served to state the meaning of denominationalism as a form of the church. It conceived the quite real and existing distinctions of doctrine, practice, and government as already overcome in a unity of fundamentals and practically overcome when Christians would unite in charity. If it dealt with the religious life more in terms of the human understanding than the will, it did so in accommodation to the realities of eighteenth and nineteenth centuries. Diversity was a fact that "consent to being in general" did little to dissipate. Diversity needed to be dealt with in terms of the actualities of the religious life. Catholic Christianity, in speaking the language of the Enlightenment, possessed an appropriately practical quality.

The appeals by evangelicals such as Wesley and Whitefield to catholic unity belong as much to the tradition of catholic Christianity as they do to the tradition of toleration or voluntarism discussed by Winthrop Hudson. John Wesley might reject the notion that he owed anything to Latitudinarianism. He protested vigorously that the catholic spirit was not "speculative latitudinarianism" of "indifference to all opinions," nor "any kind of practical latitudinarianism" of "indifference as to public worship," nor a latitudinarianism of "indifference to all congregations."[38] The debased latitudinarianism rejected by Wesley would be rejected alike by the

---

38. Wesley, Sermon 39, "Catholic Spirit," in *Works*, 2:92–94.

catholic Christians. In degenerate eighteenth-century form, it deserved repudiation. But to the seventeenth-century tradition Wesley (on this matter)—despite his disclaimer—did indeed belong. More significant than such explicit restatements of catholic Christianity by the revivalists was its more general appropriation as part of everyday evangelical life. That appropriation was evidenced at several levels in the American religious reorganization of the eighteenth and nineteenth centuries that was productive of the denominations. It was evidenced on the level of ideas in the appeal to catholicity already discussed; it was evidenced in structure by the growing similarity of denominations. It was evidenced in policy by the myriad acts of cooperation often at congregational level that took place among the several denominations. It was evidenced, most importantly perhaps, in program by the common drive to Christianize the nation and the world in terms by which the denominations understood their mission.

The "catholic" conception of American denominationalism was forthrightly stated in the several volumes of sermons produced in 1791 under the title, *The American Preacher or A Collection of Sermons from Some of the Most Eminent Preachers, Now Living, in the United States, of Different Denominations.*[39] Among its objects were:

> By uniting the several most important denominations in one work, to open the door for the most extensive exercise of CHRISTIAN CHARITY among CHRISTIAN BRETHREN
>
> To direct the present prevailing disposition to liberality in matters of religion, into a proper channel; and open the door for Christian communion, upon principles ACKNOWLEDGED AND UNDER-STOOD. To lay a foundation for the universal agreement of the Christian Church, when the high prospects of futurity shall be unfolded.[40]

The backers quite correctly saw themselves as beginning a work that would in achieving some unity affect significantly the political interests of this country. The numerous contributors, at this stage, represented the dominant denominations. Among its more notable backers were John Witherspoon, Presbyterian; John H. Livingston, Reformed; Benjamin Moore, Episcopal; and Joseph Lathrop, Congregational. Moreover, in recognizing the catholicity of the several denominations, they laid the ground work for what James F. Maclear has called "The 'True American Union' of Church and State," Robert Handy, "A Christian America," and Martin Marty, "The

---

39. *American Preacher.*
40. *American Preacher,* 1, preface, iii, vi.

"Catholic" Protestantism and American Denominationalism

Righteous Empire." It was an informal Protestant establishment, a unity of evangelical denominations whose "catholic" dimensions James Dana delineated in a sermon titled "Christian Union." Dana's language suggests the synthesis of the voluntaristic and catholic strains:

> Let every man be fully persuaded in his own mind. This is the unalienable right and duty of every Christian. Certainly then they may be differently persuaded. Notwithstanding this difference, they must keep the unity of the spirit in the bond of peace. This they will do, if they are meek and lowly, and possess Christian charity. Religion is a reasonable service: It is founded in personal persuasion.
>
> It is a material branch of charity, to entertain candid sentiments of different denominations; to believe that they may have the presence of Christ as well as we.
>
> What the apostle exhorts to is, union in affection, in endeavors to promote the spirit of Christianity; not uniformity of outward profession; not perfect agreement in sentiment. The fundamentals, according to our apostle, are faith towards God, as propitious through a Mediator; repentance from dead works; the admission of Christianity, upon the confirmation of it by the Holy Ghost sent down from heaven; joining ourselves to the body of Christ by baptism; the resurrection and judgment . . .
>
> Whosoever consents not to these is unsound in the faith. Whoso-ever consents to them, and doth not contradict them in his life, is fundamentally right. He embraces sound doctrine, according to the scriptures. He may not, therefore, be excluded from our charity.[41]

Dana, appealing to the three main features of the catholic posture, understood individuals and denominations to possess different gifts, all of which are needed to make one whole—the various organs of one body. He foresaw a catholic Protestantism. Ecumenicity (catholicity) was the basis for denominationalism. So also was toleration.

---

41. Dana, "Christian Union," in *American Preacher*, 3:59, 60, 63.

2

Toleration, Denominationalism, and Eighteenth-Century Dissent

THE FAILURES AND ACCOMPLISHMENTS of eighteenth-century Dissenters need to be understood in relation to the congregationalism imposed on Dissent after the passage of the Toleration Act. The Dissenters, whether Presbyterian or Independent (Congregationalist), Baptist or Quaker, suffered under legal and societal pressure to limit the horizon of their religious vision. And that limitation materially affected how Dissenters lived with their denominational identity and why many invested heavily in their common status as Dissenters. Toleration, ironically, both proved to be one of the preconditions for denominationalism, as Winthrop Hudson has argued, *and* could under some circumstances inhibit its full flowering.

The force of this limitation may, for some, be difficult to appreciate, since many commonly assume religion to be an individual affair. But the limits on the eighteenth-century Dissenters' religious contrasted sharply to the visions of their mainstream Puritan ancestors. The Presbyterians and Independents had sought to participate in God's eschatological activity, redeeming England, creating a realm of visible sainthood, beginning a whole new world. They rendered ecclesiologies as visions—visions of an England reformed by presbyterial order or the collectivity of congregations of visible saints. Their hopes were global: their political and ecclesiastical programs intersected eternity. By opportunity and circumstance they were given England on which to plot, but as citizens of Christ's new realm they hardly limited their horizons so geographically. Theirs was the revolution of the saints. Their religion was a national, corporate, eschatological affair.[1]

By 1689 the presumptions on the Holy Spirit, the visions of Christ's rule, the energies of total obedience to God had been convincingly repudiated by England. Enthusiasm, eschatology, Puritanism, had run their course. The Church of England had been restored. And thirty years of intermittent persecution disillusioned the Puritan visionaries, who, along with English society generally, longed for and accepted a new age. The radical character of this cultural transformation, wrought by the Glorious Revolution, has been frequently described. It needs to be kept in mind when eighteenth-century Dissent is discussed. The Dissenters were saints whose prophecy had failed, now confined, because of the transgressions of their earlier prophetic enterprise, to being a second-class subcommunity.

To be sure, the Toleration Act exempted Dissenters (or Nonconformists) from 'the penalties of certain laws'. But the limits of this toleration, sporadic harassment which would increase in Occasional Conformity (1711) and Schism (1713) Acts and societal suspicion, effectively confined and reshaped their religion. The burden of this chapter is to suggest that their religion was now given a narrow confinement, the congregation or chapel. The piety-and-polity framed and invigorated with visions of a nation and national church wholly reformed, indeed Reformed or Calvanized, now found itself limited within the four walls of a chapel or meeting house. This chastened congregationalism the Independent had not espoused nor the Presbyterian refined with presbyteries and synods. The story of eighteenth-century Dissent and of the 'three old denominations,' and theme of this chapter, is one of gradual adjustment to a limited religious world.

THE LAW, DENOMINATIONS, AND THE STRUCTURES OF DISSENT

Law and its long-term effects administered the *coup de grâce* to the seventeenth-century Puritan parties. For the law gave no status to parties or denominations. What the law recognized were the properties, meeting houses, and the ministers of Dissenters.

> Under the Act of Toleration the 'dissenting interest', as it was then called, acquired definite forms and a recognized place

---

1. Walzer, *Revolution*; Wilson, *Pulpit*; Lamont, *Godly Rule*; Hill, *Antichrist*.

> among the institutions of the country. The meeting-houses of the Dissenters were registered, and thus, by legal formality, placed them under the protection of the king's courts. Their property given for religious uses was secured by trust deed which the legal authorities recognized and enforced. Their ministers, duly licensed and solemnly sworn, were legally invested with a sort of clerical character, and exonerated from many services to which laymen were subject. While the Quakers were regarded as a distinct community, with whom Protestant Dissenters had neither legal nor religious connection, the three denominations, whatever differences may have prevailed among themselves, were, in the estimation of the law, one community, whose ministers, meetinghouses, and trusts were subject to the same authorities, governed by the same rules, restricted to the same uses, exonerated from the same burdens, and entitled to the same privileges. Their ministers carrying on no trade save that of a schoolmaster, although elsewhere known as Presbyterians, Independents, or Baptists, were recognized in law equally and only as licensed teachers.[2]

The laws, observed one historian, while "designed to extinguish all Nonconformity . . . were devised with peculiar ingenuity to break in upon the system of the Presbyterian order of Church rule and render it unworkable."[3] Whether really so designed or not, the law had the effect of forcing all the Dissenters, the Presbyterians particularly, "into the Independent principle of self-government," into congregationalists. So complying with law, the Presbyterians organized themselves by congregations.

The Presbyterians experienced the most dramatic violence to their polity and because of their social standing were to be the most pressured by the new social-legal realities of the eighteenth century. The Baptists (General, Particular, and the few remaining Seventh-Day) were to be the least affected. However, they were not immune to the pressures of law and society. Their perception of themselves as separate, as we note in the next chapter, did work to quarantine them and to preserve their distinctiveness. And sharing with the Independents a congregational understanding of the church and of polity, Baptists did not experience the quasi-congregationalism implicit in the Act of Toleration as denominationally destructive in the way that the Presbyterians did. The law had its effect on polity, even on Independents and Baptists; so argued

2. Halley, *Lancashire*, 2:292; Drysdale, *Presbyterians*, 546–48.
3. Drysdale, *Presbyterians*, 546–47.

nineteenth-century historian Robert Halley. The fact that ministers and trustees alone had status before the law as representative of congregations gradually moved the Independents towards what might be deemed presbyterial internal (intrachapel or intrameetinghouse) self-government. Law ostensibly protecting the Dissenting interest from penalties penalized their polity—providing no legal standing for denominational structures and reshaping intrachapel governance as well.[4]

Laws encouraged the surrender of distinctive Puritan ideas and structures by forcing the Dissenters into cooperation. The *Heads of Agreement* of 1691 under which London Presbyterians and Independents temporarily united has been understood as involving the compromise of distinctive ideas and institutions by both parties. Edmund Calamy, a contemporary to the union, observed that "'Heads of Agreement' were in 1691 assented to by the body of the United Ministers in London, in order to accommodate matters between the Presbyterians and Independents; but doctrinal differences remained, and were warmly agitated, both in the pulpits, and in conversation."[5] In *An Historical View of the State of the Protestant Dissenters in England*, Joshua Toulmin, the Unitarian, writing from the vantage-point of 1814, affirmed Calamy's view that, while doctrinal differences remained, the two parties each sacrificed distinctive institutional ideas. The Presbyterians compromised by relinquishing the notions that assemblies, synods, and church courts were indispensable for church order; that local churches and ministers were subordinate to larger ecclesiastical bodies; and that the visible church should be national. The functioning church was recognized as that particular society of visible saints joined under Christ for communion. Independents agreed to relinquish the concept of the church covenant and the indispensability of the congregational call of ministers to ordination.[6]

The explicit reformulation represented by the *Heads of Agreement* and the effects of legal provisions conspired both to reduce and to expand polity and denominational self-understandings. The grand visions and protocols for restructuring Church and Nation represented in Puritan polity gave way to survival strategies under the Act of Toleration. The vesting of property-holding in trustees and of preaching in the licensed ministers undermined and displaced the functions and rationale for denominational polity structures. Gradually polity was congregationalized,

---

4. Halley, *Lancashire* 2:414ff.
5. Calamy, *Historical Account*, 1:323 n.
6. Toulmin, *Historical View*, 101ff.; Walker, *Creeds*, 440–62, esp. 457.

PART ONE: The British and Dissenting Origins

reduced to that necessary for maintaining the meeting houses. However, common status before the law resulted in similar self-understandings for the three old denominations and, though the Heads of Agreement did not sustain a common Dissenting interest, other initiatives did.

Congregation and Dissent

Eighteenth-century Dissent was defined sociologically by a number of institutions. The major ones were the congregation or chapel, the academies, the ministerial associations or assemblies, the Dissenting Deputies (a body organized to defend Dissenting liberties), a variety of trusts and funds, and a leadership party, the Middle Way Men. Lacking institutional character but an aspect of the social reality of Dissent were denominational affiliations. Historical accounts of Dissent or, as it was called, the Dissenting interest, deal with these institutions and their functions.[7] Collectively these institutions constituted the Dissenting interest, that party of Englishmen willing to suffer the disabilities of dissenting from the Church of England.

Of these institutions, the one most basic to the social reality of Dissent and most significant in the sustenance of individual Dissenters' identity was the congregation, chapel, society or meeting. These terms with their separate connotations point to the social organization most distinctive of Dissent. To belong to Dissent was to associate with one or more of these small institutions. Chapel histories provide intimate access to their story and, like other forms of local history, provide a test or corrective to more general historical efforts. Their utility, of course, is not limited to the eighteenth century. However, for the eighteenth century they have particular importance. They examine the fundamental institution of Dissent. It is possible to see in the adequate and self-contained understanding of Dissent provided by chapel histories how very fundamental and independent the chapels were in the eighteenth century.[8]

The chapel, empowered by law to possess corporate status, to act as owner of property through its trustees and to carry on the work of a church through its minister, was fundamental. Other Dissenting institutions can

---

7. Routley, *English Religious Dissent*; Lincoln, *English Dissent*; and Lloyd, *Protestant Dissent*.

8. See Wilson, *Dissenting Churches*; Nightingale, *Lancashire Nonconformity*; and the Unitarian, Congregational, Presbyterian and Baptist magazines and historical society transactions.

Toleration, Denominationalism, and Eighteenth-Century Dissent

be seen as having the purpose of sustaining the congregations and their ministry. The trusts and funds supported congregations, the academies provided their leadership, the Dissenting Deputies labored to defend Dissent, the Middle Way Men strove to bind Dissenters together, and the Assemblies and Associations were gatherings of ministers which functioned to further the ministries of individual ministers and congregations. To be sure, the denominational affiliations—Presbyterian, Independent, Baptist (General and Particular) of the three old denominations—served to remind Dissenters of the larger agendas entertained by their ancestors. But as the following section will show, denominational identifications and affiliations were of less consequence in the eighteenth century than they were in either the seventeenth or nineteenth century. In the main, the religious life of Dissent was confined within the chapel.

Corresponding to this limited religious horizon was a similarly limited conception of the role of religion in human affairs. In repudiation of warfare and persecution for religious causes and in accordance with notions of enlightenment, England with Locke declared religion to be an individual affair. This was for Dissent an appropriate definition, for that was about the limit of religious expression allowed them. The piety that had sought the reformation of England now contented itself with the adornment of individuals and the national aspirations of the Dissenters were couched increasingly in liberal political rather than religious terms. This shift in the conception and limitation of the expression of piety almost destroyed Dissent. Adjustment was difficult. The persecutions and threatened persecutions of the Restoration period, the energies expended in chapel building in the two decades after 1689 and the Tory and High Church resurgence under Queen Anne permitted the Dissenters to evade the questions of their role in society, their religious identity, the purposes of continued dissent. But in the second and successive decades of the eighteenth century the question, why dissent? became unavoidable. For some there came no answer. Wealthy laity, especially, and even ministers found their way into the Church of England. By the 1730s the decline in Dissent, evidenced in chapel closings and decreased chapel membership, became a matter of comment and concern.[9]

The alarm over decline was raised in 1730 by Strickland Gough, anonymously, in *An Enquiry into the Causes of the Decay of the Dissenting Interest*. Philip Doddridge offered an alternative analysis of the decline

---

9. Bebb, *Nonconformity*; Gough, *Dissenting Interest*; Doddridge, *Works*, 4:292, 211, 207ff., 213ff.

PART ONE: The British and Dissenting Origins

in *Free Thoughts on the Most Probable Means of Reviving the Dissenting Interest. Occasioned by the late Enquiry into the Causes of its Decay*. Decline continued to be a topic of concern. In 1746 Nathaniel Neal produced *A Free and Serious Remonstrance to Protestant Dissenting Ministers, On Occasion of the Decay of Religion*. And in 1766, the Independent, Samuel Newton of Norwich, examined the *Causes and Reasons of the Present Declension among the Congregational Churches in London and the Country*. Sometimes Congregationalist and Baptist historians bemoan the fact that their eighteenth-century brethren discovered so belatedly the solution to the problem provided by the Methodists. This is a determinist reading of history which faults early eighteenth-century Dissenters for failure to anticipate the solution to the decay of Dissent adopted in the late eighteenth and early nineteenth centuries. The Dissenters were not unconcerned over the decline. Indeed, their preoccupation with it may have furthered their retreat into the congregations. Their analyses of the problem and their remedy were not that discovered by the later evangelical Dissenters. Gough, for instance, a good Whig, understood the essence of Puritanism and Nonconformity to be the spirit of liberty. He attributed the decline in Dissent, therefore, to the inattention to the principles of Dissent. As an antidote he proposed rational worship and rational education (including subjects like classics, Belle Letres [sic] and dancing). Doddridge agreed that inattention to principles, unscriptural impositions, uncharitable contentions and the bigotry of the rigidly orthodox were sources of Dissent's weakness. He opposed the appeal to learning and politeness and the elevation of the gentleman as a "wild and chimerical" solution. He looked rather to the strengthening of Associations and a revival of piety founded on catechizing and evangelical, experimental, plain, and affectionate preaching as the best designs for reviving Dissent. Doddridge's evangelical or Pietist counsel might have provided Dissenters with new meaning for Dissent and might have arrested the decline. The beliefs and structures of Dissent, confined in chapel and congregation, proved incapable at that time of grasping new conceptions of purpose and commitment. Efforts like that of Richard Davis, whose missionary and expansive activities played their part in the disruption of the Happy Union, were the exceptions that proved the rule. Such unwillingness to confine himself to his own congregation and to respect his "brother" minister was seen as disruptive of Dissent. With Samuel Newton, Dissenters opposed evangelicalism's most public face, Methodism. He thought it promised only ignorance and enthusiasm and he even ascribed the decline of congregationalism to Methodist influence and prevalence.[10]

Not until Dissenters appropriated evangelicalism were there ideological resources for putting this spatial limitation of religion into a significant and larger spiritual context and thereby providing new meaning to the question, why dissent? In the later decades of the eighteenth century evangelicalism did fill the void left by the loss of the Puritan aspirations for a society ruled by saints. Then the confines of the congregation and the relative insignificance of denominations were overcome by the vision of an invisible kingdom built in human hearts.

Until the impact of evangelicalism was felt, however, the Dissenters struggled to sustain within chapels a religious life that, under Puritanism, had been born of efforts for national reformation and the bringing in of the kingdom of God.

Denominational Self-Consciousness

The centrality of chapels and congregations in eighteenth-century Dissent owed in no small part to the very limited significance afforded denominations and denominational affiliations. Denominational identities can be established for most ministers and congregations, denominational funds functioned throughout the century, and denominational associations were maintained among the Baptists throughout the century and among the London Independents after 1727. Nevertheless, in the main, denominational structures did not drive Dissenting life, and denominational identity itself depended upon and a remained a function of the religious life of individual congregations. The meaning retained in the early part of the century for denominations was largely due to the conserving of self-consciousness by individual congregations. That hampered Presbyterians more than Baptists and Independents, whose self-consciousness was intrinsically congregational. So there were differences of degree in denominationalism. Still, the trend in the early eighteenth century was away from denominational or party identity. An anonymous observer of the London scene in 1730, for instance, could only generalize about the differences between Presbyterian and Independents on the basis of practice by chapels. The Independents, he observed, continued the custom of ordination after call; the restriction of the pastor's right to administer the Lord's Supper to his own congregation; and the presumption of the right of the whole

10. Bolam et al., *English Presbyterians*, 115ff.; Jones, *Congregationalism*, 14ff.

membership to take part in congregational decisions including the election of a pastor, admission of new members and administration of discipline.[11] Distinctive Presbyterian features were also, in the main, preserved within the congregations. The observer found "the modern Presbyterians" to have disclaimed the Presbyterian system of church courts that ran from pastor and elders to presbyteries to synods to general assemblies, and to have assented "to the congregational order."[12] Their distinctiveness then rested in greater freedoms or prerogatives allowed to the minister-to be ordained before he was called, to administer the Lord's Supper where not pastor, to admit members-and in their indifference to matters of discipline and membership.

Denominationalism then functioned mainly on the congregational level. Furthermore, outside of the metropolis, for which the above distinctions may have been valid, denominational factors seem to have been less important, even within congregations. The exigencies of country life, unions between congregations, short-lived congregations, social intercourse among ministers and congregations nearby, occupancy of pulpits by men of different denominations, all had the effect of undermining denominational self-consciousness.[13] Robert Halley observed that in many parts of England, particularly in Lancashire and Cheshire, "the distinction of the two denominations was practically obliterated," the remaining difference being that in congregations "originally Independent there was a traditional disposition of the members to interfere in ecclesiastical matters, while in those originally presbyterian the traditional disposition was to acquiesce in the proposals of the ministers and managers of the meeting-house."[14] Congregations, then, rather than denominations were foundations in which Dissenting life and identity were built.

Financing Dissent

The precarious financial situation in which many Dissenting chapels found themselves had an important effect on the life of Dissent. Outside the growing urban areas, societies often struggled for survival. The search for support and the management of resources came to have an undue

11. "An Account of the Presbyterian and Independent Ministers in London about the year 1730," in James, *Litigation*, 701ff.
12. James, *Litigation*, 700–701.
13. See Richey, "Effects," 356 n.
14. Halley, *Lancashire*, 2:384ff.

prominence within the life of Dissent. The procuring of monetary support from the wealthy of the neighborhood or afar and/or the obtaining of assistance from one or more of the Funds brought with it certain forms of scrutiny or advice.[15] Significant, in consequence, were the roles played by and influence of persons of wealth within a congregation. The wealthy laity as donor and often as trustee functioned as has been so often the case in the history of Christianity, frequently in a position of authority. Their feelings and their theological opinions were catered to As Dissent became divided into orthodox and rational parties, the wealthy laity's position became increasingly important. R. Tudor Jones called Congregationalism "the religion of the economically independent," boasting in the towns a solid core of gentlemen and tradesmen and in the country farmers and yeomen. His assessment of the Congregationalist congregation would hold for the Presbyterians as well. The Baptists, on the other hand, could claim less economic and social eminence.[16] The laity's hand, strong because of the chapel's financial straits, was given further sanction in law. By law, the chapels' property-owning function was conferred on trustees. Trusteeship became often a self-perpetuating autocracy in the chapels. The trustees' position was solidified by their control over endowments.[17] Thus authority in the chapels was established not by spiritual, leadership or theological but by economic considerations.

An incident in a chapel in Plymouth provides a graphic illustration of the usurpation of authority by trustees. In 1768 a meeting of "Trustees and other of the Contributors" to the society of Protestant Dissenters, apparently a meeting of the congregation, nominated a committee to revise the rules for governance of the society. The result was the widening of participation in the running of the church—every person who contributed seven shillings annually was declared to be a voting member of the "General Vestry." The committee in democratic mood proposed that even women contributors should be allowed a proxy vote (though not membership). The trustees as a body quickly reacted to this coup. They informed the contributors that "they [the contributors] have no business with nor have any power to act as a Trustee, and that therefore any regulations they

---

15. Ibid., 2:311ff.

16. Jones, *Congregationalism*, 125ff.; Drysdale, *Presbyterians*, 513–14; *UHST* 6: 116–29; *UHST* 11:1–31; Richey, "Effects," 357n16.

17. Clark, *English Nonconformity*, 2:126–27, 176; Drysdale, *Presbyterians*, 510–13; Halley, *Lancashire*, 2:311ff.

PART ONE: The British and Dissenting Origins

have made and inserted in their new book which relates to the Trustees, we hereby declare to be null and void."[18]

The case of Pinners' Hall represents a more common result of such wealthy leadership. Among its members were some of the most prominent laymen in Dissent: the Hollis family, noted for financial support of the Dissenting cause, universities, and liberty; and Lord Barrington, erratic member of Parliament, rational Christian and prime mover of the anti-subscription forces at Salters' Hall. In addition to liberal and wealthy laity, it enjoyed the ministerial leadership from 1707 to 1778 of three capable and liberal clergymen, Jeremiah Hunt, then James Foster, and finally Caleb Fleming. Under combined liberal lay and ministerial leadership the chapel moved towards rational Christianity. When Fleming died, the chapel died. The course of such chapels was charted by a liberal leadership with apparent indifference to the views, interests, and needs of the populace of Dissent. John Shute Barrington may have been the extreme example of the lay manipulator. He was an insistent voice against subscription. When controversy broke at Exeter, he was apparently instrumental in having the matter brought before the London Dissenters. Thus was made national what might have remained a Devonshire dispute. In some instances orthodox leadership operated in just as high-handed a manner and with similar results. An orthodox layman of similar importance in rallying Dissenters around the orthodox banner was William Coward.[19]

A late eighteenth-century layman who exercised an informal authority in Dissent was Thomas Bentley, the partner of Josiah Wedgewood. He played an important part in the formation of the Octagon Chapel, where a rational liturgy was used for worship. Bentley had much to do with its becoming a rational chapel. As a member of the committee to form the chapel, he wrote to John Seddon, a Socinian, a tutor at Warrington Academy and a fellow committee-member. Bentley expressed concerned about the liberality of one of the candidates for minister of the chapel, Nicholas Clayton. Bentley sought assurance from Seddon that Clayton was not one of the orthodox who "never do keep to practical points, but think it their Duty to wander into Mysteries."[20] The Hollis family, Lord Barrington, Bentley perhaps represent an extreme in lay power. But they serve to

18. *UHST*, 11:186–88.

19. Wilson, *Dissenting Churches*, 1:212; 2:249ff.; Underwood, *English Baptists*, 143ff.

20. Octagon Chapel MS. XXIV, quoted in Holt, *Unitarian Contribution*, 142–43.

illustrate the trend-the re-ordering of congregational life in response to the struggle for congregational survival.

THE MINISTER IN RELATION TO CONGREGATION, DENOMINATION, AND DISSENT

During the century the role of the minister and the relation of the minister to the congregation, denomination and dissent underwent alteration as well. The religious life of Dissent was transformed as much by this reconception of the Puritan ministry as it was by the loss of Puritan piety. The *Heads of Agreement* insisted of the ministry: "They who are called to this *Office*, ought to be endued with *competent Learning*, and *Ministerial Gifts*, as also with the Grace of God, sound in Judgment, not Novices in the Faith and Knowledge of the Gospel; without scandal, of holy Conversation and such as *devote* themselves to the Work and Service thereof.[21] This recasting of the Puritan ideal remained aspirational. But the conditions upon which it had rested in Puritanism changed. Dissenting ministers could no longer dream of leading the nation. Ministry was effectively confined by law inside the congregation. The minister could not operate with a parish/presbytery model as Presbyterians had hoped, nor could they really operate with the ideal of a visible congregation of saints, separatist or not, called out of the world. From the perspective of the nineteenth and twentieth centuries it seemed that the Dissenters lacked an evangelical, missionary understanding of the ministry and only succeeded in achieving such an understanding late in the eighteenth century. So Geoffrey Nuttall traced the gradual alteration in the eighteenth century in terms of the slow disburdening by orthodox Dissenters of the Calvinist and mission-inhibiting understandings of election and perseverance and their slow appreciation of Methodist and evangelical notion that invitation must be extended to the unregenerate.[22] Such analysis, fair if descriptive, seems anachronistic if offered as a critique expecting early eighteenth-century Dissenters to have appropriated ministerial self-understandings out of keeping with what they deemed the law to permit. To Dissenters then ministry seemed to be explicitly constrained from just such expansive, out-of-the-chapel, missionary activity. The chapel-delimitation symbolized and enforced a static early eighteenth-century Dissenting ministry.

21. Walker, *Creeds*, 458.
22. Nuttall, "Northamptonshire."

PART ONE: The British and Dissenting Origins

The Dissenting ministry was thus confined, at least in its purely religious activities. As compared to the leadership, influence and normative functions of the Puritan ministry and to contemporary clergy of the Established Church, Dissenting ministers exercised a much reduced role and experienced a decline in status.[23] Concurrently, as we have noted, Dissent as a whole suffered a decline—decline in members, decline in chapels, decline in the percentage of time Dissenters were willing to devote to religion, decline in morality, and, most important, decline in financial support. Dissenters did undertake some chapel building and created funds for support of poor congregations, ministers and students in the late seventeenth and early eighteenth centuries. Thereafter such enterprises decreased. Monetary support for Dissenting ministers, made precarious by ejection and by the necessity of finding voluntary support, was rendered even more precarious by the declining numbers of adherents or givers. And low salaries forced ministers frequently to seek alternative sources of income.

Many ministers in the tradition of the Puritan lecturers and in accord with their legal standing, became school teachers, providing a primary education for the children of their neighborhood. Others were taken on by persons of wealth to serve as tutors to their children and family chaplains. Nathaniel Lardner, for instance, served as chaplain to Lady Treby from 1713 to 1721.[24] Early in his career Isaac Watts had served as a tutor in the family of Sir John Hartopp, an alderman who bequeathed £10,000 for education of Dissenting ministers. Watts spent the last thirty-six years of his life with the family of Sir Thomas Abney, a Lord Mayor of London.[25] Joseph Priestley became librarian to Lord Shelburne in 1772, a post which he held until 1780.

Representing similar losses to the active Dissenting ministry were those who drifted into business or medicine.[26] Throughout the century still others would choose the route made glamorous by bishops Thomas Secker and Joseph Butler, fellow-students at Tewkesbury, the Dissenting academy, of accepting preferment in the Church. Few possessed the industry of Robert Robinson of Cambridge (1735–90) who, though building up his congregation, found its resources inadequate to his needs. To supplement his income he farmed, purchased several copyhold houses

23. Richey, "Effects," 359n23.
24. Kippis, *Life*; Kippis, *Lardner*, 1.
25. Wilson, *Dissenting Churches*, 1:295ff.
26. Halley, *Lancashire*, 2:226.

and lands, made alterations and improvements, operated a ferry across the river adjoining his house, dealt in coals and corn and engaged in other rural industries.[27]

Reconception of the Ministerial Agenda

The occupation most frequently followed by Dissenting ministers to supplement their income was that of tutor, teacher or schoolmaster. For that role their training made them most qualified. And the various educational roles they could easily pursue along with ministry. Indeed, especially among the ministers inclined towards rationalism but also among the orthodox, not only were the two occupations, teaching and ministry, frequently pursued together, but also the ministry came increasingly to be understood as a form of education. Betraying their Puritan heritage which had esteemed lectures but distinguished the ministerial offices of teacher and preacher, the Dissenters collapsed ministry into teaching.

The alteration was predicated upon the Lockean conception of religion as "the inward and full persuasion of the mind."[28] The conviction spread that any truth must necessarily cohere with the Christian religion or, as the growing community of rationalists expressed it, that there existed a harmony between natural and revealed truths. The exploration of the new science and of the new worlds opened by reason both encouraged and was encouraged by the reconception of the ministry as teaching. While this reconception especially informed the growing rational community in early eighteenth-century Dissent, it was not foreign to the more orthodox. The orthodox Isaac Watts thought it hardly necessary to inform his readers "that the foundation of all religion is laid in knowledge." He continued: "We must not worship an unknown God, nor pay him service without understanding."[29] And he affirmed that while no one "is obliged to learn and know everything . . . for it is utterly impossible: Yet all persons are under some obligation to improve their own understanding, otherwise it will be a barren desert, or a forest overgrown with weeds and brambles."[30]

Watts was probably as important as any Dissenter in forging the relationship between reason and revelation. His highly esteemed and widely used *Logick* (1724) bore the subtitle "The Right Use of Reason in

---

27. "Memoir," in Robinson, *Works*, 1:xxix–xxx.
28. Locke, "Letter Concerning Toleration," in *Works*, 2:235.
29. Watts, "Instruction by Catechisms, in *Works*, 3:199.
30. Watts, "Improvement of the Mind," in *Works*, 4:185.

PART ONE: The British and Dissenting Origins

the Enquiry after Truth." In both the *Logick* and the supplement to it, *The Improvement of the Mind* (1741), Watts laid down rules for knowledge. He insisted that reason is not "the mere faculty of reasoning, or inferring one thing from another, but includes all the intellectual powers of man."[31] Beyond these efforts to show the working of reason to be harmonious with Christianity, Watts endeavored to establish that the harmony need not be at the expense of revelation. In *A Rational Defence of the Gospel* he repudiated the Socinian who would reduce the gospel to 'the dictates, and hopes of the light of nature." In *The Strength and Weakness of Human Reason* he presented four conferences or debates on the sufficiency of reason." In The Rational Foundation of a Christian Church he established the reasonable character of Protestant institutions. Confident in the harmony of reason and revelation, Watts encouraged ministers into the task of education.[32]

It took only a short step for Dissenters to come to an understanding of the minister's relation to his congregation as "their religious guide, instructor, and friend."[33] Religious instruction became all too frequently the purpose of the ministerial office and the ministerial charge became keeping the congregation abreast of the advances in religion and nature. John Prior Estlin epitomized this reconception of ministry. At his ordination in 1778 he affirmed the end of ministry to be "my own moral and intellectual improvement, and the intellectual and moral improvement of others,"[34] This reconception of ministry accompanied and justified the departure from orthodoxy by certain Dissenters. Sustained by Lockean thought and confident in the educational role thrust upon him, the Dissenting minister who was threatened with loss of status and financial disaster possessed a new source of esteem. In a society which both formally and informally questioned the validity of his ministry, a redefinitional response was perhaps natural. Thus ministry became education and the gospel became reason. The sacral realities upon which English society claimed to rest were repudiated by Dissenters who became increasingly heterodox. To be sure, all Dissenters did not follow this course. Orthodox Calvinists repudiated the excessive reliance upon reason. But their defense against the world of reason became itself rational and their ministry also a form of teaching. Their unyielding maintenance of Calvinist doctrine took on a scholastic tone which merited the label 'Hyper-Calvinism.' The orthodox undertook

31. Watts, *Logick,* in *Works,* 5:5n.
32. Watts, *Works,* 1:163; 2:315–425; 5:669–802.
33. Estlin, *Sermons,* 193.
34. Enfield, *Principle and Duty,* 39.

to teach Dissenters the true Calvinist doctrine. William Coward to this end established a series of lectures in Paved-Alley, Lime Street, which ran from 1730 to 1731 and were then published. These lectures came to be "'esteemed among the best defences of Calvinism."[35] The Dissenting congregation became all too often subscribers to a lecturer. The Puritan office of teacher, sustained by eighteenth-century ideas of education, became the sum of the Dissenting ministry.

The Lectures

Expressive of changes in the ministry and in the content of the message were alterations in architecture and worship. The modesty of the chapel building—while perhaps an expression of Puritan aversion to extravagance and dictated by financial and legal restraints—symbolized the place of Dissent in English society and its own self-conception. Within the chapel the century witnessed increased prominence of the pulpit, leading to the employment of the octagonal shape (which was adopted by Wesley) in Norwich, Liverpool, and elsewhere, and which permitted all the congregation to face the minister.[36] For a London Dissenting minister to be chosen lecturer—to preach to one of the regular services at Salters' Hall or Weigh-House was a source of esteem, (though perhaps not as much esteem as Puritan lectureships).[37] The lecturers at Salters' Hall held various theological views. Those attending heard Calvinists, Arminians, Arians and Socinians. One set of lecturers included the orthodox Robert Bragge and Thomas Bradbury and the heterodox Philip Furneaux, Abraham Rees, and Hugh Worthington. But whatever the theological position, the lectures became, befitting their name, dry rational and ethical discourses.

The Polarization of Dissent

The Dissenting ministers, as well as the chapels, possessed an independence and self-sufficiency which left them to be buffeted by intellectual and social storms. Being themselves their reason for existing and called to no higher purpose in an ecclesiastical structure but to Dissent, the Dissenting ministers at best served the congregation; too frequently they

---

35. Wilson, *Dissenting Churches*, 1:212.
36. See Richey, "Effects," 362 n.38.
37. Again see expansive note in Richey, "Effects," 362 n.39.

PART ONE: The British and Dissenting Origins

reflected the interests of its patrons or trustees. Forced, therefore, to search for meaning to their existence, the Dissenting ministers of the eighteenth century grasped at ideological self-justification. They yoked themselves in service to Calvinism or Rationalism and divided accordingly into two camps. The polarization was expressed also in chapel splits and in discord between neighboring chapels. An example of the former was the chapel at Walsall where the Arianism of the minister and the majority of the congregation led to the withdrawal in 1763 of twenty-eight members and two deacons who were Calvinist. A notable instance of the latter occurred in Nottingham. There the Independent chapel of Castle Gate and the Presbyterian chapel of High Pavement found themselves enough in accord for both to extend an invitation to Dr. Doddridge to become minister. Their amity disappeared when a Scot came who preached in defense of the Trinity and the divinity of Christ. Subsequently an Arian was discovered (at Castle Gate), and Castle Gate became suspicious of the orthodoxy of High Pavement. Finally in 1737 Castle Gate resolved not to accept members from High Pavement except those received by the former pastor or those coming by relation of experience. Theological conflict descended to the physical level in the struggle over Walmsley chapel late in the century. There the orthodox ministers of the neighborhood attempted to wrest control of the chapel from Unitarians by gaining control of the keys, pulpit and trust deed. At one point a foot race between a Unitarian and three orthodox ministers determined who would conduct a funeral.[38] It was in the chapels that the fate of Dissent rested in the eighteenth century.

Conclusion

Our theme, the limitation of Dissenting religious life, only begins to touch on the larger and more complex story of the transformation of eighteenth-century Dissent and of the changes that congregations and ministers underwent. Some of that we explore in other chapters. Clearly there are many dimensions of ministerial role and congregational life that need to be discussed to sustain the argument for the congregationalizing of Dissent. This treatment has concentrated on the limiting effects of the toleration laws on eighteenth-century Dissent. A fuller picture would require attention to the significant details—biography, social status, roles, beliefs of ministers; nature, composition, functions of congregations; the complex interplay of Dissenting institutions; the varying roles of Dissenting

38. See Richey, "Effects," 363 nn.40, 41, 42.

denominations. This chapter, it is hoped, will occasion the larger task by pointing to the quiet congregational interlude between the highly developed and organized revolution of the saints and the evangelical conquest of the world. The Toleration Act that governed life in this interlude permitted the continued existence of the three old denominations. But vigorous denominationalism? That blossomed under evangelical cultivation. In the eighteenth century, chapel contained much of the religious life. And Dissenting not denominational structures served the common good of Presbyterians, Independents and, to a somewhat more limited extent, Baptists.

3

Baptist Denominationalism in Eighteenth-Century Dissent

DENOMINATIONAL IDENTITY OFTEN VIES with a shared Protestant or Christian identity in the lives of individuals and congregations. At times, groups and movements vest heavily with other Christians in common endeavor, as did Protestants in the long campaign for a Christian America. During moments of this quest, Protestants so affirmed their shared evangelical and evangelistic purposes and so joined together organizationally that they seemed one body.[1] At other points, denominational or sectarian concerns or agenda loomed large for these same Presbyterians, Methodists and Baptists and competition between and among them became fierce. Then these communions or at least their most boisterous leaders would all but unchurch one another. So my Methodists forebears resorted to name-calling, vicious debates and even camp meeting fisticuffs with Baptist or Presbyterian competitors and received back the same.

The tensions for individuals and groups between denominational membership and more inclusive Christian or Protestant association are important aspects of larger issues of freedom and authority, of conscience and consent, of individual integrity and shared beliefs and values, of pilgrim's progress and kingdom building. Such tensions shape religious life on several levels—minister and congregation, congregation and association, association and Protestantism (denominationalism and ecumenism). Self-contained and sufficient citadel? An open marketplace? Between

1. Baird, *Religion in America*.

these two extremes, somewhere in the middle, denominations typically function. But also there may not be consistency across a church's regional expanse or up and down its leadership levels. So a denomination may not be entirely at the same place with respect to this tension; and between those extremes at any given time, its activities, commitments, and leadership at national, regional, and local levels sometimes tending in quite different directions. That said, denominationalism, sometimes virtually equated with sectarianism and so taken to stand for the separatist pole of this tension, actually embraces this tension in its very nature, as our first chapter endeavored to show.

BAPTIST OR DISSENTER?

Baptists have sometimes been seen as living closer to the sectarian edge and indeed at times have earned such a perception. This chapter treats one such moment in Baptist life in particular: the English Baptists in the eighteenth century. It posits that the Baptists located themselves in the tension been denominational and associational identity.[2] Sociologically this tension was expressed as separateness (or sectarianism, to use sociological language) versus community with other Protestant Dissenters (Presbyterians and Independents). It might have been experienced as the question, were the Baptists a community unto themselves, a member of the larger community of dissent, or both? The tension was expressed psychologically as a problem of identity. In question form: Were they Baptists, Dissenters, or both? From where were the beliefs, symbols, and institutions for religious life to be derived? From the Baptist tradition or from Dissent? The answer, we suggest, is from both.

Even when the Baptists most seem a separate people as in eighteenth-century England, their separateness was the accented polarity of a tension. Further, in understanding sectarianism and denominationalism, the relation to the larger religious community needs to be discussed, since the relation forms part of the sect or denomination's identity. In the eighteenth century, as Robert Halley indicates, the significant pressure for Dissenting unity derived from societal perception, expressed in repression and persecution, and embodied in law.

> Under the Act of Toleration the 'dissenting interest,' as it was then called, acquired definite forms and a recognized place

---

2. Harrison, *Authority and Power*; Conner, "Early English Baptist Associations."

PART ONE: The British and Dissenting Origins

> among the institutions of the country. The meeting-houses of the Dissenters were registered, and thus, by legal formality, placed under the protection of the King's courts. Their property given for religious uses was secured by trust deed which the legal authorities recognized and enforced. Their ministers, duly licensed and solemnly sworn, were legally invested with a sort of clerical character, and exonerated from many services to which laymen were subject. While the Quakers were regarded as a distinct community, with whom Protestant Dissenters had neither legal nor religious connection, the three denominations, whatever differences may have prevailed among themselves, were, in the estimation of the law, one community, whose ministers, meeting-houses, and trusts were subject to the same authorities, governed by the same rules, restricted to the same uses, exonerated from the same burdens, and entitled to the same privileges. Their ministers carrying on no trade save that of a schoolmaster, although elsewhere known as Presbyterians, Independents, or Baptists, were recognized in law equally and only as licensed ministers.[3]

The history of the interaction of Puritan groups and the very identity of Baptists as separatists, naturally would have led to Baptist separation. But as belonging to a group perceived by English society to be distinct (Dissenting) and treated as such, the Baptists (General and Particular) were pressed towards unity with other Dissenters. They were, in fact, Dissenters, suffering the same disabilities and sharing the same legal status with the Presbyterians and Independents (Congregationalists). Societal pressure rather early resulted in Presbyterian and Independent cooperation and varying degrees of Baptist participation therein.

Dissent or Nonconformity

The Happy Union under the Heads of Agreement (1691), though eventually aborted, set the pattern for county associations that continued to function throughout the eighteenth century. The need for cooperation, particularly for a common defense, drove Baptists into cooperation only a decade later. Edmund Calamy recorded that the Three Denominations made the first joint address to the Crown, an act symbolically significant, in 1702. By that year, London Baptists were participating in the Body of

---

3. Halley, *Lancashire*, 2:292.

the Three Denominations.⁴ This alignment set the stage for Baptist participation both formally and informally in various Dissenting activities and institutions, particularly in London. Most important, Baptists were included in a General Body of Dissenting Ministers of the Three Denomination and were represented by the Dissenting Deputies, both of which organizations undertook the guarding of the Dissenting interest. These institutions actually and symbolically maintained Dissenting unity.

Baptists shared also informally in Dissenting activities. Most significantly they exercised lay and clerical leadership in Dissent. The Hollis family, patrons of Pinners' Hall in London, were benefactors of and provided leadership for Dissent as a whole. The liberal cause in Dissent was advanced by the writings and labors of John Gale (1680–1722), James Foster (1697–1753), and Joshua Toulmin (1740–1815), all General Baptists, and Robert Robinson (1735–1790), a Particular Baptist. Highly revered for their roles in the defense of Calvinism, on the other hand, were the Particular Baptists John Gill (1697–1771), John Brine (1703–1765), and Andrew Fuller (1754–1815). These leaders helped to make the Baptist experience in the eighteenth century typical of Dissent as a whole. So the Baptists anticipated the polarization of Dissent into Liberal and Calvinist interests. The General Baptists drifted toward Socinianism and the Particular Baptists toward Hyper-Calvinism. Baptists shared in Dissent beyond ideological skirmishes and on lower levels as well, by participating in lectures, exchange of pulpits, and even ordinations. They were part of the Dissenting flux in which denominational affiliations of congregation and ministers were uncertain and subject to change.[5]

Baptists Distinctiveness

While Baptists were Dissenters, they also regarded themselves and were regarded as distinctive. Their sectarian or denominational self-consciousness was markedly different from the Presbyterian and Independent self-consciousness. A contemporary noted this distinctiveness when he described Dissenters as "this odd mixture of contradictions in three distinct classes . . . distinguished under the well-known denominations of Quakers, Anabaptists and Presbyterians."[6] Other Dissenters were lumped

---

4. Calamy, *Historical Account*, 2:460.
5. Tibbutt, "Pattern of Change," 166ff.
6. Joseph Smith, *Modern Pleas for Schism and Infidelity Reviewed* (3rd ed.; 1717) in James, *Litigation*, 95.

PART ONE: The British and Dissenting Origins

together as Presbyterians and the Quakers and Anabaptists were seen as separate.

The theological convictions and sociological differentia which had prompted separatism in the previous centuries remained salient. While sometimes still voicing the broader critiques of the Church and concerns about the vacillation of their fellow Puritans that had prompted the Separatist movements, eighteenth-century Baptists laid much of the explicit defense of distinctiveness in terms of that rite which symbolized separation. Namely believer's baptism, baptism itself. One bond, then, which united Baptists and separated them from others was their disavowal of infant baptism and vigorous distinctive practice of reserving baptism for those who could confess sin and profess belief. In the eighteenth century other Dissenters attacked, and the Baptist defended the practice of adult (believer's) baptism. In 1726 John Gill wrote *The Ancient Mode of Baptizing by Immersion Maintained*, which occasioned responses in 1727 by M. Maurice, *Plunging into Water, no Scriptural Mode of Baptizing*, and by J. Cogan, *Some Remarks upon J. Gills Defence of Plunging*. Gill then rejoined with *Defence of the Ancient Mode*. Again in 1749 Gill drew fire with his *The Divine Right of Infant Baptism Examined and Disproved*, which brought M. Towgood to answer anonymously in 1750 and 1751, *The Baptism of Infants a Reasonable Service*, and *Dipping Not the Only Scriptural and Primitive Manner of Baptizing*, and C. Fleming to write *Plain Reasons for Infant Baptism*. Gill in 1752 replied in *Anti-Paedo-baptism*. Such writing continued throughout the century.[7] While it differentiated Baptists from other Dissenters, the exchanges themselves might be read as indicators of the importance Dissenters put on trying to come to more common mind or at least to ways of understanding one another. To put it another way, the debate showed that Dissenters mattered to one another.

Baptists manifested self-consciousness as Baptists also in the Baptist histories produced during the eighteenth century. Thomas Crosby took four volumes to narrate wrote *The History of the English Baptists from the Reformation to the Beginning of the Reign of King George I*, all appearing between 1738 and 1740. In 1790, Robert Robinson published *A History of the Baptists*, a volume he had been commissioned to undertake.[8] These histories were produced at a time when Independents and Presbyterians were identifying themselves as Dissenters by tracing the historical background of Dissent. So Edmund Calamy published *An Abridgement of Mr. Baxter's*

---

7. Dexter, *Congregationalism*; the appendix lists books by year.
8. Ivimey, *English Baptists*, 4:48ff.

History of his Life and Times in 1702. The "abridgement" required two volumes and he published it again in 1713. Daniel Neal took four volumes for *The History of the Puritans, or Protestant Nonconformists* (1732–38). He also republished this in 1754 but in 2 volumes. Samuel Palmer edited and republished Calamy's *Abridgement* as *The Nonconformist's Memorial* in 1775.

Baptist distinctiveness is not to be explained solely in religious terms. Certainly the gulf between Baptists and Paedo-Baptists was, in part, social. While Independents, particularly in urban areas, and Presbyterians more generally found their constituency becoming increasingly middle class, the Baptists seem to have maintained their position among lower class and rural peoples. Their ministers were correspondingly, for the most part, poorly educated.[9] Both Particular and General Baptists resisted the impulse to found their own academies until late in the century. Some few Baptists received education at the various Dissenting academies. However, on the whole they were an uneducated people with an uneducated ministry. Further testimony to the socioeconomic status of the Baptists is given by the Baptist historian W. T. Whitley who discovered only one Baptist who had qualified for an office under the Test and Corporation Acts and his church, said Whitley, "at once dealt with him."[10] This was at a time when occasional conformity had become accepted practice through which those who dissented from the Established Church could nevertheless play a part in English society.

The sectarianism of the Baptists was recognized by other Dissenters. For instance, an anonymous observer of the London scene in 1730, after having described the Presbyterians and Independents, turned to the Baptists. He noted three types of Baptists—Seventh Day, General, and Particular—and various theological orientations among them: "There are Arminians and Socinians, Calvinists and Antinomians, and Ranters and Libertines." There was also, he thought, a "greater disposition to changes and divisions than amongst either of the before-mentioned denominations of Protestant Dissenters." But despite the fact that "Both ministers and people are much divided in their sentiments," the Baptists were still united in sectarian consciousness—it may be allowed plunging under water has a cementing quality." (The Seventh Day Baptists were a small group and in decline.) In 1730 London boasted only two Seventh Day

---

9. Bogue and Bennett, *History of Dissenters*, 3:298; Underwood, *English Baptists*, 126ff., 128ff.

10. Whitley, *English Baptists*, 196.

PART ONE: The British and Dissenting Origins

Baptist Ministers. By contrast there were eight General Baptist and fifteen Particular Baptists. By 1754 the Seventh Day Baptists had apparently died out).[11]

General Baptists

The rigidity of divisions among Baptists, especially between the two major groups, the General and Particular Baptists, is open to question. However, both groups developed internal stabilizing forces which served to distinguish them from one another and to preserve some degree of isolation from the rest of the Dissenters. Such stabilizing forces were less consistently developed or used among the Independents and Presbyterians. The General Baptists were what Underwood calls "connexionalists rather than Independents."[12] After the passage of the toleration act they reinstituted Presbyterian-like ecclesiastical government. Such association was to characterize their corporate life throughout the century.[13] Associations were established on regional and national levels. The formula of unity was

> The General Assembly of Messengers, Elders & Brethren, Representatives of the Several Churches of Baptized Believers, constituted according to Heb. 6, 1, 2, and owning ye doctrine of Universal Redemption now met at Whites Alley May 16–17: 1733.

This formula expressed their doctrine and practice, commitment to universal redemption, and understanding of polity. Among the regional associations were the Western Association, The Midland Association, the Lincoln Association and the Lancashire Association. These met (though there is some question about the latter, in whose records there are gaps) throughout the century. They paralleled the dissenting associations.[14]

The *Minutes* of this "General Assembly," which cover the century provide an illuminating picture of the General Baptists, their struggles for self-definition, their relations with the Particular Baptists and their general decline.

---

11. "An Account of the Presbyterian and Independent Ministers in London about the year 1730," in James, *Litigation*, 703.
12. Underwood, *English Baptists*, 119.
13. Whitley, *Minutes*.
14. Ibid., 2:16.

Their unity, at any rate, was thus established upon a modest amount of theological agreement. One treaty of unity, for instance, drawn up in 1704 included seven points. Of these, two dealt with belief in God and Christ. The rest outlined procedures for association, basically calling for exclusion of controversy and permission of silent dissent. Unity upon fundamentals, the course attempted within Dissent as a whole soon thereafter, proved productive of all manner of theological diversity. By 1731, the General Assembly, reaffirming the formula of unity, agreed "that no preacher or Member of the Churches . . . shall Preach, Write or Urge, in discourse, such controversie about the Doctrine of the Holy Trinity, which shall be unto the Disturbance of the Churches Peace, and naturally hath tendency to cause Divisions and Offences Rom 16, 17." The treaty made provision for declaring disorderly and dealing with accordingly any who so trespassed.[15]

Institutional factors operated to hold the General Baptists together. The ministerial messengers, though nominally delegates, functioned as church officers. They maintained the denominational machinery and assisted the elders and deacons of local churches. Certain distinctive practices such as foot washing, anointing the sick, refraining from eating blood, marrying within the communion (which was encouraged by the General Assembly until 1744) undoubtedly had the effect of maintaining General Baptist Separateness. There was also a General Baptist Fund (created in 1726 in response to exclusiveness on the part of what came to be known as the Particular Baptist Fund) which helped to sustain some of the weaker Churches. In functioned also to unify the General Baptists, but the help was only temporary.

The decay of the General Baptists has been frequently attributed to their Socinianism. Whether or not that was a sufficient explanation, it was early a matter of record that there was decay. (However, in Sussex between 1725 and 1760 almost all the new growth—sixteen registrations of chapels in Lewes Archdeaconry—was General Baptist).[16] The Assembly sent out a Circular Letter in 1724, signifying "the Sevall [sic] Complaints that have been made of the great Decay of Religion & the generall [sic] want there is of a Ministeriall [sic] help in many Churches," and proposed lest "the Cause & Interest of the gospel" be irrecoverably lost, the appointment of fast days, meetings, Scripture reading and instruction of the young in "the

---

15. Whitley, *Minutes*, 2:2, 15.
16. Underwood, *English Baptists*, 127; Caplan, "Sussex Nonconformity," 188ff.

PART ONE: The British and Dissenting Origins

Ministeriall Work," in order that God would send laborers.[17] Their prayers apparently went unanswered. The continued calls for fast days and the appointment of special committees did not prove sufficient to stave off the general erosion of membership or the growth of Socinianism in General Baptist ranks.[18] Separation was not sufficient to exempt the General Baptists from one of the general trends in Dissent, towards rationalism and a certain kind of religious indifference.

Particular Baptists

The Particular Baptist experience differed. Like the Independents they disclaimed "superiority or superintendency over the churches."[19] They could not rely on national organization to maintain separateness and unity. Despite their allegiance to congregational polity, they did feel compelled to create certain structures that served their common interests. In 1704 an attempt was made to found a London Association. By 1714 a Particular Baptist Society was meeting at Hanover Coffeehouse. The year 1717 saw the creation of a Particular Baptist Fund. But in the first two-thirds of the eighteenth-century theology, not structure, kept the particular Baptists united. Cohesion came through allegiance to Calvinism and Calvinism as defined by the Synod of Dort. Under the leadership of John Gill and John Brine and in reaction to the currents of rationalism in Dissent, Particular Baptists became ever more rigidly attached to and defined by their Calvinism.[20] In the theological defenses of Calvinism both Particular Baptist distinctiveness and Dissenting Orthodoxy were served. Other Dissenters, laymen like William Coward, cooperated in this defense of the faith. The Particular Baptists in these efforts to sustain their own unity found themselves the archdefenders of the orthodoxy and very much a part of the second trend in Dissent.

Evangelicalism

The tension between separateness and association is evident finally in Baptist appropriation of evangelicalism. It was well after midcentury when the

---

17. Whitley, *Minutes*, 1:142–43.
18. Ibid., 2:67, 144, 149, 159.
19. Underwood, *English Baptists*, 129.
20. Toon, *Hyper-Calvinism*, 49ff.

Baptists were touched by the evangelical revival. The Methodist-inspired revival of experimental religion spread among the General Baptists in Leicestershire under the leadership of Dan Taylor (1738–1816). In 1770, a New Connexion of General Baptists formed, an orthodox alternative to the then largely Socinian General Baptist associations. Evangelicalism also spread into the Particular Baptist Churches. From this point the organization which is typical of the modern denomination began to appear among the Baptists. Under Taylor, Andrew Fuller, and William Carey, Baptists committed to self-propagation, and propagation of the gospel created academies, annual associations, district conferences, periodical literature and hymnals, Sunday schools, and supportive funds.[21] Evangelically inspired purposiveness and organization then supplanted rigid Calvinism as the central principles of the Orthodox Baptists. In such commitments, they tracked Dissenters equally dedicated to evangelicalism and orthodoxy.

It is interesting to note in this regard that Baptist historians, particularly Whitley and Underwood perceived their history in terms of the norm of evangelism. They faulted early eighteenth-century Baptists for Socinianism and Hyper-Calvinism. Both they regard as antithetical to evangelism. Underwood joined the early Nineteenth-Century Baptist historian Joseph Ivimey in decrying the Hyper-Calvinist commitment to predestination and final perseverance, the "non-invitation, non-application scheme" which "devitalized evangelistic preaching and effort, depriving men of any kind of feeling of responsibility for extending the Kingdom of God."[22] On evangelical purposiveness and organization a distinct Baptist denominationalism was built.

But Baptist separateness was also strengthened by joining in the larger evangelical movement within Dissent and thereby reshaping Dissent as well. Out of a desire for evangelical effectiveness came structures for mission, both at home and abroad. These structures evolved into the unions and missionary societies whose purposes centered in the winning of the lost to Christ and the consolidation of the churches and their institutions.

IRONIES

Ironically, even in their attempts to sustain their distinctiveness and separateness, Baptists typified Dissent. General Baptists engineered separation

21. Underwood, *English Baptists*, 154.

22. Whitley, *British Baptists*; Underwood, *English Baptists*, 134; Ivimey, *English Baptists*, 3:267.

PART ONE: The British and Dissenting Origins

by polity, by elaborating their own church government. Nevertheless, many tracked Dissent's appropriation of liberal views and Enlightenment agendas. They participated in and contributed to the Dissenting trend toward Unitarianism. Eventually some of their cohort—ministers and congregations—embraced Unitarianism. The Particular Baptists strove for theological self-definition. In so doing they became important defenders of Calvinism and played their own role in invigorating Dissenting orthodoxy. Even in their efforts to be separate, then, Baptists were shaped by and shaped larger Dissenting religious patterns.

The irony also worked the other way. When the Baptists (and Independents) became influenced by and part of English evangelicalism, partners in the common evangelical mission to Christianize the world, they created the missionary structures and imbibed the spirit foundational for modern religious distinctiveness—denominationalism. In this way association (with other Protestants) in evangelicalism produced distinctiveness.

Dissenters created their early common organizations—the Happy Union, General Body of Dissenting Ministers of the Three Denomination, Dissenting Deputies—for defensive purposes. So Dissenters sought to safeguard their rights, their properties, and their license to practice the faith under the Act of Toleration. The Dissenting organizations initially looked outward to protect what was inward. By the late eighteenth century, as we note in other chapters, the Dissenting Deputies and outspoken Dissenters went on the offensive—for liberty, toleration (for themselves and others), reform—becoming critics of British policy toward the colonies and eventually champions of the American Revolution. Some of the participants in this Whiggish or liberal campaign led also in the theological transformation of Dissent that produced Unitarianism. In this liberal "offense" General Baptists may have been bit players, but they played. So also Particular Baptists played roles in the "offense" known as evangelicalism and in its primary vocation: missions. Primary actors in the first cause—the Joseph Priestleys, Richard Prices, John Adamses, Thomas Jeffersons—thought theirs would win the nineteenth century. They bet wrong. But at the time, English Presbyterians and General Baptists shared that bet and in the cause. So also the Independents and Particular Baptists in the campaign that would indeed conquer in the nineteenth century. Eighteenth-century Baptists make an interesting study in the tensions between denominational formation and transition and larger association.

4

Denominations, British Radicalism, and the Changing Rationale of Dissent

UNTIL THE EXPLOSION OF nondenominationalism, the emergence of megachurches, new affinities based on these and parachurch connections, and alignments along cultural war lines, denominational identities, loyalties and labels, at least in the U.S., seemed very durable.[1] Presbyterian or Lutheran or Mennonite membership transferred from one generation to the next, much like political commitments. Now these several religious relatively new patterns, the growth of the nonchurched population, the expansion of non-Western religions, and continued switching between and among religious options point, for some interpreters, to an American society in a new, postdenominational phase. In making sense of the atrophying of denominational identity in supposedly postdenominational America, we may find it instructive to revisit a period of predenominationalism. So in this chapter as in this section generally, we explore the time in English religious history when denominational identities vied with the alternative religious self-understanding of Dissenter.

DISSENT AND LIBERTY

The eighteenth-century English Dissenters' involvement in and contribution to the cause of liberty is well established. Possessed of an insecure

1. Greeley, *The Denominational Society*.

PART ONE: The British and Dissenting Origins

toleration, still victimized by the Test and Corporation Acts and subjected to sporadic persecution, the Dissenters fought a century-long campaign for religious and civil liberties.[2] During the course of the campaign the cause of liberty gradually expanded to include liberties of all varieties and liberty for others as well as Dissenters. To Joseph Priestley the dynamics of the generalization of the cause appeared obvious: "So long as we continue Dissenters, it is hardly possible that we should be other than friends to civil liberty, and all the essential interests of our fellow-citizens."[3] By their steadfast advocacy of liberty key leaders among the Dissenters played a role in the rise of British radicalism[4] and in the ongoing shaping of the intellectual radical tradition of Whiggery.[5]

With other true Whigs the Dissenters transmitted the Commonwealth or republican vision adapting it to meet new realities. The Dissenters and the changes in Dissent discussed in this chapter are but part, then, of this larger movement that remained loyal to and propagated the true Whig or Commonwealthman views of James Harrington, Marchmont Nedham, John Milton, Algernon Sidney, Henry Neville, and John Locke. *Liberty,* their watchword, meant individual freedom, freedom of thought especially; religious toleration, the right of resistance to tyrants; parliamentary reform, including a broadened franchise, reallocation of seats in the interest of fairer representation, shorter parliamentary terms and the end of placement; separation of powers; secularization of education; and social transformation. This true Whig ideology inspired the Dissenters' political efforts in their own behalf, in others' behalf and in behalf of the colonies.[6] Their writings and advocacy encouraged their colonial American religious compatriots to adopt and adapt the Commonwealthman vision and so become ideology for the American Revolution and resource for reform and radical agendas.[7]

---

2. Watts, *Dissenters,* 1; Haykin, and Stewart, *Advent of Evangelicalism;* Wolfe, *Evangelical Faith;* Noll et al., *Evangelicalism;* Noll, *Rise of Evangelicalism;* Lincoln, *English Dissent;* Barlow, *Citizenship and Conscience;* Hunt, *Two Early Political Associations;* Henriques, *Religious Toleration.*

3. Priestley, "A Free Address to Protestant Dissenters, As Such, By a Dissenter (1769)," in *Works,* 22:263.

4. Maccoby, *English Radicalism;* Christie, *Wilkes, Wyvill and Reform;* Cone, *English Jacobins;* Brown, *Chathamites;* Halevy, *Philosophical Radicalism.*

5. Robbins, *Eighteenth-Century Commonwealthman.*

6. Bridenbaugh, *Mitre and Sceptre.*

7. Bailyn, *Pamphlets,* 1:viii–ix, 28–29; and Bailyn, *Ideological Origins;* Wood, *Creation;* and Wood, *Empire of Liberty.*

Denominations, British Radicalism, and the Changing Rationale of Dissent

This chapter seeks further explanation for the Dissenters' radical credentials and the existential attachment to the cause of liberty described by Priestley. In particular it will examine the Dissenters' own self-understanding as it was expressed in their explanations of and apologies for their Dissent. It is, then, a study of the area in theology called apologetics and an examination in psychology of the problem of identity. The Dissenters' growing attachment to the cause of liberty, we suggest, brought about and in turn was fostered by a restatement of the rationale for Dissent and a new self-understanding. Thus the Dissenters' contribution to radicalism and reform evolved, at least in part, in the changing meaning they gave to Dissent or Nonconformity. Ideology and identity relate closely and prove to be best understood in their interrelation.

Explaining Dissent or Nonconformity

When eighteenth-century Dissenters sought to explain why they dissented from or refused to conform to the Church of England, they touched on matters of great importance, personal urgency, delicacy, and even danger. They and their Anglican critics might recall a long history which remembered pre-Protestant reformers, Protestantism under Henry VIII, Elizabethan Puritanism, theological wars of the seventeenth century, the killing of the king, persecutions during the Restoration, an enforced uniformity, the Glorious Revolution, and the ecclesiastical and theological differences dividing the Dissenters. Their reasons for being required Dissenters to meet the challenges from Anglicans, to honor their forebears, and to make clear to themselves and others why they continued in their nonconformity.

In explaining their continuation as Presbyterians, Independents (Congregationalists), Baptists, or Quakers, the Dissenters opened old wounds, revived old controversies, and caused the air to be filled once again with the charges of treason and schism. So Edmund Calamy discovered when he published *An Abridgment of Mr. Baxter's History of His Life and Times* in 1702 with a chapter reciting "The Grounds of the Nonconformity of the Ejected Ministers." Even historical reference to the reasons for nonconformity proved highly controversial. Before the air had cleared, numerous attacks on the Abridgement had been published, including three from Benjamin Hoadly (later Bishop), including *Reasonableness of Conformity to the Church of England* (1703) and three from John Ollyffe, including *Defence of Ministerial Conformity* (1703). Calamy answered with a three-volume *Defence of Moderate Nonconformity* (1703–5). Calamy's

PART ONE: The British and Dissenting Origins

Abridgement and the ensuing controversy was an important event for the Dissenters. The comity among Dissenters and Churchmen that had effected the Glorious Revolution and had been expressed in the Act of Toleration had dissolved under Anne. The next decade was marked by the war with France, Tory resurgence, High Church politics, harassment of the Dissenters, and national indecision about the status of Dissent. Similarly, within the community of Dissenters the mutual acceptance and tolerance that had given birth to the ill-fated Happy Union of London Independents and Presbyterians gave way to a more cautious exploration of what it meant to Dissent. At this juncture Calamy's *Abridgement* appeared.

Calamy set his statement of the rationale for Dissent within the context of a life of Richard Baxter, an important link with Puritanism but one markedly Presbyterian and compromising. Calamy, cut of the same cloth, thus narrated the case for eighteenth-century Dissent in terms of Baxter's commitments and agenda—charity, unity, reason, and Scripture being its identifying features. Calamy recognized, to be sure, that a diversity of sentiments had existed within late Puritanism and that among others the grounds of nonconformity differed from those identified with Baxter. He simply set forth "the reasons of those who were the most moderate, and least fond of separation, and which, for the most part, were common to them all."[8] Calamy consecrated this Baxterian foundation for Dissent with an account of the sufferings of the ministers ejected after the Restoration. So he created for Dissent what John Foxe had earlier achieved with his *Book of Martyrs* for English Protestants generally, a pattern of history sanctified by the blood of martyrs.

By grounding the reasons for Dissent or Nonconformity in a history of suffering faithfulness to a grand cause, Calamy transformed criticisms of and objections to Anglicanism and the required conformity into the mandate for a new community, Dissent. The objections to Anglicanism and conformity had become so ritualized that Calamy could outline and number them. First, Dissenters objected to the reordination required by the Act of Uniformity for those not episcopally ordained. Second, they had scruples about the required "unfeigned assent and consent" to everything prescribed by the *Book of Common Prayer* and about subscribing to the proposition that the *Book of Common Prayer* conformed to the Word of God. Calamy rehearsed the list of the Dissenters' objections to the Book of Common Prayer, touching here and elsewhere on episcopal government; convocation; vestments, discipline; faults in liturgy; and such particulars

---

8. Palmer, *Nonconformist's Memorial*, 1:37.

Denominations, British Radicalism, and the Changing Rationale of Dissent

as the use of godparents as sponsors in baptism; the doctrine of real baptismal regeneration; the baptism of only those sponsored; the sign of the cross in baptism; kneeling in communion; the recognition of bishops, priests, and deacons as the three orders in the church; the indiscriminate pronunciation of all communicants as saved; the false rule for Easter; the Apocryphal lessons; mistranslations in the Psalter; and the Athanasian Creed, with its damnations; and the exclusion of the unconfirmed from communion.[9]

Third, Calamy explained, Dissenters could not comply with the oath of canonical obedience and the swearing of subjection to an ordinary. Among the items in the canons objected to were the use of excommunication to enjoin uniformity and regularity, the wearing of the surplice, baptizing of all children presented, the prohibition of private fasts, the claims that convocation was the true Church of England, and the inadequate representation of clergy and lack of representation of laity in convocation. "Another capital reason why these ministers scrupled taking the oath of canonical obedience was, that they found the episcopal government managed by chancellor's courts . . . where laymen exercise authority, by decretive excommunications and absolutions."[10] Fourth, for various reasons they objected to abjuring the Solemn League and Covenant. And fifth, Dissenters perceived in the declaration that resort to arms against the king was unlawful, made in connection with the Oath of Allegiance and Supremacy, potential jeopardy to their rights and liberties as Englishmen. In addition Calamy recited reasons why laymen dissented. Laity dissented believing in the right of laity to select ministers, in objecting to a national establishment, in perceiving a lack of discipline in the Established Church, and in holding important various matters of belief and order.[11]

Having legitimized dissent, Calamy then defended the Dissenters against the charge of schism. Schism according to scripture, he insisted, consisted not in differences of opinion or practice or even in separate worship, but rather in the lack of love and charity. On those grounds, not the Dissenters but the Churchmen proved to be the schismatics. Besides, the Dissenters' separation was involuntary. "They were cast out of the church by her impositions, and excommunicated by her canons . . . if there were a schism, it lay at their door who laid the foundation of it by their impositions." Turning the screw tighter, he insisted that the schismatics were

9. Calamy, *Abridgement*, 1:196–237. Cf. Palmer, *Nonconformist's Memorial*, 1:38–43.
10. Calamy, *Abridgement*, 1:238–53, 253; Palmer, *Nonconformist's Memorial*, 1:47.
11. Calamy, *Abridgement*, 1:258–73.

PART ONE: The British and Dissenting Origins

those who add "other conditions of Church-Communion than Christ hath done." The moderate Dissenters for their part were united to the Church in faith and doctrine and willing to demonstrate their love and charity by occasional communion with her.[12]

New Use for an Old Narrative

Calamy's apology for Dissent struck no new chords. "The Grounds of the Nonconformity" were essentially those of Richard Baxter, echoing Baxter's *Narrative of his Life and Times* and *Nonconformity Stated and Vindicated*, and as such a "moderate" statement of objections to Anglicanism that were as old as Puritanism itself (*The Abolishing of The Book of Common Prayer, by reason of above fifty grosse Corruptions*).[13] And Calamy by no means enumerated all the Puritan objections, intending to state the main reasons for Dissent and not all the corruptions of the *Book of Common Prayer*. Nor did Calamy's defenses against the charge of schism break radically new ground. The Independents and Separatists had long made a specialty of speaking to this point. And the nature of schism had been exhaustively canvassed after the sermon by Edward Stillingfleet, Dean of St. Paul's (later Bishop of Worcester), "The Mischief of Separation," preached in 1680. A nineteenth-century editor commented, "Perhaps no sermon has ever given rise to a controversy in which a greater number of writers has appeared on both sides; and among these were names signally eminent for worth and learning." Twelve for Dissent and five for the Church! Among the most eminent of these exchanges were Richard Baxter (*Answer to Dr. Stillingfleet's Charge of Separation*), John Howe (*A Letter written from the Country to a Person of Quality in the City*), and John Owen (*A Brief Vindication of the Nonconformists from the Charge of Schism*) for Dissent; and for the Church, Stillingfleet and William Sherlock (later Dean of St. Paul's). Owen's work was but one of several of his devoted to the matter of schism. *Of Schism* published in 1657 was the most extensive. The case that he and other Independents had made for Independent congregations then came to serve Dissenters as a whole against the charge of schism.[14]

---

12. Ibid., 1:280–85.

13. Nuttall and Chadwick, *From Uniformity to Unity,* 157–58; Davies, *Worship of the English Puritans*, 58.

14. Goold, *Works of John Owen*, 13:304, in a "Prefatory Note" to Owen's response to Stillingfleet.

While therefore the arguments against Anglicanism and in definition of Nonconformity were very much part of a continuum that ran all the way back to the troubles in Frankfort in the time of Mary, in terms of their context and function they were new. Early Puritan aspirations for a remade Church and redeemed England envisioned such reforms as a realization of the last days of the book of Revelation. The differing Puritan programs and critiques of Anglicanism presumed millenarian outcomes. By the late seventeenth and early eighteenth centuries, however, the Dissenters had disavowed their revolutionary intentions to remake England and repressed the millenarian commitments. They clung to their ecclesiologies and their critiques of Anglicanism as elements of the past vital to their identity as Nonconformists. Repressed were the once millenarian-revolutionary context of this Puritan platform and the instrumental role entertained for it as a means of bringing in the kingdom of God. Calamy and his contemporaries faithfully recorded the grounds of nonconformity as their charter, their constitution, their reason for being. What had been instrumental to the kingdom of God became venerated in its own right.

In testimony to the importance of Calamy's work and the fidelity of his statement of the rationale for Dissent, Dissenters for the next hundred years faithfully rehearsed these grounds of nonconformity and reenacted the great battle against Anglicanism in minor dramas on the eighteenth-century stage. Among the most notable of these performances: James Peirce required three volumes for *A Vindication of the Dissenters* (1717). Samuel Bourn produced *A Vindication of the Principles and Practice of Protestant Dissenters* in 1747. In 1753 Micaiah Towgood published *Dissent from the Church of England Fully Justified*, which was many times republished and acclaimed as the best statement of the rationale for Dissent. Micaiah Towgood insisted that the Dissenters separated themselves from the Church of England only in "that which she separates herself ... from the Church of Christ ... To every impartial judge, our dissent from the Church of England will appear, nothing but a protest ... against A New Edition of Christianity." Joseph Cornish followed with *A Serious and Earnest Address to Protestant Dissenters* in 1772. Robert Robinson, composer of the hymn "Come, Thou Fount of every blessing," published *A Plan of Lectures on the Principles of Nonconformity* in 1778, and by 1797 it had gone through six editions. At the end of the century, David Bogue and James Bennett revisited the grounds for nonconformity in their *History of Dissenters*. They divided "Reasons for Dissent" into two sections, "General Principles on which Dissent is founded," and "Particular Reasons of Dissent." They render both of these in the first person, leading one to assume that the authors are speaking through the ancestors, or that the ancestors are speaking through the authors. The "Particular Reasons" essentially track those outlined by Calamy. The "General Principles" represent a later and more Independent rendition of the principles of the ancestors. They also counter the charge of schism.[15]

The recitation of the objections to Anglicanism had became a common litany, even a liturgy, which Dissenters professed or confessed and which gave definition to the community of Dissent. To be sure, denominational reasons for Dissenting did not completely disappear. Calamy, Peirce, Bourn, Towgood, and Cornish were Presbyterians, and not all Dissenters shared Calamy's and Peirce's sentiments about moderate Nonconformity, or Calamy's justification of occasional conformity, or Calamy's, Peirce's, and Towgood's confidence in Presbyterian ordination, or the liberal theology of Towgood and Cornish. Nor were the clearly Independent principles of Dissent enumerated by Bogue and Bennett entirely shared by Dissenters. But in the main, these defenses reflected a common mind, suggested in the popularity of Baptist Robinson's work and in the commendation of Presbyterian Towgood's work by Bogue and Bennett.[16] The Dissenters defined themselves as they were defined in law and in the eyes of English society, in terms of their repudiation of Anglicanism.

An Unstable Identity?

Such a self-understanding was peculiarly unstable. It was essentially negative (a definition over against the Established Church). It was also historic in character. That is, implicit in Calamy's rendering of the principles of the ejected ministers and made more explicit as the Dissenters came to see Puritanism as history was a sense of distance from one's purpose and principles. In Daniel Neal's *History of the Puritans*, 1517–1688 (1732–38) Dissent separated itself from its past even as it kept it in memory. To balance this negative and historic statement of identity Dissenters required some more positive self- affirmation. For some Dissenters, notably the varieties of Baptists, sectarianism provided positive identity. An observer of Dissent in 1730 noted that the three types of Baptists-Seventh Day, General, and Particular—were divided in theological sentiments: "There are Arminians and Socinians, Calvinists and Antinomians, and Ranters and Libertines."

15. Towgood, *Dissent*, iii–v; Bogue and Bennett, *History of Dissenters*, 1.
16. Bogue and Bennett, *History of Dissenters*, 3:206–7.

Denominations, British Radicalism, and the Changing Rationale of Dissent

But despite the divisions "it may be allowed plunging under water has a cementing quality."[17] To some extent a sectarian self-consciousness persisted among the Independents and to a lesser extent the Presbyterians. But such sectarianism militated against the unity needed for a common defense, the unity felt by Dissenters, the unity expressed in their identity as Dissenters and also in an ideology of unity known variously as Baxterianism, Catholic Christianity, or the Middle Way which stressed oneness, charity, and love among Dissenters.[18]

The instability of the identity as Dissenter, and this tension between identity as Dissenter and the sectarian or denominational identity, drove the Dissenters, already in Calamy's time, into search for a positive statement of their self-understanding. This they found in Whiggery and the cause of liberty. And this gradually emerging Whiggish self-understanding tended to displace both sectarian and the anti-Anglican statements. It remained a central source of identity until the end of the century. Then ideological warfare disturbed Dissenting unity and a denominationalism invigorated by evangelicalism provided new resources for identity. Before then, Dissent united in commitment to liberty.

The Dissenters' commitment to liberty was not without precedents. On liberty of conscience and toleration by the state the Dissenters could look back to certain of their Puritan forebears—the John Miltons and Roger Williamses—for both nonseparating Independency and the radical sects had come to this position.[19] But in many ways the eighteenth-century Dissenters' advocacy of toleration and liberty was quite different. Liberty for Dissenters no longer figured as part of the divine drama for the millennium and the redemption of the world. It became but a human ideal. It could be enjoyed as a civil right, not reserved as a prerogative of the community of saints. It presumed religious pluralism rather than divine election. Dissenters advocated liberty not so much as the obedient response to a sovereign God but as a very human quality. It rested on human ability rather than divine grace.

The place of liberty within religious the array of religious beliefs was new too. So recognized Henry W. Clark a century ago. Toleration came to be championed as the central and defining feature of the Dissenting

---

17. James, *Litigation*, 703.

18. Doddridge, "Christian Candour and Unanimity," *Works*, 3:277; Nuttall, *Philip Doddridge*; Nuttall, "Philip Doddridge"; Nuttall, *Richard Baxter and Philip Doddridge*; Gordon, *Philip Doddridge*.

19. Nuttall, *Visible Saints*, 101–30. Woodhouse, *Puritanism and Liberty*.

PART ONE: The British and Dissenting Origins

community's self-understanding. After the Toleration Act, Congregationalists through their fight for greater toleration and freedom, came to confuse this ideal with their identity. "In reality Independency," he insisted, "was no affair of self- government, or of decisions taken through a majority vote: it was a matter of a united submission to the Spirit of the Church's Head, followed by a united translation and declaration of that Spirit communicated to one and all alike . . . But now, with Congregationalism bent upon that freedom which was democracy's ideal, and with Congregationalism already democratic to the outward eye, the idea that congregationalism stood for the democratic method applied to Church affairs found its chance and slipped quickly and easily in as at an open and unguarded gate."[20] Clark deplored the fact that the Congregationalists themselves and most historians have been so misled as to overlook the significant change and, from his viewpoint, essential prostration of the Congregational ideal. Our argument here represents a broadening of Clark's analysis, insisting that the new ideal came to animate all Dissent and to serve as a source of self-understanding for Dissenters. (In so doing, we also reject, as we elaborate in a later chapter, Clark's characterization of Presbyterianism as being too rigidly attached to Presbyterial polity and too early tainted by heresy.[21]

LIBERTY

What had once been one of the theological affirmations of Independency had become the central feature of the religious experience for a significant portion of Dissent. The clearest statement of the new ideal was made in *The Occasional Papers* published from 1716 to 1719 by Dissenting ministers and dedicated to "the best of Causes; the Cause of Truth, Liberty, and Catholic Christianity."[22] Opposed to persecution, bigotry, partisanship, and sectarianism, these papers championed a moderate Nonconformity whose very essence lay in its espousal of "LIBERTY, within the Bounds of Reason and Religion." One author, summing up his sentiments, identified the faith with the cause of liberty:

> I have exprest my Concern for Religious Liberty, though I have at the same Time guarded against all the Abuses of it. In

---

20. Clark, *English Nonconformity*, 2:127.
21. Ibid., 2:127, 126–29, 131, 138.
22. *Occasional Papers*, 1: Advertisement to Paper 1.

Denominations, British Radicalism, and the Changing Rationale of Dissent

> vindicating this Freedom, I have (in mine own Opinion at least) been contending for the Faith. For if a Man must not judge for himself, he may be a Papist, a Lutheran, a Calvinist, or of what Name and Party he pleases; but he can't be a Christian: Since every Disciple of Christ must have a Reason to give for the Hope that is in Him. He must first be persuaded of the Truth of the Christian Revelation, and then act according to what he (himself, and not Another) apprehends to be the sense of it.[23]

On the basis of a sharp distinction of "Things Sacred and Civil," largely borrowed from Locke, the rejection of the magistrate's authority in all matters of conscience where clear endangerment of the state could not be demonstrated, and affirmation of the ability of individuals to know and choose the truth, these Dissenters professed their faith in liberty.

The self-identification was cautious and tentative and was made with Queen Anne days a very present memory. But by 1730 this memory, the unsuccessful appeals to Parliament to rescind the Test and Corporation Acts, growing interest in liberal theological doctrines, and, perhaps most importantly, the controversy over heresy at Salters' Hall and the specter of creeds imposed by Dissenters on themselves had more firmly wedded at least a significant portion of the Dissenting community to the cause of liberty. Dissent by the 1730s was bent on liberty. It rejected attempts to force subscription. And concerted efforts were made for Parliamentary relief, an association dedicated to that end, the Dissenting Deputies, being formed. Thus when Strickland Gough published anonymously his *Enquiry into the State of the Dissenting Interest*, he spoke the mind of Dissent by affirming: "The fundamental principle of the dissenters is . . . a liberty for every man to form his own sentiments, and to pursue them by all lawful and regular methods; to disclaim the impositions of men, and to worship God according to the dictates of his own conscience."[24]

Gough wrote to determine the reasons for the decay in the Dissenting interest and capitulation of its prominent and educated laity into the Church. His conclusion was most revealing: these lapses occurred because the laity were unaware of the principles of liberty upon which Dissent was based and took their dissent to derive merely from the opposition to the surplice, bowing, and the like as sinful. (Gough later conformed, a reflection perhaps on his attachment to the very Dissenting principle he espoused or was it to the instability of this new ideal?)

23. *Occasional Papers*, 3:3–4.
24. Gough, *Enquiry*, 6, 25–26.

PART ONE: The British and Dissenting Origins

Philip Doddridge responded to Gough and rejected Gough's prescriptions for halting the decline, prescriptions which would have made Dissent a rational religion for the educated and cultured. Doddridge called instead for spiritual, evangelical, and experimental preaching which would move the people's hearts. But he agreed with Gough "that our interest has received great damage from our acting in a manner directly opposite to our principles, by unscriptural impositions, and uncharitable contentions with each other."[25]

Doddridge's agreement with Gough indicates that for the moderate and liberal segments of Dissent a new basis for identity was operative. For many Dissenters, like Doddridge, the commitment to liberty was held in tension with evangelical, sectarian, doctrinal, or anti-Anglican sentiments. Samuel Bourn, whose *A Vindication of the Principles and Practice of Protestant Dissenters* (1747) cited the usual objections to conformity and the Established Church, affirmed the distinguishing characteristic of Protestant Dissenters to be "their declaring for a Scripture Religion and the Rights of Conscience, in Opposition to the Lordship of Man in the Kingdom and Church of Christ, and all their arbitrary Impositions."[26] Similarly Towgood, Cornish, and Bogue and Bennett characterized Dissent negatively by its opposition to the Church of England and positively by its rejection of subscription, its affirmation of religious liberty, and its commitment to the right of private judgment.[27] But in most such statements, clear emphasis was given to Dissent's unique attachment to the cause of liberty.

Even where the old identity formulas were retained, the emphasis had shifted to the new expression of identity. Andrew Kippis writing in 1772 was precise and forthright about the shift in self-understanding. Referring to the Dissenters' Puritan forebears, he affirmed:

> We do not dissent so much as they did, on account of scruples with regard to certain ceremonies, habits, and modes of government and discipline; nor do we dissent solely on account of

---

25. Doddridge, "Free Thoughts on the Most Probable Means of Reviving the Dissenting Interest," in *Works*, 4:202.

26. Bourn, *Vindication*, 2–3.

27. See Towgood, *Dissent from the Church of England*, esp. 8, 21, 109, 116, 133, 266; Joseph Cornish, *Serious and Earnest Address*, esp. 58; and Bogue and Bennett, *History of Dissenters*, 1:287–311. Bogue and Bennett call these "General Principles on which Dissent is founded." The "Particular Reasons of Dissent" are those objections to the Church of England and Conformity already discussed. Here then the tension is made explicit.

some objections which may be urged against the Liturgy and Offices of the church of England. It is true that we have difficulties on these heads ... We found our dissent on what appear to us to be most important general reasons. We dissent, because we deny the right of any body of men, whether civil or ecclesiastical, to impose human tests, creeds, or articles; and because we think it our duty, not to submit to any such authority, but to protest against it, as a violation of our essential liberty to judge and act for ourselves in matters of religion. We dissent, because we apprehend that the church of England, in the requisition of a subscription to her doctrines and ceremonies, claims and exercises a power which we look upon as derogatory to the honour of our great Master, the sole legislator in his own kingdom.[28]

Dissent had become in one sense an end in itself, in that the Dissenters rejected conformity because they stood for liberty in matters of conscience. They Dissented to proclaim their right to dissent. Yet in that affirmation Dissent was once again made instrumental—now not to the kingdom of God but to the cause of liberty.

Dissenters affirmed this new identity and purpose most forcefully in the decade of the 1770s when they again made a concerted effort to gain parliamentary relief from the Test and Subscription Acts, when Dissent rallied to the defense of the colonies, and when Unitarianism became a self-conscious and public movement. Then key Dissenters dedicated themselves and the community of Dissent itself to liberty. They voiced their commitment to liberty. They also threw themselves into activities in the causes of liberty. So Robert Robinson began *A Plan of Lectures on the Principles of Nonconformity: For the Instruction of Catechumens* (1778) with "The doctrine of free religious inquiry stated, explained, and vindicated." So Richard Price in his commentary on the American Revolution, *Observations on the Importance of the American Revolution, and the Means of Making It a Benefit to the World*, spoke of the religion that would most serve America and mankind: a rational and liberal religion supported solely by the light of truth and the individual conscience, free of the tyranny of civil authority, respecting the rights of private judgment, "a religion that the powers of the world know little of, and which will always be best promoted by being left free and open."[29] These Dissenters were Whigs by conviction and their convictions were Whiggish. Liberty was their God, or as they preferred to put it, their God was liberal, benevolent, rational,

28. Kippis, *Vindication*, 25–26.
29. Price, *Observations*, 23, 26, 31, 34, 35.

moral, and trustworthy. They understood their God as they understood themselves, as working for human liberty.

Such a self-understanding was both a product of and an incentive to radical activity. Its raison d'ê'tre lay in the traditions and in the social position of Dissent. Once, however, the Dissenters had come to understand themselves as advocates of "the rights of Men and the privileges of Christians,"[30] to remain consistent with this self-understanding, they threw themselves into fighting for others as well as themselves. Their identity required action in behalf of liberty. The Dissenters identified with the American cause, many identified with the French revolutionaries, and in someone like Priestley they could rise above vital historic antipathies enough to identify with Roman Catholics and support their right claims to religious freedom.

Denominationalism

Dissenting radicalism, the celebrated Nonconformist conscience, then, was, at least in part, the product of a new and Whiggish sense of Dissenting identity which emerged during the eighteenth century. Dissent had come into being in loyalty to Puritan ideals and Puritan objections to Anglicanism. Dissenters continued to rehearse the Puritan apology. But in the course of the century the language used in self-defense, the language of the Toleration Act, of Locke and of Whiggery, came gradually to displace the objections to Anglicanism. Dissenters internalized this language as a self-understanding and thereby transformed the identity of Dissenter. The Dissenting radicalism of the late eighteenth century was then a working out of new roles consistent with the new sense of identity. Yet this new identity was as unstable as the one it had displaced. Despite its rootage in radical Puritanism, the Whiggish sense of identity broke too dramatically with the Christian heritage to satisfy all Dissent. Denominationalism was revived. Thereafter radicalism would be one identity, one role among several, open to Dissenters. Among its institutional expressions? Unitarianism. A denomination.

---

30. Toulmin, *Present and Future State*, 14n.

5

Enlightenment Denominations in Transition

Did the English Presbyterians Become Unitarian?

AMONG THE PROBLEMS POSED to one interested in Unitarianism is to explain why it was that Unitarianism evolved out of Presbyterianism in England while it emerged out of Congregationalism in the United States. The problem of the origins of Unitarianism is in this way fashioned into denominational questions. Why did English Presbyterianism become Unitarian? What explains the appearance of Unitarianism in New England Congregationalism? The purpose of this essay is to examine the denominational understanding of the genesis of English Unitarianism.

In abbreviated form the denominational argument holds that after the passage of the Toleration Act and the closure of any real hope for being comprehended in the established church, and either during the Happy Union with the Congregationalists (1691–1695) or soon afterwards, the English Presbyterians began a slow drift into rational or liberal sentiments. The extent of Presbyterian departure from Calvinism became first apparent in the Salter's Hall controversy (1719). Then, a case of Arianism in Exeter, referred to the London Dissenters meeting at Salters' Hall, disturbed the accord among Dissenters. In the decades after Salters' Hall, Arianism and rationalism spread rapidly among Presbyterians. During this same period Presbyterianism experienced a nationwide decline in numbers. In the final quarter of the century heretical Presbyterians came to avow Unitarianism openly. English Presbyterianism had become Unitarian.

77

PART ONE: The British and Dissenting Origins

The Orthodox Analysis

Some students of English Presbyterianism and English Dissent begin with the assumption that English Presbyterianism became Unitarian. For them the real question is why? The quest for a solution, especially among orthodox historians, employs images which suggest an organic relation between Presbyterianism and Unitarianism. The evolution from Presbyterianism to Unitarianism is typified as a process of decline, decay or dry rot.[1] Some orthodox historians in explaining this decline have resorted to the standard Christian shortcut to analysis, a fall. Thus Thomas M'Crie attributed the eighteenth-century Presbyterians' "descent from the highest Arianism to the lowest Socinianism" to the "religious declension," "spiritual blight," and "doctrinal laxity" which overtook much of Protestant Christianity in the eighteenth century. M'Crie saw the cause of this fall as "the withdrawal of God's Spirit from the churches of the Reformation."[2] It is perhaps understandable that a Calvinist might explain history in such a way. But such explanations are really unsatisfactory. For change is both inexplicable (wrapped in the mysteries of predestination) and its own explanation (the Unitarians fell because they fell; how else could one explain the abandoning of Presbyterianism?).

Other historians, while not fully expunging the theological explanation of history, have undertaken the equally Calvinist task of analyzing the secondary causes. Of these, A. H. Drysdale's analysis in *History of Presbyterians in England* remains important and instructive. By 1720, he suggested, the "Insidious Tendency to Arianism" had infected the Presbyterians, "Philosophic Rationalism" had displaced "Puritan enthusiasm," and "the reign of cold indifferentism to the higher interest of spiritual religion [had] now set in." What had caused this state of affairs? He recognized that the spirit of the times was finally to blame. But the Presbyterians succumbed to it. The Presbyterians became enamored of speculation. They made their religion into intellectual exercises: "Christian doctrine ceased to be held as a living faith or conviction, and degenerated into a mere set of scheme of 'opinions.'" The Presbyterians championed the rights and interests of free inquiry in religion. Unmindful of the consequences, they followed speculation into Arianism and Pelagianism and finally Unitarianism. Then the

---

1. Bogue and Bennett. *History of Dissenters*, 2:343; Drysdale, *Presbyterians*, 549; and Wilson, *Dissenting Churches*, 4:554–55.
2. M'Crie, *English Presbytery*, 297–98.

"icy hand was on its vitals; inner declension was attended with outer decay. Many Presbyterian congregations were dissolved."

Why was it that the Presbyterians were "especially liable to fall victims to any fungus that might alight"? Why was it that the Presbyterians accepted the rational and philosophic spirit and permitted it to define their religious life? What did they possess or lack that the other denominations, the Congregationalists and Baptists, enjoyed? The fall was attributable to the nature of the eighteenth-century Presbyterian denomination. The failure of the Presbyterians to be properly Presbyterian occasioned their downfall. By the strictures of the Toleration Act they had been robbed of the distinctive Presbyterian synodical government upon which order, discipline, and doctrine rested. Without Presbyterian polity and lacking the fixed standards of doctrine that prevailed among the Congregationalists, without these rudders, the Presbyterians were left to shift with the tides. The congregations and ministers were on their own. Moreover, the congregations had no control over the academies in which their ministers were trained. Consequently, persons leaning towards rationalism and latitudinarianism who made themselves tutors were free to guide students. The rational spirit of the age enticed tutors and pupils into deeper and deeper heresy. Not only did Presbyterianism suffer from its few constraints, but also within the congregations the trend was away from order and discipline. Congregations abandoned subscription to confessions and creeds as an infringement of freedom of thought and substituted human authority for the authority of Scripture. Congregational discipline over minister and members deteriorated. By the Toleration Act authority had been taken from the congregations and vested in the minister and in trustees. The latter, thereby made legal owners of Dissenting property, came to constitute a monied and liberal oligarchy that often encouraged defection from rigorous Calvinism. Finally, many congregations (and other Dissenting institutions) were sustained by endowments, an underwriting which allowed the ministers to preach their sentiments unrestrained by the suasion of declining membership. Without the sustaining presbyterial structures the Presbyterians were for the most part lost to heresy.[3]

A twentieth-century explanation of the decline of Presbyterianism into Unitarianism by J. C. Spalding also invokes the structural argument. Employing an understanding of eighteenth-century Presbyterianism similar to Drysdale's, Spalding adopts a comparative approach to the problem. He seeks to determine why the English Presbyterians degenerated into

3. Drysdale, *Presbyterians*, 550, 520, 550, 508, 509–14; James, *Litigation*, 41ff.

PART ONE: The British and Dissenting Origins

Unitarianism while the Congregationalists, the Scottish Presbyterians, and the Anglicans did not. All were subjected to the currents of rationalist thought and religious indifferentism of the eighteenth century. The other communions possessed, he found, features conservative or protective of theological orthodoxy. Among these he enumerated a fixed liturgy, stable form of government, commonly accepted creed, unifying hymnody (the Congregationalists especially) and conservative membership. The eighteenth-century Presbyterians lacked all of these. Accordingly the largely middle-class Presbyterians capitulated to the spirit of rationalism; their "tradition had become rationalism."[4] This structural analysis has much to recommend it. Its description of the decline of Presbyterianism is particularly valuable. Its weakness, aside from its obvious normative and denominational biases, lies in its static conception of institutions and theology. By rejecting with derogatory religious epithets both purposiveness and direction in the abandonment of orthodox tradition and institutions, it fails to accomplish its end—that of explaining why Presbyterianism became Unitarian. We shall also find reason to question its operating assumption, the relation between Presbyterianism and Unitarianism.

A second orthodox analysis reverses the structural analysis and assigns the decline of Presbyterian structures to the prior failure of their religious life. It was classically stated by the eyewitness Walter Wilson: "The result of a departure from the doctrines of the gospel," he insisted, "has been the declension of the Presbyterian interest, and in many places its total extinction. Indeed the name is now retained only by a few Arian congregations which scarcely exist, and are hastening to a dissolution."[5]

An elaboration of this argument, though beset with the same difficulties suggested above, was suggestively stated by H. W. Clark in *A History of English Nonconformity*. Spalding and Drysdale looked on eighteenth-century Presbyterians in terms of the patterns of nineteenth-century and twentieth-century denominationalism; Clark employed a romantic notion really more applicable to the Puritans than to eighteenth-century Nonconformity. He regarded a church idea or ecclesiology as fundamental for Nonconformity as it was for Puritanism. Expressed in its most general form, this church idea or Nonconformist principle, he felt, would hold "that life comes before organization, that the making of a Church can only rightfully proceed from and by the manifestation of inward spiritualities, that all the external arrangements of Church order and discipline and

4. Spalding, "English Presbyterians."
5. Wilson, *Dissenting Churches*, 4:555.

creed must be the spontaneously produced and correspondent issue of vital processes within." The religious life or *Geist* is thus the grounds for not conforming and the source of religious self-understanding and religious organization. Clark contended that after the Toleration Act and under toleration the Dissenters lost the Puritan church idea. From that naturally followed a religious decline. He argued, for instance, that under the Act of Toleration the Congregationalists became intrigued and enticed by the possibilities of toleration into reinterpreting their own distinctive polity in terms of the ideal of toleration. Clark observed:

> In reality Independency was no affair of self-government, or of decisions taken through a majority voice: it was a matter of a united submission to the Spirit of the Church's Head, followed by a united translation and declaration of that Spirit communicated to one and all alike . . . But now, with Congregationalism bent upon that freedom which was democracy's ideal, and with Congregationalism already democratic to the outward eye, the idea that Congregationalism stood for the democratic method applied to Church affairs found its chance . . . [This was] really an intrusion of the Conformist spirit into a Church professedly consecrated to the Nonconformist spirit and idea.

Following this rejection of the true Congregational church idea, Congregationalism fell into heretical doctrines; piety and members declined; and compromises of ecclesiological principles were made in occasional conformity and in association with the Presbyterians and Baptists. The Presbyterians, Clark found, had suffered an even worse fate. They abandoned their peculiar church idea, their principles of presbyterial government, without having found, as did the Congregationalists, a viable if transformed idea to replace it. Thus their loss of Presbyterian ecclesiastical principles led to a total repudiation of Calvinism. From the "slack gripping of the primary church idea" followed "slack gripping of that Calvinistic faith which had put iron into the Church's blood." While the Congregationalists, though stained, nevertheless persevered in the Calvinist way, the Presbyterians, descending from higher to lower religious ideas, were reprobated to Socinianism.[6]

---

6. Clark, *English Nonconformity*, 2:159–60, 127, 152, 197.

PART ONE: The British and Dissenting Origins

The Unitarian Self-Understanding

Unitarians have also argued for an organic relation between English Presbyterianism and Unitarianism. They reject, of course, the image of the fall employed by the orthodox in favor of the biological image of evolution and the Whiggish notion of the travail of liberty. They see Presbyterianism moving "progressively" from Calvinism through Arminianism, through Arianism, to Unitarianism in gradual acceptance of humanitarian principles and the freedom of conscience. A twentieth-century statement of this argument and for long the best study of English Unitarianism is the collaborative effort titled *The English Presbyterians*. The subtitle *From Elizabethan Puritanism to Modern Unitarianism* indicates the general thesis, but they authors carry it through with significant qualifications. They recognize that the Unitarian movement of the late eighteenth century was heir to intellectual ferment that had stirred all Dissent; boasted leadership, membership and chapels from all three Dissenting denominations; and gained immensely from the defection of clergymen of the Church of England. For instance, among the leaders of Unitarianism in the late eighteenth century were Theophilus Lindsey and John Disney who resigned from the Church of England, the General Baptist Joshua Toulmin, the former Independents Joseph Priestley and Thomas Belsham and the Particular Baptist Robert Robinson. The authors establish, furthermore, that during the century the meaning of denominational labels was altered. And they recognize how very fluid Dissent remained through most of the first half of the eighteenth century. They make clear, as well, that the fundamental division in Dissent that gave rise to Unitarianism, that which was precipitated by the Salters' Hall controversy, was not denominational. Despite these qualifications, they find appropriate and meaningful the Presbyterianism-to-Unitarianism scheme. They suggest, these significant qualifications notwithstanding, that a denomination persisted through the century which can be called Presbyterian, and that by century's end it was Unitarian.

The English Presbyterians is but a recent example of literature which advanced the right of the Unitarians to the name Presbyterian. In the nineteenth century such literature played an important apologetic role for Unitarianism, when between the Trinity Act of 1813 (which made Unitarianism legal) and the Dissenters' Chapels Bill of 1844 there was an "Evangelical Declaration of War Against the Unitarians" and attempts through Court and Parliament to take from the Unitarians the properties that had once been orthodox.[7] By the parliamentary action in 1844 the Unitarians were allowed properties for which they could show twenty-five years' possession. An important aspect of the Unitarian argument both in stating their case and in compliance with the 1844 bill was the insistence that Unitarianism was the legal heir to Presbyterianism. The force of the argument rested on the fact of possession. The Unitarians were in possession of many formerly Presbyterian properties. They had to demonstrate the legitimacy of their possession and counter the orthodox contention that the properties and trusts had been established in the interest of orthodoxy. Both sides appealed to the spirit of the ancestors. The Unitarians invoked the open-trust myth, which some later Unitarians even concede as specious. Noting that many of their trust deeds contained no creedal tests, the Unitarians insisted that their Presbyterian ancestors, unlike the Independents, had put their property in open trust in anticipation that their children by the advance of truth and liberty would progress to new opinions.[8] The Unitarians founded in 1834 an "English Presbyterian Society," whose purpose was the vindication of this historical self-understanding and thereby their rightful inheritance of Presbyterian properties. Thus Unitarian denominationalism came to be bound up with claiming its Presbyterian roots and gave that expression in a denominational historiography which linked Presbyterianism and Unitarianism.

Presbyterianism-to-Unitarianism Reconsidered

It might seem folly, given this concert of Unitarian and Orthodox testimony and even the imprimatur of the English Parliament, to assail the Presbyterianism-to-Unitarianism argument. The property issue aside, a strong case for the Presbyterianism-to-Unitarianism scheme can be made. In its favor, in addition to the aforementioned authorities, certain inescapable facts loom. From the late seventeenth century through the eighteenth century there was a high incidence of theological liberalism among those called Presbyterian. Then and thereafter, the name *Presbyterian* became associated with theological liberalism, rationalism, and, for the orthodox, heresy. Quite clearly, in the very late eighteenth century and early nineteenth century many Presbyterian ministers and congregations assumed the name Unitarian. And well into the nineteenth century Unitarians

7. Wilbur, *Unitarianism*, 344–62; Lloyd, *Protestant Dissent*, 83–98; James, *Litigation*.

8. Lloyd, *Protestant Dissent*. 28, 191ff.; Wilbur, *Unitarianism*, 358ff.; James, *Litigation*, 49–60, 65–66, 70–71.

PART ONE: The British and Dissenting Origins

claimed rights and properties which bore evidence of being originally Presbyterian. Thus the association of Unitarianism and Unitarian congregations with the Presbyterian name continued into the nineteenth century and apparently in some instances still continues. Yet the adequacy of the historiography on the premised connection deserves some testing.

One problem in the Presbyterianism-to-Unitarianism scheme lies in the ambiguity of names. The names *Presbyterian* and *Unitarian* in the twentieth century were terms for denominations. When these names (or, for that matter, the word *denomination*) are employed to describe the religious life of the eighteenth century, they suggest to modern readers something comparable to the highly structured and organized modern denomination, self-conscious in its sense of identity and boundaries. The Presbyterianism-to-Unitarianism scheme suggests a denominational continuity, a continuity of the social organization, the self-understanding, the identity of a denomination, from Presbyterianism into Unitarianism. Is this Presbyterianism-to-Unitarianism scheme an entirely apt, useful and accurate account of the demise of 'Calvinistic' Presbyterianism or the rise of Unitarianism? Did Presbyterianism as such, as a denomination in the modern sense of that phenomenon, become Unitarian? Or does it make sense, as we argue also in the next chapter, to see Dissent itself as the better intellectual and social context for the emergence of Unitarianism? That position—that Unitarianism evolved out of Dissent rather than Presbyterianism—Robert Halley advanced in the mid- and Walter Lloyd proposed in the late nineteenth century.

Neither the decline of Presbyterianism nor the existence of ministers and congregations called Presbyterian can be denied. The decline of the Presbyterians is beyond dispute. Surveys of Dissenting congregations were made for the period 1715–1729 by Daniel Neal and John Evans and in 1773 by Josiah Thompson. Drysdale, using these surveys, arrived at these figures:

1689	Presbyterians 500	Independents 250
1715	Essentially the same	
1773	Presbyterians 302	Independents 400[9]

Just as real was the use of the self-designation *Presbyterian*. The London associations were unions of ministers from denominations. The Heads of Agreement and the Common Fund of 1691 brought together

9. Drysdale, *Presbyterians*, 531–32; see chapter appendix (immediately following this chapter).

Presbyterians and Congregationalists. When this Happy Union broke down in 1695, the Congregationalists established a denominational fund: the Congregational Fund. Similarly, the General Body of the Three Denominations, which began informally in 1702, was explicitly composed of Presbyterians, Congregationalists, and Baptists. Its committees were composed of a specified number of members from each denomination. Similarly, analyses of London Dissent made during the eighteenth century employed denominational labels.

THE LONDON SCENE

Why the disquiet about the denominational understanding of the genesis of Unitarianism? In the first place it posits a suspect denominational unity and coherence in a social organization and denominational consistency in ideology. Second, having credited eighteenth-century denominations with an institutional and ideological reality they lacked, it wrongly attributes the proclivity to liberalism solely to the Presbyterians. The clarity even in London is dispelled on close examination. In London, denominational consciousness did exist throughout the eighteenth century, and the denominational identity of ministers and chapels is apparently fairly clear.[10]

On closer scrutiny, however, denominational identity and denominational lines prove to have been tentative and changing. This is most apparent in the frequency with which ministers apparently of one denomination were associated with another. Thomas Ridgely, DD, tutor with Isaac Chauncy in the Congregationalist academy at Moorfields, and minister at the Congregationalist Three Cranes Chapel, was also lecturer at the prominent Presbyterian Old Jewry Chapel. John Evans, assistant to the "bishop" of the Presbyterians, Dr. Daniel Williams, and then minister at the Presbyterian congregation of New-Broad-Street, Petty France, received a call to join his father in ministry to a Congregationalist congregation. Samuel Harvey, assistant from 1722 to 1729 at Presbyterian Poor Jewry Lane, was prevented only by death from becoming minister of the Congregationalist Chapel at Sudbury, Suffolk. John Allen, MD, once minister of the Congregationalist chapel at Shrewsbury, served from 1730 to 1758 as minister of the Presbyterian congregation of New-Broad-Street, Petty France, in London, and thereafter as pastor in a Presbyterian congregation in Worcester. Among other examples is John Fuller, educated at the strictly Calvinist King's Head Academy at Mile-End, who served

10. Wilson, *Dissenting Churches*.

PART ONE: The British and Dissenting Origins

an Independent congregation at Kettering, been for a time a sub-tutor at the Independent academy at Daventry, and became an assistant at Presbyterian Carter-Lane, London, from 1778 to 1783. Samuel Morton Savage studied with the Independent tutor John Eames, served as tutor with Dr. David Jennings in the same academy, later with Abraham Rees and Andrew Kippis in the orthodox Coward's academy of Hoxton, then assisted the Independent Samuel Price, but became afternoon preacher from 1759 to 1766 and Thursday lecturer from 1760 to 1767 in the Presbyterian congregation in Hanover-Street. Finally, Hugh Farmer, immensely popular afternoon preacher at Salters' Hall (Presbyterian) during 1761 to 1762, remained an Independent all his life.[11]

The openness and fluidity of eighteenth-century Dissent was symbolized in the lecture at Salters' Hall, London. Auditors heard from that one pulpit Presbyterians and Congregationalists, Calvinists and Arminians, Arians and Socinians, staunch champions of orthodoxy and subscription like the Independent Thomas Bradbury and rationalists of the stamp of Philip Furneaux, Abraham Rees, and Hugh Worthington. One must conclude with the Unitarian historian Alexander Gordon that the denominational labels of early eighteenth-century Dissent were "little more than nugatory." He continued: "Where they had any real meaning they referred . . . to differences of internal management; the Independents maintaining among themselves the cohesion of autonomous church association, while the Presbyterians were rather in the position of subscribers to a lectureship, leaving matters of business in the hands of a self-elected body of trustees, or a lay committee of management. The denominational names were revived at a later date, and without much reference to the history of congregations, in the interest of that redistribution into doctrinal parties which Doddridge . . . deprecated as a suicidal policy."[12]

If reservations must be made about the nature of denominational unity and coherence in the early eighteenth century, similar reservations must be made about the putative association of the Congregationalists with orthodoxy and of the Presbyterians with liberalism in the early eighteenth century. The crucial division of London Dissent at Salters' Hall was not denominational at all. For the important dispute over subscription of a creed and advice to Exeter, we have this denominational breakdown:[13]

11. Wilson, *Dissenting Churches*, 2:75ff.; 213; 1:84ff.; 2:225–26; 2:173; 1:320ff.; 2:60–61.

12. Gordon, *Philip Doddridge*, 34–35.

13. Bolam et al., *English Presbyterians*, 163n.

	Scot. Pres.	Pres.	Ind.	Gen. Bap.	Part. Bap.	????	Total
Non-subscriber	0	48	8	14	2	1	73
Subscriber	3	27	28	1	14	5	78

In the decades after Salters' Hall, London Dissent divided along ideological lines. Aligning with the three parties—Liberals, Calvinists, and a mediating party that followed in the steps of Richard Baxter and were called Middle Way Men or Baxterians—were individuals from all denominations. The Middle Way was represented by the Presbyterian Edmund Calamy (1671-1732) and the Congregationalist Isaac Watts (1674-1748). The Liberal Party included the Congregationalists Moses Lowman (1680-1752), Nathaniel Lardner (1648-1768), Jeremiah Hunt (1678-1744), Martin Tomkins (d. 1755?), Caleb Fleming (1689-1779), Philip Furneaux (1716-1793), and Hugh Farmer (1714-1787). An observer of the London scene in 1730 found nineteen Presbyterians to be Calvinist, thirteen Presbyterians to be Arminians and twelve to be Middle Way Men. He classified all Independents as Calvinist. Of the Baptists he said: "Both ministers and people are much divided in their sentiments, though it may be allowed plunging under water has a cementing quality." Whether his perception of such a low incidence of heresy among the Independents and such a mild variety among the Presbyterians (Arminianism) is to be ascribed to the author's charity or to misjudgment is not clear. By then the London picture became more murky.[14]

In the 1730s, the prevailing pattern of theological diversity in all the denominations began shifting. The King's Head Society was founded in 1730 as a fund dedicated to the sustenance of Calvinism. Soon thereafter the Congregational Fund made orthodoxy a condition of its support. A new pattern was established in which Congregationalism was associated with Calvinist orthodoxy. In the decades ahead, the orthodox tended to shift to Congregationalism and the rationalists to Presbyterianism. Nathaniel Lardner, for instance, shifted from the Congregationalists to the Presbyterians. Several comments are in order. First, it is important to recognize that the association of Congregationalism with orthodoxy and the defense of orthodoxy was new, established in the 1730s as a consequence of the ideological polarization of Dissent. Secondly, the denominational labels were applied to ideological parties, rather than ideology being assumed by denominational parties. This distinction may seem a fine one,

14. James, *Litigation*, 696-702, 703.

but it is crucial. As we have seen, previous to 1730 the denominational labels were loosely worn. When, however, Dissent divided itself along ideological lines, the denominational labels were applied to the ideological parties (Orthodox and Rationalist or liberal at that stage) and thereafter assumed a new importance. Thirdly, both the new meaning given to denominationalism and the ideological split pertained initially to London.

The Association of Country Dissenters

The history of London Dissent is often related as though it were the history of English Dissent. There is some warrant for this in that events in London and initiatives taken by London Dissenters did have their impact on Dissent as a whole. Also, without explicit "denominational" or theological sanction, London Dissenters did arrogate to themselves the right to represent Dissent as a whole. The access of the London Dissenters to Parliament and Court and the precarious legal state of Dissent made this perhaps inevitable. Further, the Londoners created institutions like the funds and the Dissenting Deputies, and undertook actions in relation to the Corporation and Test Acts, which were for the good of all Dissent. Their representation of Dissent was never formalized and was the source of some discontent.

Unfortunately, the result has been that the denominational and ideological consciousness of London Dissent (which we have seen was more tentative in the early eighteenth century than has sometimes been recognized) is prematurely, and in some cases wrongly, attributed to Dissent as a whole. The attempt at real unification of Dissent is sometimes recounted as though the short-lived Happy Union of London under the Heads of Agreement were the whole story. Actually in the matter of Dissenting cooperation the Londoners needed the instruction. Associations outside London neither began nor ended with the "Heads of Agreement." In Cheshire, Devon (later Somerset, Devon and Dorset), Gloucestershire; and neighboring counties, Lancashire, Essex, Cumberland and Westmoreland, Staffordshire and Worcestershire, Nottinghamshire, and Norfolk and Suffolk, associations continued and in some cases functioned effectively throughout the eighteenth century. Their vitality was by no means uniform, but where they were active these associations provided for interaction of Dissenters between and among the several denominations.

The associations, institutionalized meetings of ministers, made provision for the interests of Dissent. In particular they garnered support for education, weak congregations, underpaid ministers and the indigent. They served as vehicles for communication among Dissenters. They were responsible in some cases for arranging supply-ministers for empty pulpits and for permanent ministers. In a few instances they even attempted the presbyterial goal of governing the life of Dissent through care of candidates for the ministry, supervision of ordination and the exercise of discipline.

The associations gave formal expression to interaction that went on continually among Dissenters. For outside the large urban areas denominational self-consciousness proved a luxury that few could afford, something which had to be purchased at the price of friendships available among fellow Dissenters. Not surprisingly, except in some cases for the Baptists who still dwelt in sectarian isolation, Dissenters during most of the eighteenth century chose unity over denominationalism. Interaction and association took many forms: friendship, correspondence, societies, exchange of pulpits, gatherings, mutual assistance. Ordinations epitomized this interaction as, for instance, in 1757 when three Independents and two Baptists took part in ordaining a William Wells. Newcome Cappe was ordained for ministry to a Presbyterian congregation in a service which included nine ministers. For three of these the denomination is uncertain; several were Independent, several had been educated in an Independent academy but held Presbyterian pulpits, and at least one had held both Presbyterian and Independent pulpits. The pattern of interdenominational relations was represented also in baptisms. Joseph Cappe, Newcome Cappe and Joseph Priestley, who held Presbyterian pulpits, all had children baptized at Call Lane, the Independent chapel in Leeds.

The extensive interaction and association, both formal and informal, among Dissenters give some indication of the fluidity of eighteenth-century Dissent. Such evidence suggests still a type of interchange which broke down but did not finally disassemble denominational identities. In some cases, however, the exigencies of life in eighteenth-century Dissent and the resolve for unity completely eradicated denominational lines. We have already noted the fact, appealed to by nineteenth-century Unitarian apologists, that many chapels founded in the early eighteenth century lacked doctrinal or creedal formulae in their trust deeds.

Similar to this presumption of doctrinal unity operating among early eighteenth-century Dissenters was a presumption of denominational unity. Frequently chapels were created without reference to denomination at all. In many places chapels bore the designation given that in Lewes: "a Place of Religious Worshipp for Protestant Dissenters." Supporting what is

PART ONE: The British and Dissenting Origins

implicit in this, that for most Dissenters their primary self-identification was that of Dissenter (rather than a denominational self-identification), is the fact that for many chapels not so explicitly denominating themselves "Dissenter," the denominational interest is difficult to determine.

Important evidence of Dissenter's primary identity as "Dissenter" in the eighteenth century is suggested in the fact that surveys of Dissent by John Evans for 1715–1729 and by Josiah Thompson for 1773 give figures for the total number of Dissenting congregations and the total number of Baptist congregations. They recognize Baptist sectarian identity but chose not to separate Presbyterian and Independent congregations. Later efforts to derive separate figures for Presbyterians and Independents infer numbers from supposed ratios of the two denominations. Thompson's division might be related to the fact that he was a Baptist and followed the Baptist penchant for dividing Christians into Paedobaptists and Baptists. Also of importance: he did offer a breakdown for the London scene into Presbyterian, Independent and Baptist.[15]

Further indication of the insignificance of denominational labels can be found in trust deeds. The trust deed of Lincoln Chapel conveyed land and cottage to trustees for "that separate congregation or Church of Christ," a typically Independent designation, but the ministers and chapel were known as Presbyterian. At Gainsborough the chapel and endowments were held "for use of the people of Gainsborough of the Presbyterian or Independent persuasion, and their minister." At Framlingham the meeting was "to be freely used and enjoyed as a place for Divine Worship by such Protestants as shall profess themselves to be of the Presbyterian or Congregational persuasion." Deeds for chapels in Hapton, Norfolk, for Angel Street, Worcester, and for Marsh-field, Gloucestershire, also referred to "Presbyterian and Congregational, persuasion. A deed for Wingle Chapel, Lancashire, nicely symbolized the lack of attachment to denominational labels. It spoke of "Presbyterian ministers usually so called in a large sense as comprehending Protestant ministers dissenting from the Church of England."[16]

Care should be taken, no doubt, that the language of trust deeds, reflective of the life of a congregation, the requirements of law and the state of Dissent at one particular point, not be assigned too much positive value in the case against denominationalism in early eighteenth-century Dissent. They have rather a negative value as pointing to the lack of attention

---

15. See the chapter appendix on statistics (immediately after this chapter).
16. James, *Litigation*, 61–62.

to denominational matters. To that extent they contribute to the evidence against the theory that Presbyterianism as such evolved into Unitarianism.

The denominational argument has appealed to chapels' contribution to or being recipient of the Funds, the Common Fund (Presbyterian) and the Congregational Fund, as indication of denominational identity. But it was not uncommon for a chapel to receive grants from both the Common and the Congregational Funds. Joseph Priestley found this to be the case in 1755 at Needham Market. Priestley broke the tie with the Congregational Fund, a step along the way to the founding of Unitarianism.[17] His act recognized the expectations of orthodoxy and the ideological significance of alignment with a fund. Similarly illustrative, James Wood, minister of Weigh-House, Little East-cheap, from 1727 to 1742, soon after assuming office shifted his allegiance and that of his chapel from the Presbyterian Board to the Congregational Fund. Still, both in London and even later outside London the new meaning of the affiliation with a Fund functioned largely within the congregations. Neither strong denominational institutions nor significant denominational consciousness existed in the early and middle decades of eighteenth-century Dissent. The tenuous bond to a Fund, which demanded little in the way of allegiance and offered little in the way of influence, left the congregations largely to themselves.

The extent to which denominational identity derived from congregational and individual self-understanding was graphically illustrated in 1727 when the London Congregationalists attempted to organize for participation in the General Body of the Three Denominations. The gathered ministers could only agree "that every one present who chooses to be reckoned among the congregational ministers, and does not design to vote in and with the body of the Presbyterian or Baptist ministers, be allowed to vote at this meeting."[18] A more negative definition of denominationalism would be difficult to imagine. But even this measure of denominational consciousness was new. In a subsequent meeting it was suggested that subscription to the Savoy Confession should be necessary to be Congregational. However, those opposed to human standards of faith beat down the proposal. The above formula for membership in the Congregational denomination was retained. It called itself, fittingly, "a Third Body." It adopted the ad hoc and informal procedure of accepting new members on the simple basis of recommendation and personal statement.

17. Priestley, *Works*, 1:29.
18. James, *Litigation*, 89.

PART ONE: The British and Dissenting Origins

Unity in Dissent

Positive inducements to unity reinforced reluctance to separate denominationally: common status before the law, common civil disabilities, common peril from High Church Anglicanism, the necessity for unity in defense, the importance of unity for sustenance and an articulated theology of unity. Each of these deserve attention for together they functioned to create the common status of Dissenter and to confer the identity of Dissenter.[19]

The last in particular merits mention for it indicated and produced the salient identity as Dissenter and the dominant self-consciousness of Dissenters as Dissenter. The theology of unity was articulated for Dissent by Richard Baxter (1615–91), and those following him were fittingly known as Baxterians, Middle Way Men, Catholick Christians, or Mere Christians. The most eminent of these were Edmund Calamy, Isaac Watts and Philip Doddridge. During their maturity (roughly from 1700 to 1750) and under their leadership, the Middle Way functioned as a source of unity for Dissent. The Middle Way theology persisted as an ideal for the duration of the century.

The Middle Way was the Dissenting variant of Latitudinarianism. It called for moderation, unity, charity, candor, concord, eclecticism. The Middle Way put deeds over words, charity over creeds and confessions, community over parties, and Scripture over all. The Middle Way raised opposition to partisanship and divisive ideas, issues, actions and formulas to the level of religious imperative. Individuals like Doddridge abhorred bigotry and ignored denominations and parties.[20] Doddridge regretted that "Too many have from their tenderest years been taught to place a part of their religion in the severity with which they censure their brethren, and a peccant humour, so early wrought into the constitution, will not easily be subdued by the most sovereign medicines." Instead he called for a "true Catholicism of temper," which would avoid provocations and uncharitableness, heal wounds, conciliate affections, discover excellencies in others, enlarge the range and diversity of one's acquaintances and re-store the church "to a form more worthy of itself."[21] This

---

19. Richey, "Origins of English Unitarianism."

20. Doddridge, "Christian Candour and Unanimity," in *Works*, 3; Nuttall, *Philip Doddridge*; Nuttall, "Philip Doddridge"; Nuttall, *Richard Baxter and Philip Doddridge*; Gordon, *Philip Doddridge*.

21. Doddridge, "Christian Candour and Unanimity," in *Works*, 3:278–79, 271–72, 277–78.

counsel became a norm for behavior and belief for Dissent in the early eighteenth century. The compliment paid by Dr. Benjamin Grosvenor to a fellow minister, William Harris, invoked this norm: "To me he seemed to be of no party. Men might call him by what name they pleased; he was fond of no denomination but that of a Christian. Truth had him on her side, and he embraced her as heartily as if she brought along with her a dowry of worldly emolument."[22] (Benjamin Grosvenor [1676-1758] was a moderate Calvinist, lecturer at Old Jewery and Salters' Hall and political spokesman for Dissent He contributed to *The Occasional Papers* [1716-1719] and to *The Old Whig* [1735-1738].) Harris served as minister of Poor Jewry Lane from 1698 to 1740.

The unitive ideology and leadership of the Middle Way, successful in over-coming the factionalism of seventeenth Puritanism, achieved unity for Dissent for several decades. However, Dissenting institutions proved inadequate to contain the new factionalism sown in Dissent by the Enlightenment.

Unitarianism Emerges from Dissent

Two statements can now be made. First, under the leadership of the Middle Way Men the Dissenting denominations (Presbyterians and Congregationalists and to a much lesser extent Baptists) gave way as sociological entities to Dissent itself. That is to say, the Middle Way largely achieved its goal of unifying Dissent. The Dissenters became in the early part of the eighteenth century one community, defined in law, sharing common interests and common status. Denominational names were continued in some places. But they were just that, names, denominations. They retained a certain historic significance. They lacked, however, strong correlation with beliefs or institutions. Instead, it was Dissent which provided the ideological and institutional life for the Dissenters. There is, consequently, some real merit in both the structural analysis of Drysdale and Spalding and the ideological argument of Clark. They show that Presbyterian structures disintegrated and that the historic Presbyterian self-understanding dissipated. They fail to appreciate the important Dissenting structures and self-understanding that were inducement to the abandonment of Presbyterianism and its replacement. Presbyterianism is somewhat unfairly charged with being the reason for its own demise. In fact the Middle Way carried on much for which Presbyterianism had stood. These authors also

22. Wilson, *Dissenting Churches*, 1:70.

fail to see what Bolam and others point to in *The English Presbyterians*: that between the Presbyterianism of the seventeenth century and the Unitarianism of the eighteenth lay the community of Dissent. This brings us to the second point.

Second, Unitarianism was the child of early eighteenth-century Dissent, not of Presbyterianism. To be sure, in the ideological polarization of Dissent in the decades after 1730 the Congregational name did become associated with orthodoxy and Presbyterianism with liberalism. But this new meaning of the word "denomination" should not obscure the manner in which Dissent itself nurtured liberalism into Unitarianism. I have already mentioned that the Unitarian movement attracted ministers from all the denominations including some from the established church. Unitarian chapels were also of diverse origins. There were many formerly Presbyterian and General Baptist chapels in the Unitarian fold. There were also Congregational chapels, like those in Gloucester, Allostock and Yarmouth, and chapels with both Presbyterian and Congregational ties, like those of Toxteth, Leicester, and Chester.

Dissenting institutions, in particular the academies, proved determinative in the evolution of Dissent towards Unitarianism. The institutions of Dissent—the academies, the assemblies, the funds and trusts, the Dissenting Deputies and even the chapels—were created to sustain the Dissenting interest and were shaped under the Middle Way leadership so as to minimize or avoid partisan factionalism. Guided by the *moderating spirit* of the Middle Way and alert to the scientific and intellectual advances of the Enlightenment, the academies—as we noted in earlier chapters—gradually, increasingly embraced the *inquiring spirit* of the Age of Reason. And as some Dissenters, searching the Scriptures guided by the light of reason, broke ever more sharply with their Calvinist past, Dissenting institutions provided no stay against the growing heterodox sentiment. Individual chapels were the most conservative institutions, but in many cases the congregation could exercise little control over minister or trustees. The debacle at Salters' Hall, following an equally unsuccessful effort in the Exeter Assembly to deal effectively with the case of Arianism in Exeter, illustrated the powerlessness of assemblies. The creedal requirements, made conditional for support by certain funds, proved significant over time, but which had little power to counteract the growing rationalism that other funds sustained. And of all the institutions of Dissent the academies, the least subject to denominational controls and the most subject to the new currents of thought, had perhaps the most influence in shaping ideas, worldview and ideology. (Two studies of the academies did not attempt denominational classification of the academies. One addressed classification explicitly and insisted that denominational classification of the academies, except in the case of the Baptists, is "doomed to failure." Neither study attributed any significant role to denominational factors in the early history of the academies.[23])

The restraints on the academies were minimal. Without bulwarks against liberal sentiments, the academies and their tutors were left to drift with the breezes of rationalist learning from the Continent, Scotland and England, with the result that the academies tutored Dissent to liberalism. The King's Head Society and the Coward Trust made valiant efforts to stem the tide by making their support conditional upon proof of orthodoxy. Despite such efforts, the Congregational academy in which the strictly orthodox Isaac Chauncy had labored came ultimately into the hands of Abraham Rees and Andrew Kippis, tutors from 1762 to 1785, both markedly heterodox. And in 1789 the Coward Trust saw its tutor in the Daventry Academy repudiate Calvinism, profess Unitarianism and resign.

That Unitarianism was a child of Dissent and not of Presbyterianism is perhaps best illustrated by the case of Doddridge's Academy at Northampton and its successor at Daventry, both nominally Congregationalist. Doddridge, though dedicated to evangelical and spiritual Christian life, sought to instill in his students the love of truth and the spirit of free inquiry. The students were referred to writers on all sides of issues. This enlightened educational philosophy laid the foundation for Unitarianism. Doddridge's academy and its successor at Daventry produced men of both the orthodox and rational persuasions. Together, however, these two academies produced twenty-six rationalist tutors, a significant part of the leadership of rational Dissent, the tutors who carried Dissent from Arminianism into Unitarianism.[24] Among them were Job Orton, John Aikin, Caleb Ashworth and Andrew Kippis (tutors trained by Doddridge), and Joseph Priestley, William Enfield, Hugh Worthington, Timothy Kenrick, and Thomas Belsham (tutors trained at Daventry). These Dissenters, trained in a Congregationalist context, together with clergymen like

---

23. Smith, *Modern Education*, 3; McLachlan, *English Education*; Griffiths, *Religion and Learning*.

24. Smith, *Modern Education*, 147ff.; McLachlan, *English Education*, 149–52; Griffiths, *Religion and Learning*.

PART ONE: The British and Dissenting Origins

Theophilus Lindsey and John Disney from the Church of England, led Dissenters into profession of Unitarianism.

CONCLUSION

Despite the fact, then, that the denominational name "Presbyterian" became associated with Unitarianism, the social and ideological base for Unitarianism lay in the larger community of Dissent, not solely in Presbyterianism. And if one were to examine Dissent further for causes or conditions for Unitarianism, he/she would find not denominational factors but socioeconomic matters like congregational wealth, urban situation, educational level of clergy and congregation to be most intimately related to the emergence of Unitarianism. Therefore the invocation of denominationalism to explain the rise of Unitarianism is not finally edifying.

Chapter Appendix: Congregational Statistics

Drysdale used the Evans and Thompson figures (see above), which combine Independents and Presbyterians. Employing ratios for the denominations used to determine representation in the Dissenting Deputies, he came to the ratios listed. These figures, others argue, should be used with caution. Roger Thomas in "The Evans List: The Hidden Neal List," *Congregational Historical Society Transactions* (Hereafter *CHST*) 19 (1961) 72–74, posits that the composite upon which Drysdale worked was a conflation of surveys of Dissent by John Evans for the Three Denominations and Daniel Neal for the Independents made by Josiah Thompson in 1773. The Thompson List with county-by-county figures of congregations from the Evans List is reproduced in "A View of English Nonconformity in 1773," *CHST*, 5 (1911–1912) 205–22, 261–77 and 372–85.

Uninterpolated the statistics follow:

1715–1716	1,182 congregations of which 283 were Baptist
1773	1,080 congregations of which 374 were Baptist (353 of 1,052 ministers)

B. D. Bebb used these lists and other material to assess the position of Dissent. He found a general decline of Dissent with some significant regional and denominational countertrends.[25] The general decline was also a sub-

25. Bebb, *Nonconformity*, 30–57.

ject of contemporary discussion. Strickland Gough, *Enquiry into the State of the Dissenting Interest* (1730); Philip Doddridge, *Free Thoughts on the Most Probable Means of Reviving the Dissenting Interest* (1730); Nathaniel Neal, *A Free and Serious Remonstrance to Protestant Dissenting Ministers, on Occasion of the Decay of Religion* (1746); and Job Orton, *Letters to Dissenting Ministers* (written in the eighteenth century but published in 1805) all concerned themselves with the decline.

6

From Puritanism to Unitarianism in England

A Study in Candour

ENGLAND GIFTED THE WESTERN world with denominations and denominationalism. It did so as it struggled with the place of diversity and dissent in a society and political order needing unity. The robust confessional identity, missional commitments, and patterns of association often taken to be definitive of denominationalism emerged rather more gradually then sometimes supposed and were not the immediate product of the Glorious Revolution and Acts of Toleration. Indeed, England took the better part of the eighteenth century to perfect the denominational form of the church. The community of Dissent or Nonconformity provided the context within which much of this experimentation went on. And as other chapters in this section as well as this one show, for much of the century the "three old denominations"—Presbyterians, Congregationalists (or Independents), and Baptists—toyed with the notion that their common status as Dissenter or Nonconformist served better to protect and enhance their marginal status than did their separate confessional identity. This chapter explores, as did the last, insights into the nature of denominationalism by charting the emergence within Dissent of the Unitarian denomination.

Unitarian Historiography

The history of English Unitarianism has been written from a variety of perspectives. One standard conception is theological, identifying the heterodox traditions that over several centuries and in various contexts rejected the orthodox doctrine of the Trinity and proclaimed the unity of God.[1] Thereby the defining doctrinal commitments of Unitarianism are given rootage in the Radical Reformation, and distinct phases of the English movement are recognized: Arminian, Arian, Socinian. The insufficiency of a narrative framed only in relation to such a heterodox tradition is suggested by the treatments of Unitarians and of their contributions to English intellectual life rendered by the many students of the English Enlightenment, English church history, and eighteenth-century English radical and reform activity. These histories rightly acknowledge that the individuals, commitments, movements, and ideas that produced Unitarianism also contributed to and drew upon the English Enlightenment. So also these dynamics informed English liberal politics and reform, especially those associated with radical Whiggery. But for the gains from appreciation of the multiform contributions of Unitarianism and proto-Unitarianism, its character as a religious movement can be obscured.

A partial corrective is provided by the histories that find a social basis for Unitarianism in Presbyterianism, from which a significant portion of heterodox leadership and congregations were drawn.[2] The theory purchases simplicity in understanding the social context of Unitarianism at the cost of some of the movement's richness. Despite a certain incidence of Presbyterian properties (chapels and trusts) among those claimed by the Unitarians in the nineteenth century, there is reason to suspect that the scheme Presbyterian-to-Unitarian has served the cause of polemics better than the interests of history. Unitarian membership and leadership came from all three of the so-called old denominations (Presbyterians, Congregationalists, Baptists). Some of its leadership came out of the Established Church. Many of its most prominent leaders were nurtured in the Congregationalist academies of Philip Doddridge and his successors. Further, there is reason to question whether denominations (as we know them today) were significant as social units or means of identity for most of the eighteenth century. My contention is that the denominations and particularly the Presbyterians yielded their place as the primary religious

1. Wilbur, *Unitarianism*.
2. Bolam et al., *English Presbyterians*.

PART ONE: The British and Dissenting Origins

unit and source of identity to Dissent itself. For the better part of the eighteenth century the Nonconformists (excepting some of the Baptists and of course the Quakers) spoke of themselves as Dissenters. (This essay tends to employ *Dissenter* rather than *Nonconformist*—terms both used to identify the Protestant religious movements that did not conform with the Church of England).

Recognizing the social and intellectual base as Dissent or Nonconformity, the larger community of which Presbyterianism was part, facilitates rather than frustrates attention to the other explanatory approaches to Unitarianism.[3] Within Dissent, we would suggest, Enlightenment ideas, preeminently those of John Locke, gradually eroded and displaced the system of orthodoxy and produced that movement which shares the central theological commitment with Unitarians generally. And Dissent incubated reform and radical agendas: the political outworkings of Enlightenment commitments. The transformation of segments of once-Puritan Nonconformity into theological and political radicalism occurred gradually.

Four general phases in the transformation, each marked by a distinctive style of leadership and community self-understanding, have been recognized. In the first phase, terminated by the Act of Toleration, Puritan ideals and leadership were slowly displaced by the passage of time, the failure of comprehension, and the exigencies of conflict and persecution. In the second phase, inauspiciously inaugurated by the short-lived Happy Union of 1691, unity was the counsel for survival, the catholic spirit of Richard Baxter generally prevailed, and the Middle Way Men dedicated to unity in Dissent provided leadership. The third phase saw enmity sowed by an Arian controversy at Salters' Hall gradually divide Dissent into orthodox and liberal wings. A Lockean or Rationalist leadership developed for the latter. And in the final phase, beginning roughly in 1760, the liberal wing of Dissent metamorphosed into Unitarianism under the leadership of Joseph Priestley. Traditionally, these phases have been comprehended under a sequence of theological options: late Puritan orthodoxy, Arminianism, Arianism, and Socinianism. It is the purpose of this chapter to augment those categories with others derived from and also appropriate for understanding the transformation of Dissent into Unitarianism.

---

3. Watts, *Dissenters*, 1; Haykin, and Stewart, *Advent of Evangelicalism;* Wolfe, *Evangelical Faith;* Noll et al., *Evangelicalism;* Noll, *Rise of Evangelicalism;* Lincoln, *English Dissent;* Barlow, *Citizenship and Conscience;* Hunt, *Two Early Political Associations;* Henriques, *Religious Toleration;* Lloyd, *Protestant Dissent;* Halley, *Lancashire.*

The Commitment to Candour

Adequate examination of the rise of Unitarianism requires careful attention to the manner in which the Dissenters through their primary institutions and activities came to appropriate Enlightenment ideas in place of Calvinist orthodoxy as the way of comprehending and interpreting their place within English society. One can observe the dynamics of this transformation by focusing upon a central liberal commitment, an almost universal virtue in eighteenth-century life. Dissenters shared with Englishmen generally a commitment to candour. In the course of the eighteenth century the meaning or emphases of this word underwent a series of changes. These linguistic and value changes were not unique to Dissent. Important if not absolutely unique was the tenacious hold this ideal of candour had on the Dissenting mind. In consequence, the evolution in the meaning of candour illustrates the principal intellectual and emotional postures of the eighteenth-century Dissent under the impact of liberalism and it tracks the transformation of Dissent into Unitarianism.

Employing *candour* as an appropriate historiographical category for exploring the origins of Unitarianism is not exactly a new idea. Very early, indeed almost at the point that Unitarianism emerged as a denomination, its commitment to candour was fingered as a culprit. At the turn of the nineteenth century, David Bogue and James Bennett, in their *History of Dissenters*, observed:

> The misapplication of the word candour was more injurious in its effects on religious sentiments, than can now be well conceived. It was supposed to possess indescribable virtues. Candour was sounded from many a pulpit; and like charity, it was supposed to hide a multitude of sins. An orthodox minister who had candour, was to believe that an arian or socinian was a very good man; and that if he was sincere in his opinions, and not rigid in condemning others, he ought not to be condemned himself. The influence of this idea was exceedingly pernicious; for it led to an indifference with respect to truth and error, which depraved both their sentiments and dispositions, which relaxed the springs of Christian integrity and conduct, and gradually brought them to call good evil and evil good, to put light for darkness and darkness for light. This was another of the arian idols.[4]

---

4. Bogue and Bennett, *History of Dissenters*, 3:384.

PART ONE: The British and Dissenting Origins

Another opponent of the Unitarians, Andrew Fuller, writing in 1793 and responding to Joseph Priestley among others, characterized the Rationalists or Unitarians in relation to their appeal to candour. "It has long been observed," he stated,

> of writers of that stamp, that they exalt what are called the *social virtues*, or those virtues which respect society, to the neglect and often at the expense of others which more immediately respect the God that made us. It is a very common thing for Socinians to make light of religious principle, and to represent it as of little importance to our future well-being. Under the specious name of *liberality of sentiment*, they dispense with that part of the will of God which requires every thought to be in subjection to the obedience of Christ; and, under the guise of *candour and charity*, excuse those who fall under the divine censure.[5]

These orthodox contemporaries of the Unitarians realized that the appeal to candour to be fundamental to the emergence of Unitarianism. Unhappily their acute suggestion as to the importance of candour as an interpretive category has not received extensive attention.[6]

Candour, an eighteenth-century ideal, a principle of the eighteenth-century mind, an accepted grace of polite society, as these opponents of Unitarianism made clear, came to have an ever-increasing significance among certain Dissenters, a significance that bordered on idolatry. This strong commitment to candour by Dissenters helps explain the emergence of English Unitarianism. The change emphases that *candour* underwent serve as a kind of linguistic history of Dissent. Four meanings of *candour* approximated the four above-mentioned distinct phases of Dissenting life. These were candour as: (1) "stainlessness of character; purity, integrity, innocence"; (2) "freedom from malice, favourable disposition, kindliness; sweetness of temper, kindness"; (3) "freedom from mental bias, openness of mind; fairness, impartiality, justice"; and (4) "freedom from reserve in one's statements; openness, frankness, ingenuousness, outspokenness."[7] In abbreviated form candour as purity, kindness, openness of mind, and outspokenness represented respectively the essential character of Dissenting life in its late Puritan, Middle Way, Liberal, and Unitarian phases. In this

---

5. Fuller, *Calvinistic and Socinian Systems* 346 (italics original).

6. But Drysdale, *Presbyterians*, 520; Barlow, *Citizenship and Conscience* and Chaplin, "Theology of Joseph Priestley," employ *candour* in important chapter titles.

7. Murray, *Dictionary on Historical Principles*, definitions 2–5 with 3 and 4 interchanged.

way the category of candour summarizes the development in Dissent from Puritanism to Unitarianism. Our attention here will be on the Middle Way, Liberal, and Unitarian stages when candour did become almost an idol, and when the shift in meanings best illustrates an important transformation that has been represented doctrinally as the shift from Arianism to Unitarianism. Candour did become an idol for the Rational or Liberal Dissenters. They worshipped candour. But it was also in candour that they came to refuse worship to Christ.

Candour as Purity and Kindness

The choice of the first meaning of *candour* as purity to represent Dissent in the late seventeenth century is in a sense arbitrary in that the word itself does not seem to have been popular. Seldom in the eighteen volumes of Milton's *Works* is *candour* employed. In a discussion of the various virtues Milton noted, "Candour is usually spoken of under the general name of charity or love."[8] Milton associated with it equity, moderation, "simplicity, faithfulness, gravity, taciturnity, courteousness, urbanity, freedom of speech and the spirit of admonition." He opposed to candour evil surmising, fault finding, tale bearing, calumny, slander, contumely, litigiousness, flattery, and unmerited praise or blame. It was, however, apparently not a defining category for him. But if the word *candour* was not in vogue, its synonym (the ideal of purity) was very much. From the Puritan agendas and impulses for individual purity, a purified church, and a redeemed nation came their nickname. As Leonard Trinterud insisted, the preoccupation with purity was definitive of Puritanism.[9]

The turmoil that an agenda of purifying and redeeming England produced, and that continued up to the Glorious Revolution, disenchanted the English and even the Puritans with their vision. Puritans and especially the Presbyterians and Congregationalists who pursued purification with politics and violence settled for the sheer survival promised in the Act of Toleration. The exigencies and difficulties of adjustment under continuing social and political disabilities yielded a religious and social self-understanding altered to suit the changed realities. A new vision of the religious life was summarized by a second meaning of the word *candour*: "kindness." The ideal specified the unifying relations Dissenters should maintain with one another. It could also apply to proper attitudes towards

8. Patterson, *John Milton*, 17:311ff.
9. Trinterud, *Elizabethan Puritanism*.

PART ONE: The British and Dissenting Origins

all Christians, especially those in the Established Church who proved more open and friendly.

This new understanding of the religious life served in some ways as a Dissenting version of Anglican Latitudinarianism. It was prophetically stated for Dissent by the eminent Richard Baxter. Baxter established a program for unity in Dissent, a personal religious posture and a style of Dissenting leadership which was to continue well into the eighteenth century. Appropriately those who shared his ideals earned the name Baxterians. They were also called Catholic Christians, mere Christians and Middle Way Men.[10] Baxter, as his eighteenth-century followers saw him, stood for an eclectic theology, religious seriousness, unity among Christians, the Scripture as alone authoritative, concord upon agreement in fundamentals of the Christian faith, opposition to the divisiveness of sects and parties and dislike of creeds and other imposed formulas.[11] Baxterian or Middle Way men counseled a personal religious style of moderation. In the generation after Baxter, his attitudes and agenda found exemplars and Dissenting leaders in Edmund Calamy (1671–1732) of Westminster and Philip Doddridge (1702–1751) of Northampton, especially the latter. Some interpreters insist that the Baxterian or Catholic label should be applied only to Baxter and Doddridge who fully lived up to the ideal. While these two may have most fully exemplified the ideal, they sought nonetheless to make it the standard for Dissent and encouraged other to follow according to individual interpretation and ability.[12] So Doddridge charged an association of ministers meeting in Northampton:

> Let us be greatly upon our guard that we do not condemn our brethren, as having forfeited all title to the name of christians, because their creeds or confessions of faith do not come up to the standard of our own. Yea if it were in a matter which seemed of so great importance as to give us some room to suspect that the mistake were fatal, (which surely nothing can be that does not greatly affect men's temper and conduct towards God, and each other) even that consideration should engage us to gentleness and tenderness, rather than severity to them.

---

10. On the Middle Way Men see Bolam et al., *English Presbyterians*, 134–40, 178, 180, 185–91, 202–3, 207–8; Nuttall, "Philip Doddridge"; *Puritan Spirit*, 146–69; *Philip Doddridge*; and *Richard Baxter and Philip Doddridge*; and Gordon, *Philip Doddridge*.

11. Nuttall, *Richard Baxter and Philip Doddridge*, 2–6; Nuttall, *The Puritan Spirit*, 104ff.

12. Nuttall, *Richard Baxter and Philip Doddridge*, 29 n. 71.

Preaching on Philippians 2:1-2, Doddridge exhorted the ministers in the words of Paul, "be like-minded, having the same love, being of one accord, of one mind." He titled this discourse "Christian Candour and Unanimity." In his advice to the ministers he permitted himself some freedom with the text. He insisted that "common sense will not allow us to understand it as an exhortation, to be entirely of the same opinion in every religious sentiment... For considering the diversity of men's capacities, and opportunities of improvement, that is absolutely impossible." He advocated neither unity nor like-mindedness in doctrine or opinion but unity in love despite differences in opinion and even in practices. Love was the meaning of *candour* for Doddridge. Pride and bigotry and name-calling would be overcome. In love the true unity, unity of spirit, would be achieved. It was the character of the Christian—the love of God, the acceptance of his truth, the obedience to his precepts—which constituted the candour upon which Christian unity could be predicated.[13]

Consistent with this understanding of the Christian faith, Doddridge provided Dissent effective leadership and sought continually to strengthen the community by bringing Nonconformists together in unity. He advocated associations of Dissenters as long as they stopped short of becoming Presbyterian synods. He maintained an important and influential school at Northampton characterized by free and open inquiry of all theological questions and which proved a training ground for both the subsequent liberal and orthodox parties. Doddridge's writings carefully avoided doctrinal controversy and encouraged serious religion in the interest of the revivification of Dissent. So he wrote on *The Rise and Progress of Religion in the Soul* (1745); *Sermons on the Power and Grace of Christ, and on the Evidences of His Glorious Gospel* (1741); *Sermons on Regeneration* (1741); and *The Family Expositor*, a six-volume paraphrase of the New Testament. But above all Doddridge maintained friendly relations with Dissenters of all the various groups and theological positions. He kept up an extensive correspondence. Through his many activities he exercised an informal leadership in Dissent, actively implementing his own prayer that God "would raise up in all the churches a generation of faithful and laborious, serious and spiritual, candid and evangelical ministers."[14]

---

13. Doddridge, *Works*, 3:267, 264, 261ff.

14. "The Temper and Conduct of the Primitive Ministers of the Gospel" (1737) in Doddridge *Works*, 3:189-90. See the already-cited works by Nuttall and particularly "Philip Doddridge."

PART ONE: The British and Dissenting Origins

Doddridge continued to work for unity in Dissent though the seeds of the division in Dissent had been sowed by the Dissent-dividing Salters' Hall Arian controversy of 1719. The Middle Way ideal of candour continued to have its appeal even after a party of Rational Dissent had become a reality and was already tending towards Unitarianism. As late as 1787 John Disney, an important Unitarian spokesman and colleague of Theophilus Lindsey in the first explicitly Unitarian chapel, published *A Friendly Dialogue, between a Common Unitarian Christian, and an Athanasian*. In this the spokesman for Rational Dissent or Unitarianism pled the Middle Way ideal:

> I will never cease to pray to almighty God, that the same love of truth, and the same candid and charitable temper may universally prevail among all the different denominations of christians; being fully persuaded that until we can agree to entertain different opinions upon religious subjects, with perfect harmony and love, we shall never discover the truth, or be capable of receiving it.[15]

The social organization and the religious ideals of Dissent evolved slowly and gradually. The Puritan parties committed to the purification and redemption of England gave way to Dissenting denominations loosely united under the Middle Way leadership and the ideal of candour (as love or kindness). Puritanism's eschatological drive for purity transformed into the Dissenters' essentially bourgeois ideal of charity. The behavior called for was similar, but the context within which the behavior was put and the role that it played changed drastically. The cohesion sought by Middle Way leadership faltered, and this led to gradual polarization along ideological lines. A John Disney could lay claim to the Middle Way understanding of candour even though he operated out of a Rational Dissenter framework, and a Philip Doddridge could be deemed responsible for the Rational Dissenter ideal even though it contravened the ideal for which he stood.

CANDOUR AS OPEN-MINDEDNESS

The responsibility of Doddridge for this second transformation and for the third religious ideal and third meaning of *candour* grew out of his role as tutor. Doddridge's academy at Northampton was but one of a number of Dissenting academies that during the eighteenth century exposed

---

15. Disney, *Friendly Dialogue*, 33.

Dissenting clergy and laity to the new trends in science and philosophy as well as to the classical and Calvinistic studies. Such academies provided Dissenters with the education they could not obtain at Oxford and Cambridge. As one of the major institutions of Dissent and a primary source of religious values, these academies profoundly shaped the community of Dissent and played no small role in the reconception of the religious life along educational lines—thus creating the foundation for Unitarianism. Doddridge carried on the educational style of his own tutor, John Jennings, which Doddridge characterized in this way:

> Mr. Jennings encourages the greatest freedom of enquiry, and always inculcates it as a law, that the scriptures are the only genuine standard of faith. He furnishes us with all kinds of authors upon every subject, without advising us to skip over heretical passages for fear of infection.[16]

Doddridge instilled this spirit of free inquiry into his students. He also trained nine tutors who were so imbued with this spirit as to be called Rational Dissenters. The academy at Daventry carried on the Doddridge tradition and educated seventeen Rationalist tutors among its students. (Many of Doddridge's students including some who became tutors did not become Rationalists. Our interest here is in those that did.) In this way Doddridge who himself held to the ideal of candour as love as the Dissenting way tutored a generation which came to a new understanding of the purpose of Dissent and a new meaning of candour.

The third meaning of candour—open-mindedness, freedom from prejudice—came gradually to characterize Dissent. The gradualness of the change obscured, no doubt, how drastically the Dissenters were departing from their Puritan forefathers. Many indeed dedicated themselves to free enquiry, following in the trajectory from Doddridge, and in so doing implicitly substituted the spirit of the Enlightenment for the Puritan Holy Spirit. The new self-identification and self-understanding is apparent in Edmund Calamy's signature: "Sincere, Disinterested, Universal Admirer and Pursuer of Truth and Love."[17] Here were the synonyms for candour which spelled a new program for Dissent. The Puritan forefathers had esteemed a godly and learned ministry. Their children seemingly now equated *godly* and *learned* and increasingly employed the latter term to denote the Christian life.

---

16. Humphreys, *Philip Doddridge*, 1:155, 198.
17. Calamy, *Thirteen Sermons*, preface.

PART ONE: The British and Dissenting Origins

Heralding this new day was a short-lived Dissenting periodical, the *Occasional Papers* (1716–1719), whose authors were the Dissenting ministers, Benjamin Avery, Benjamin Grosvenor, Simon Browne, Samuel Wright, John Evans, Jabez Earle, Moses Lowman and Nathaniel Lardner. Their purpose was "to do the best Service . . . to the best of Causes; the Cause of Truth, Liberty, and Catholick Christianity." One of the author's wrote:

> In this Design as he knows who are like to be his Enemies, and defies beforehand the narrow-soul'd Bigot, the Party-man, the affected Sectarian, the lewd Profaner of the Name of Free-Thinker; so he promises himself the Assistance of those Gentlemen who shine in the Opposite Character; the Lovers of Truth wherever they can find it, of the Liberties of Mankind and their dear Country, where Truth and Liberty are yet preserved; and of real Goodness, and Religion without Distinction of Parties.

Their ideals and ideas were those of John Locke—liberty and toleration within the bounds of reason and religion, opposition to bigotry and party spirit, distinguishing between the provinces of church and state and a rational religion. Their indebtedness to Locke was expressed in sentiments, analogies, even language: "'Tis not the Diversity of Opinions (that cannot be avoided) but the Refusal of this Liberty to those that are of a different Opinion, (which might have been granted) that has produced all the Bustles and Wars, that have been in the Christian World, upon account of Religion."[18] This particular paper echoed Locke's "A Letter Concerning Toleration" throughout and in places reproduced Locke's phrasing, conceptions and imagery.

The *Occasional Papers* provide evidence of how appropriate to their circumstances the Dissenters found Locke was and how readily they appropriated his thought. However, Locke was one of several intellectual influences on the Dissenters, moving them in a rational direction. The Dissenters or at least the liberal-tending wing thereof were part of the whole tradition of Commonwealthmen from Henry Neville, James Harrington and Algernon Sidney on. They very much admired the Dutch Arminians and the Latitudinarians. Some were influenced by the Cambridge Platonists. And many were impressed by the Scottish philosophers and particularly at this time Francis Hutcheson. From these diverse sources the Dissenters received the banners of free enquiry and private judgment around which at least part of the community of Dissent came to rally.

18. *Occasional Papers*, 1: Advertisement to Paper 1; I, No. 4.

Henry Grove (1684-1738), tutor at Taunton and contributor to the *Spectator*, was one who thought both individuals and Christian societies should have the right of private judgment. "In religion," he proclaimed, "every man hath a natural right to examine and judge for himself; and, in all things not inconsistent with the good of society, to follow that judgment." Moreover, involuntary errors were no grounds for excluding anyone from a congregation. Heresy and division, the grounds for exclusion according to the New Testament, pertained, according to Grove, not to opinions but to bad character.[19]

John Taylor (1694-1761), who disposed of the Calvinist doctrine of original sin in his *Scripture Doctrine of Original Sin* (1740), was of much the same sentiments. An important purveyor of rational doctrines from his pulpit at Norwich, he later became divinity tutor at Warrington Academy. Like Doddridge's, his understanding of theological education invoked the ideal of candour and free inquiry. He charged his students to attend to the evidence of Scripture and to guard against imagination and "ill-grounded conjecture." They were to assent to no idea not appearing to them to be supported by Scripture and to reject any teaching which they might come to find false. He charged them: "keep your mind always open to evidence ... labour to banish from your breast all prejudice, prepossession, and party-zeal ... study to live in peace and love with all your fellow-christians ... and steadily assert for yourself, and freely allow to others, the unalienable rights of judgment and conscience."[20]

Gradually free inquiry came to be seen as one of the purposes of Dissent itself. William Enfield (1741-1797) had been trained at Daventry, the successor to Doddridge's academy, under Dr. Caleb Ashworth. He became rector and tutor in belles-lettres at Warrington Academy and was a contributor to the *Monthly Review*. To him the rationale for Protestant Dissent was bound up with free inquiry. In speaking to ministers gathered for the ordination of John Prior Estlin, he observed:

> We have then, my brethren, two grand objects of attention as Protestant Dissenters, the support of the right of private judgment, and the advancement of moral and religious knowledge in the world. Amidst all the diversity of our opinions on subjects of speculation, these important objects ought to form an inseparable bond of union amongst us, and engage us to a zealous

---

19. "The Terms of Communion," in Grove, *Works*, 4:148, 153, 147, 164, 167, 181.

20. Watson, *Theological Tracts*, 1, quoting the "Preface" to John Taylor's *A Scheme of Scripture-Divinity*.

attention to our common interests, and a warm attachment to each other as brethren.[21]

With this ideal of candour the Rational Dissenters committed themselves to free investigation—free examination of the Scriptures, for instance. They felt confident that from this process truth would emerge, the truth at least for the searching individual. Thus Joseph Priestley found the division of Christians into sects and parties and the diversity of opinion among Christians as tolerable, inevitable and God-willed. For him as for Lessing the pursuit of truth was esteemed:

> Let every question be proposed to the freest examination; and, without indecent passion, or personal animosity, (which are equally a disgrace to us as men, or as Christians), let us weigh the merits of every cause; and, without concealment or reserve, advance every thing that occurs to us in support of our respective opinions. If the pure love of truth influence us, we shall, in this way, much sooner find it. And, especially, being each of us conscious of the uprightness of our own intentions, let us not easily admit a doubt of the sincerity of others.[22]

It was such a Rational Dissenting notion of candour, as open-mindedness and sincerity, of which Bogue and Bennett and Fuller complained. In such a spirit the examination of the orthodox doctrines of anthropology, Christology, regeneration and the Trinity had proceeded, to the detriment of each. Under such an ideal the alien from orthodoxy could operate without challenge. With this understanding Priestley called his congregation at Mill Hill "candid and generous-minded," spoke of their candor and indulgence, and in his address to the congregation in Birmingham on assuming the pastoral office relied on their candour to indulge him in the beliefs in which he might be mistaken. Priestley regarded it as a mark of a Christian to "put the most candid construction upon the conduct of others."[23]

Here was a significant restatement of the religious ideal for Dissent. The Middle Way had professed candor as kindness and love, an ideal of unity for Dissent. This liberal ideal presupposed the mutual acceptance and respect. Now knowledge or truth trumped unity. These liberals continued to respect the Dissenters who loved their religious compatriots,

21. Enfield, *Principles*, 14.

22. Priestley, "Consideration on Differences of Opinion among Christians (1769)," in *Works*, 21:308–9.

23. Priestley, *Works*, 15:7, 9, 44; 22:424.

but they seemed to respect more the Dissenters sincere in their beliefs, who had freely inquired after truth, and who now held to articles of faith by conviction not because of imposed creeds. The style of leadership had been correspondingly altered. It was now, in Calamy's words, the "Sincere, Disinterested, Universal Admirer and Pursuer of Truth and Love" who led and led increasingly only the portion of Dissent which was coming to call itself Rational Dissent.

The Rational Dissenters tried to lay the onus of division on their orthodox brethren. The responsibility was really a shared one. Both the orthodox and the Rational Dissenters had altered the terms of communion. The orthodox in the 1730s were beginning to demand explicit avowal of creeds which had long since become formulas rather than a living faith. The Rationalists had followed the Middle Way in rejecting a creedal basis of unity but had now proceeded beyond the Middle Way to make a dogma of rejecting creeds. As a consequence there were now two Dissents, the orthodox and the Rationalist. On the horizon ahead lay even a third, a new evangelical Dissent whose orthodoxy was revivified by the Wesleyan movement. In the final quarter of the century, the Rationalists whom we are examining had to contend with two opposing parties, the older orthodox and the new evangelicals. The increasing self-consciousness of all parties furthered the division.

Candour as Open Avowal

The person most responsible for eliciting the self-consciousness of the Rational Dissenters and leading Rational Dissent over to Unitarianism was Joseph Priestley. His advocacy in religious, educational, and political arenas, posthumously yielding twenty-five volumes, effected yet another intellectual transformation in Dissent. In one of his early writings he summarized the Rational Dissenting ideal:

> So long as persons are sincere in their profession of any form of religion, they are certainly entitled to our candour and respect. Integrity is the chief excellence of every moral agent, and claims our esteem and veneration, even in a Papist, a Mahometan, or a Heathen. The man who loves and seeks after truth, and who conscientiously obeys it, wherever he but thinks he has found it, will, no doubt, be accepted of God, though his faith should happen to be ever so erroneous, and his practice, founded upon it, ever so absurd. And without the Christian virtues of mutual

PART ONE: The British and Dissenting Origins

> love, candour, and forbearance, the soundest Christian faith will stand for nothing.[24]

On the basis of this belief, really a summary of both the Middle Way and liberal or Rational Dissenting notions, Priestley led the Rational Dissenters to a new religious ideal—the fourth meaning of *candour*—candour as open avowal: the frank, open, even outspoken statement and defense of one's opinions. The shift from candour as free inquiry to candour as open avowal marked a fundamental change in mood, a new mind-set and in some sense a repudiation of the older ideals. The shift marks the change from Rational Dissent to Unitarianism, from recognition of the partiality of all truths to profession of an explicit set of opinions.

Again Bogue and Bennett in History of Dissenters were alive to the way in which Priestley violated "the unholy league" which had existed between truth and error. They spoke of "Socinianism having now dropped the mask of candour, and avowed its hostility to almost all that was dear to thousands." Of Priestley, they affirmed, "With a very just and inviolable attachment to liberty of opinion, unfettered by interference of the civil power, he displayed in advancing life a zeal for his peculiar principles which broke all terms with those who opposed his creed." They continued, "Dr. Priestley's zeal exposed the folly of the orthodox in being induced by the sounds of charity, candour, and forbearance to tolerate fatal errors; for they saw him charitably pronounce believers in the Trinity and deity of Christ tritheists and idolators, candidly avow that unitarians were the only rational dissenters, and with much forbearance express his pity for the ignorance and bigotry of those who adhered to the horrible doctrines of Calvinism." It was as they saw it, "From this time dissenters ceased to seek an equivocal middle course; for they saw that there was no neutral ground for any one to stand upon."[25]

The Unitarian J. P. Estlin, alluding to the two meanings of *candour*, indicated where Unitarianism departed from the older ideal:

> But just and rational sentiments only, on subjects of religion, will not secure us the divine approbation. If we have not the courage and integrity openly to avow our principles, and to bear our hottest testimony to the truth, the extent of our knowledge will serve only as the measure of the depravity of our hearts.[26]

---

24. Priestley, "A Free Address to Protestant Dissenters (1769)," in *Works*, 22:267.
25. Bogue and Bennett, *History of Dissenters*, 4:380–81.
26. Estlin, *Sermons*, 100–101.

Thomas Belsham (1750-1829), an orthodox tutor at Daventry Academy, took such advice seriously, and therefore resigned when he became Unitarian. His candour later gained him the mantle of Unitarian leadership. Speaking with the force of his own example, he gave express formulation to the new mood. At the ordination of Timothy Kenrick he charged the latter: "Be not ashamed of avowing, upon every proper occasion, those principles which you hold to be true and important."²⁷

Of course, a dialectic had existed and continued to exist between investigation and formulation. However, in terms of emphasis—as revealed in the new meaning of *candour*—forthright expression had supplanted the right of free inquiry. The search was over: truth had been found. The Unitarian movement had begun.

Fearless and open avowal was the Unitarian trademark. Unitarians took active part in the intellectual ferment in education, philosophy, science, social reform and political reform. Among the most outspoken defenders of liberty, they became perennial critics of government and society. During the American revolution and in the decades leading up to it, they served as active spokespersons for the American cause and outspoken critics of administration policy. In the decade following the American revolution, the Unitarians led the Dissenters' fight for relief from the Test and Corporation Acts. Early champions of the French Revolution, they suffered in the popular backwash when that followed.

Most characteristically, however, Unitarian candour and open avowal meant open profession of their doctrine and denunciation of Trinitarianism. Belsham captured this central concern of the Unitarian movement in the title and content of a sermon. In 1790 he addressed the supporters of the covertly Unitarian college at Hackney on "The Importance of Truth, and the Duty of Making an Open Profession of It." Belsham observed that "truth is an object of inestimable value, and then insisted, "it is the indispensable duty of all, as far as ability and opportunity permit, to bear testimony to it by diligent inquiry after it, courageous profession of it, faithful adherence to it, and by using every faith and honorable means of promoting its progress in the world."²⁸ In such a spirit Unitarians carried on their research and publications. In that spirit they intrepidly attacked the doctrine of the Trinity and advanced 'the truth' of the proper unity of God.

27. Belsham, "A Charge . . . at the Ordination of the Rev. Timothy Kenrick at Exeter," in Thomas Jervis, *A Sermon Preached* (London, 1785), 18.
28. Belsham, "The Importance of Truth," 9.

PART ONE: The British and Dissenting Origins

Candour drove them naturally into reformation of liturgy and worship as well. Worship was in their view a form of communication in which candour was imperative. Hence Joseph Bretland (1742–1819), Dissenting minister and tutor in Exeter preached to his congregation on "The Necessity and Importance of Forming Right Notions of the Object of Worship."[29] Public worship, Unitarians thought a religious activity whose essence was open avowal. Hence the great pain experienced by Rational Churchmen and Dissenters obliged to use forms which made them profess what they did not believe. The movement for liturgical reform, ongoing since the earliest days of Elizabethan Protestantism gained advocates among the Rationalists or liberals in the eighteenth century in both the Church of England and Dissent. Although all such the experimenters did not gravitate into Unitarianism, the movement was intimately related to Unitarianism. Many of the specific reforms had been urged earlier, some advocated ever since the earliest days of Elizabethan Puritanism. All the reforms were now presented as means of making the Liturgy more acceptable to Rationalists who scrupled Trinitarian doctrine.[30]

As in their tracts, so also in their worship, the Unitarians were in quest of candour. Indeed, as a form of communication among men and between men and God, the Unitarian worship was candour. Candour stood between them and God; candour stood between them and other persons. Candour was their mediator. They needed no other. So churchman Theophilus Lindsey appealed to candour in his *Apology on Resigning the Vicarage of Catterick*.[31] As Bogue and Bennett observed, from the perspective of orthodoxy, candour "was another of the Arian idols."

CONCLUSION

The history of English Unitarianism needs to be written from a variety of perspectives and with attention to the several dynamics that informed the movement. The discussions of the Trinity, the impact of the Enlightenment, liberal political activities, the life of Dissent and the changes in Presbyterianism require attention. But too long neglected has been the inner life of liberalism, what in some Germanic work might be conceived as the quest for human self-consciousness. For Dissent in the process of

---

29. Bretland, *Sermons*, 2:3.

30. Peaston, *Prayer Book Reform*; and Peaston, *Prayer Book Tradition*; and Davies, *Worship and Theology in England*.

31. Lindsey, *Apology*, 192.

transformation into Unitarianism a focus upon candour provides access to that inner life. The successive ideals of purity, kindness, open-mindedness, and open avowal—these successive meanings of *candour*—were for Dissent the virtues of a community becoming liberalized and eventually organized denominationally. Other names, orthodox names—Puritan, Arminian, Arian, Socinian—have been given to the phases in the process of transformation. Such names point to the interplay of liberalism with orthodoxy and to the way in which liberalism was experienced and experienced itself in an orthodox world. But these names point away from the inner life of liberalization and to that extent away from the process of denomination-formation. The commitment to candour was the inner dynamic of that process. Or as the orthodox saw it: "The influence of this idea was exceedingly pernicious."

PART TWO

Perspectives on Denominationalism

7

The Denomination as Institution

THE STUDY OF AMERICAN religious institutions appears to be a battlefield rather than an academic field. For unlike topics or terrain on which scholars from different disciplines work collaboratively, presume one another on common ground, share the tools and the yield, and improve the theory and method in the process, this one is a contested field across which five scholarly units move, sometimes occupying, sometimes skirmishing, seldom working at peacemaking, and virtually never respecting one another's claims.

"The five scholarly claimants are denominational or confessional history; interdisciplinary discussions of voluntary association; organizational studies; the ideal typology of church, denomination, sect, and cult; and studies of religious institutions as ethnic groups. Although these approaches do, at places, draw upon one another, they tend to do so mainly on the empirical level. For theory, and hence in the conceptualization and study of religious institutions, the approaches show little attention to one another. For example, those from both denominational and organizational perspectives reject the church/denomination/sect/cult typology. Yet the typological approach may be the one that beginning students of religion first meet. J. Gordon Melton complained of its normative (rather than objective or descriptive) character and pejorative overtones and of" the lack of consensus among its users. James Beckford concurred.[1] He insists further that the revisions and reformulations indicate basic design problems and divert attention to conceptual issues so as to create a methodological

---

1. Melton and Geisendorfer, *Directory*; Beckford, "Religious Organization."

quagmire. Viewing the typology as distorted by theological and ethical concerns and as anachronistic, he calls for a moratorium on its use.

These criticisms make the point that the study of institutional forms of religion has been fragmented into tunnel-like perspectives. The invitation to the topic beckons the student into one of the several approaches. This chapter seeks to promote scholarly conversation on the topic by highlighting the distinctive contributions and weaknesses of each approach and then suggesting possible lines of convergence.

The five scholarly trends show little sign of convergence and only modest interaction because each claims self-sufficiency. Each trend offers an interpretive model, an internally consistent method (or methods), and a language for analysis. Each boasts a sizable literature, continuing intradisciplinary discussion, and recent sophisticated restatement. The approaches vary in their capacity to analyze and assess what might be termed American organizational culture, with interactions among national bodies, with the distinct levels of organization and the relations among them, with the networks of para-denominational or quasi-denominational associations, with commonalities among national bodies, and with institutional and cultural changes over time. Even in the face of these complexities, however, each model proves sufficient to continue to claim adherents and/or users.

Here we shall briefly review each of the theories of religious institutions in the sequence in which it came to prominence in American religious scholarship; trace its emergence for the insight this provides into both the nature and changes in institutional configurations; exhibit major features of religious institutions as they are brought into relief by the theory; note primary strengths and weaknesses of each and points of convergence or dissonance among the theories; and conclude by pointing toward an evolutionary model of religious institutions that draws on all five theories.

Denominational History

Although scorned by many academic students of religion, denominational history prospers both as a mode of sustaining and renewing the self-consciousness of individual bodies and as a framework for examining religious institutions in general. Denominational studies attract amateur as well as professional historians. They are sustained by the impulse of each judicatorial or organizational level of every religious body to know and legitimize itself. Denominational histories come in every conceivable form from mimeographed handout and Sunday school literature to seminary text, TV docudrama, and university-press monograph. Denominational presses, theological school reviews, and denominational journals churn out focused, regional, biographical, and national items.

Denominational history functions like other popular forms of historical investigation—like genealogy, family narratives, obituaries, and local history—to gather and order the memories and records that belong to the past of institution, individual, or place. Its investigatory procedures do not always please the social scientists. But the latter not infrequently finds themselves dependent upon these often highly self-interested, sometimes normatively governed efforts for data. Further, denominational data lie in the hands and are at the disposal of church officials who may not be eager for sordid details of the institution's life (corruption, scandals, implication in slavery) to be given critical attention. The biased nature of much denominational history writing (especially in the past) and the "interested" charge given (some of) the guardians of church records understandably discourages academic pursuit of denominational history. Particularly university-based scholars have to calculate whether years of research on a confessional body will earn them tenure and promotion or the disdain of their colleagues. Still denominational history will continue to thrive as a means of recovering and ordering the stuff of institutional life. And the data has and can stimulate alternative and more sophisticated analyses of religious institutions, many of which belong to the four other approaches surveyed here but a few of which might be classified as "denominational studies in a new key."

Before reflecting on denominational history as a framework for critical analysis of religious institutions, we should note several characteristics of the approach that are seen most clearly in typical histories, especially the early histories, of single denominations. The very first histories are especially revealing as they typically indicate the presence of denominational consciousness as we have noted in earlier chapters. That is, such historical endeavors indicate that the religious movement which produced this history recognizes itself as conditioned by time and space (that is, as a historical not a transcendent reality), as destined for an earthly future, as related to other institutions (voluntary and governmental), and as surrounded by other religious bodies with equivalent claims to legitimacy. So, for instance, the publication of Thomas Crosby's four volumes, *The History of the English Baptists from the Reformation to the Beginning of the*

PART TWO: Perspectives on Denominationalism

Reign of King George I (1738–40) and of Jesse Lee's *A Short History of the Methodists* (1810) can be read as signs that English Baptists and American Methodists had come to understand themselves in denominational fashion. They betray then, a denominational self-consciousness and should, in my judgment, be classified as denominations.

Some of the peculiarities of denominational history derive from its role in shaping and being shaped by denominational self-consciousness. Denominational history assumes as appropriate, true, and defensible the distinctive aspects of ethos, belief, ethic, ritual, and structure defining the movement. It may, in fact often initially did, take an apologetic or defensive stance. It functions less to persuade outsiders of its truth claims than to address outside criticism in such a way that insiders remain persuaded. In so doing it may account for denominational distinctions by tracing them back into earlier history, perhaps to the period in which sacred texts were delivered. Yet such a longer historical perspective and also the comparative or critical comment on other traditions reinforces rather than abandons the internal analytical stance. Most of the other marks of denominational history follow from its both shaping and being shaped by denominational consciousness.

Denominational history, then, can be idiosyncratic, internal, continuous, self-contained, and developmental. It tends toward the idiosyncratic in that its language of analysis is the denomination's own, often heavily laden with terminology by which the movement established itself on American shores—terminology only marginally adjusted to subsequent dramatic growth, greater complexity, transformed authority systems, and changed relations to society.

While this language functions to reconnect the present-day movement with its origins, it may mask later developments. Its very familiarity to the insider, the reader typically raised on the hymns, the major themes, the unique theological formulations, and other normative characteristics may inhibit this language's value for analytical purposes. For instance, when Baptist language explains Baptist history, insiders sometimes fail to recognize their own patterns as conditioned by and shared with outside religious and nonreligious bodies. And outsiders, if they reflexively discount the imagery, symbols, and beliefs that define the movement, can fail to appreciate the functionality, variety, nuance, and evolving meaning of denominational language. Or privileging and valuing the spiritual vitality, revivalistic dynamism, and organizational strength of a movement in its early phases, both internal critics and social scientists can too readily take cheap shots at the denomination's supposedly secular, present-day bureaucracy. Mishandling a denomination's peculiar language and concerns, either by dismissing or privileging its primitive idiom, dramatically oversimplifies the ways in which the body has come to terms with change.

The fact that denominational history has traditionally been written by and for insiders (until recently mainly clergy at that), sometimes by commission, and has been made available under denominational auspices further reinforced its 'interested' and internal-biased quality. Contemporary practitioners try to eliminate or control the triumphal tone that colored earlier efforts. Although denominational history currently respects standards of historical objectivity, aims at impartiality, and often bends over backward to be self-critical, still the parochial perspective remains.

While the normative, internal quality of denominational history often reinforces the status quo, it has played and continues to play prophetic as well as legitimating roles. Indeed, reformist parties often discover imprisoned in the denominational past just the vision to which they would move. And schisms typically foster competition between mother and daughter churches to claim the record. Dramatic instances can be found in early historical accounts produced by Old and New School Presbyterians and by Northern and Southern Methodists after their respective divisions. Other schisms produced similarly 'interested' accounts on both sides.

Like Whiggish history, denominational history is presentistic in that the boundaries and constituencies of the denomination as they exist at the point of writing shape the conceptualization of history itself. The past is ordered so as to establish a continuity of denominational self-consciousness between the present denominational configurations and the accepted points of origin. 'The denominational histories of Methodism written before and after the merger of the Methodist church with the evangelical and United Brethren illustrate this reshaping of the past. Historians revised the Methodist past so as to write the Brethren into the narrative (see, for instance, our own effort, *The Methodist Experience in America: A History*). Although it is not uncommon for the largest or dominant body in a family of denominations to provide in its denominational history some attention to smaller bodies, the dominant body is still treated as self-contained. While denominational historians carefully chart change, they assume a continuity of denominational identity. The historiographical approach, then, is continuous and developmental. Even major schisms or divisions do not part the fabric of the movement but only tear away the fringe.

PART TWO: Perspectives on Denominationalism

As our discussion of other approaches will suggest, this tunnel view of history rather severely distorts the record. It minimizes discontinuities within religious traditions. It also minimizes continuities with other religious traditions and with American culture. On the other hand, for certain phases in the life of many movements—sectarian ethnic, or confessional periods—when interaction with the outside world was minimized, the introspection of denominational history has a definite but unintended utility. Then in one of its most distinctive contributions to the study of religious institutions, it exemplifies important aspects of denominational consciousness at those crucial periods in the life of the body. Denominational history then serves—perhaps best serves—as primary rather than secondary resource. It becomes data for other assessments of the movement. Often the initial assessment of a religious movement, denominational history provided one of the earliest, nontheological modes for analyzing American religious institutions in general.

So also efforts to portray the array of denominations and to sketch major moments in their history functioned as among the earliest histories of American religion. From Thomas Branagan's *A Concise View of the Principal Religious Denominations in the United States of America* (1811) through Daniel Rupp's *He Pasa Ekklesia: An Original History of the Religious Denomination at Present Existing in the United States* (1844), Peter Gorrie's *The Churches and Sects of the United States* (1850), and the thirteen-volume American Church History Series edited by Philip Schaff (1893–1897), down to Arthur Piepkorn's four-volume *Profiles in Belief: The Religious Bodies of the United States and Canada* (1977–1979) and J. Gordon Melton's two volumes, *The Encyclopedia of American Religion* (1978), Americans have surveyed religious institutions by proceeding from one national body to another. Early ventures such as Rupp's and Schaff's simply commissioned and incorporated accounts by eminent denominational spokespersons. Recent interpreters tend to content themselves with advisers from the several traditions. The important point is that like individual denominational histories, such aggregate efforts rely upon the conceptual systems generated by the bodies studied. This means that religious institutions are not so much brought within a single framework as they are juxtaposed.

To be sure, from looking at the collectivity of denominations certain important issues surface and certain findings result. Many of these were cogently stated by Melton.[2] How are religious institutions to be analyzed? Are they to be brought within some one controlling paradigm, dissected for comparison of internal characteristics, arranged in several types or classifications? Melton insists that an analytic scheme must be "empirically based," attentive to the variety of religions forms, productive of "meaningful data," and constructed in terms of "the group in itself." He posits that the shaping characteristics, "life style," "thought world," and "heritage," permit such a meaningful classification. Rejecting the church/denomination/sect/cult typology, he instead proposes the phrase "primary religious group" to cover all "associations which seek the primary religious allegiance of . . . members." "Secondary" refers to service, supplementary, or subsidiary agencies, and "tertiary" to "groups of groups." On the basis of these considerations he classifies primary groups into those persistent, largely endogamous but evolving aggregations termed "families." In some, like the Lutheran-liturgical family, heritage distinguishes. Life-style and/or religious experience mark Communal, Holiness-Pentecostal, and Psychic families. Thought-world identifies Protestants, Adventists, and Fundamentalists. Other families include Liberal, Mormon, Independent Fundamentalist, European Free Church, New Thought, Magical, and Non-Christian. Such classifications are quite common. For analogous schemes, based respectively on historical and historical-theological considerations, see below and the several volumes by Arthur Piepkorn.[3]

Among the chief virtues of this scheme, as Melton notes, is its elasticity. First, the classification is indeed open and developmental. Additional families can be readily added as they emerge on the American religious scene. In the event of major ecumenical ventures or interfamily "marriages" the scheme alters readily to fit the new pattern. It is really a classification, not a typology. Second, the notion of family permits the identification of the dominant member(s) whose size, influence, and priority establish familial image and self-image. That dominant role may shift, as has occurred within the Baptist fold with the growth to national prominence of the Southern Baptist Convention and dwindling of the American Baptists. Third, Melton recognizes an American religious establishment in which he places ten of the families. These considerations point to the value of the denominational-history approach, its continuing popularity, and its attractiveness to historians. It surveys the religious landscape, performing

2. Melton and Geisendorfer, *Directory*.
3. Piepkorn, *Profiles*.

what Martin Marty years ago termed "mapping."[4] It is geographic rather than geologic, showing interest in underlying features of the religious terrain only as they affect life on the surface. In so doing, it evidences history's sense of obligation to the topography of human experience.

Religious-studies and sociology researchers might well be appalled that Melton would gather the major world religions under a single, nonstablishment category of Classical Non-Christian Family. Yet his point is that whatever schemes may be appropriate to analysis of these religions in other contexts, their institutional life in the United States should be portrayed in appositional terms. Some bodies enjoy preeminence and some marginal status. Institutions reflect the religious power realities. However, denominational history is only one way of analyzing this dimension of religious institutionalization. Like diary or autobiography for the biographer, denominational history functions for the student of religious organization as a vital entrée to the interior world of religious groups. Whether it is a sufficient resource, we can better say after examination of other approaches.

A Study in Voluntarism

The treatment of religious institutions—from congregations and societies through denominational and interdenominational associations—as instances of the voluntary principle is, in one sense, coeval with American political consciousness. John Locke's definition of the church as a voluntary society, the reinforcement of this definition through the liberal or British Commonwealth tradition, which in recent years has been conceded as of decisive importance in shaping American political thought (Edmund Burke recognized this "dissidence of dissent" in the Revolutionary cause), its prominence in the political discourse surrounding the Constitution, and its employment as analytical tool by Alexis de Tocqueville have made voluntarism a central precept in American reflection on religious institutions and their relation to public order. Therefore, this conception has been of a piece with other aspects of American pluralism and decentralism—laissez-faire, localism, provincialism, states' rights, agrarianism, individualism.

In the nineteenth century, European visitors and spokespersons for Protestantism acclaimed the voluntary principle as the grand point of distinction for the American church. In fact, in explaining this distinguishing

4. Marty, *Nation*.

mark of American institutions, American apologists gave the concept formal analytical significance. Notably Robert Baird in *Religion in America* (1844) and Philip Schaff in *America* (1855), who wrote for Europeans, made the voluntary principle the very essence of American religion and the organizing principle of its history. Embraced by interpreters and practitioners (particularly Baptists, who proclaimed it their own), voluntarism has been featured as the American institutional principle. Twentieth-century publications exemplifying this principle include James Gustafson, Milton Powell, J. Roland Pennock/John Chapman, and Constance Smith/Anne Freedman. The monumental contributions of James Luther Adams and Winthrop Hudson to the study of voluntary associations have been celebrated and itemized in festschrifts dedicated to them and well documented by their own many publications.[5] The centrality of voluntarism to the Republican Party, symbolized in and hallowed by the memory of Ronald Reagan's presidency, should suggest both its salience in American ideology and something of its prospects for the future.

It is, in part, the longevity and vigor of this tradition that argue for the distinction of voluntarism as an approach in its own right. Some, however, would relegate the concept of voluntary association to a subcategory, subsuming voluntarism (and the study of American religion) under organizational studies. For two reasons we prefer to make voluntarism a separate theoretical option. First, the concept and topic are by no means the property of sociologists who study organization. Political scientists, social ethicists, and historians have used, and continue to use, this rubric. Their contributions to our understanding of religious institutions are not well comprehended under organizational studies. In fact, they tend to be simply ignored. Second, many who favor this rubric function at one level or another with a pluralist understanding—of truth, of politics, of society, of religion. To recognize the study of voluntarism as a distinct approach gives such visions due consideration.

One fruit of this pluralist perspective is, ironically, a kind of monism. Its advocates see Judaism and Catholicism as well as Protestantism, episcopal and presbyterian patterns as well as congregational, and bodies of' European and Asian as well as British origin adopting a common voluntaristic form. That is, so the theory goes, the American religious environment fosters institutional convergence. 'The realities of the American scene—religious freedom, separation of church and state, pluralism—condition the nature of membership, resource mechanisms,

---

5. For literature, see Richey, "Institutional Forms," 49.

authority systems, structure, internal dynamics, purpose, ethos, and leadership patterns. Some who discern the increasing uniformity of religious institutions worry that traditions, orthodoxies, pieties, and polities have been compromised. The fact that this uniformity extends beyond religion and typifies voluntary association in general increases that worry. In the individual act of joining and supporting, in the configurations of local gatherings, in the regional structures and national offices, religious patterns resemble those of the March of Dimes, the Odd Fellows, or the PTA. And societal function is assessed, as well, in similar terms. The presumption that democratic societies depend upon (indeed, must have) voluntary associations has led to concerns when joining and participating in voluntaristic activities seems to wane.[6] Frequently cited sociopolitical functions include providing smaller belonging units that mediate between citizen and centralized state or mass society; training in self-government, citizenship, and democratic values; initiating improvements in and conserving the overall quality of life; serving as basis of or reinforcement for law, order, social cohesion; shaping personal identity; and fostering communication, innovation, and planning.

Several significant aspects of religious institutions and of this approach surface in this itemization. First, as opposed to denominational history, which makes the national organization primary, this approach regards the individual act of consent and the local body that elicits that consent as the foundation of religious institutions and indeed religious life. Consent establishes religious institutions. Hence voluntarism means the freedom to join or not but also the explicit *willing* that creates institutions in the first place.

Second, institutions are stamped in subtle but important ways by consent. Consensual exigencies "distort" authority, politics, and structure. The degree to which this has occurred is a matter of some dispute. Gibson Winter once argued convincingly that the actual differences are of degree rather than kind and located religious systems on a spectrum with Roman Catholicism on the right, Protestantism in the middle, and Judaism on the left.[7] Institutional convergence, then, is partially moderated, partially obscured by polities that formally locate authority in clerical, centralized, or hierarchical fashion. Nevertheless, the prevalence of the voluntary principle and its relation to the democratic ethos of American society put great pressure on institutions, their authority structures, and their sources

---

6. Putnam, *Bowling Alone*.
7. Winter, *Religious Identity*.

The Denomination as Institution

of legitimacy. Typically, though, religious bodies have found ways of accommodating the right of consent; even those with clerical, centralized, or hierarchical authority have succeeded. The forms of that accommodation, though, have varied.

The Southern Baptist Convention has a well-earned reputation for congregationalism and individualism, is zealous for lay prerogatives as exercised by deacons, and in the past kept the barriers into ministry low, yet can lodge quite formidable power in pastors. Presbyterians, on he other hand, whose successive levels of church courts, high barriers to ordination, and framework of laws suggest more aristocratic patterns, balance structural hierarchy by including laity at every level and by carefully circumscribing clerical authority. Strains of black and white Methodism, at least in the past, vested considerable power and prerogative in episcopacy and in clergy-only conferences but fostered lay activism and preached a very empowering, free-will gospel. The Episcopal Church, in a sense, resolved the issue in the seventeenth century by learning to live with powerful lay vestries. Roman Catholicism has certainly formalized consensual practices since Vatican II (1962–1965), but, Protestant impressions to the contrary, earlier found quite subtle ways of establishing consent without altering church law, particularly by legitimating various languages and cultures. Judaism, at least in the estimation of Joseph Blau, has come to embody American institutional culture in quite striking ways. Blau proposed four terms, all consensual marks, to characterize both American religion in general and American Judaism—voluntarism, pluralism, Protestantism, and moralism.[8]

Many immigrant religious communities have felt the consensual pressures of voluntarism. That dynamic in turn thrusts itself into self-perception and historical reflection. Many histories of immigrant religious bodies make Americanization the central dynamic. The inner meaning of institutional life became progressive democratization. To Americanize meant to yield increasingly to consensualism. But does this historical commonplace exhaust the nature of consent and the meaning of America?

To illustrate, in the Delaware Valley, where toleration and pluralism prevailed, the initial phase of eighteenth-century denominational development increased authority, reversing more democratic tendencies of the European sending churches [9] Comparable patterns occurred in the same period in New England Puritanism. Furthermore, as we shall see, the

8. Blau, *Judaism*.
9. Butler, *Awash*.

organizational revolution in the late nineteenth and early twentieth centuries created powerful centralized bureaucracies in many communions. Was democratization confined to the intervening period? Was it illusory? Did it represent a nineteenth-century aberration? Not really. The force of these several apparent countertrends derives from an expectation, a highly normative, progressive conception of Americanization that is itself problematic. The historical assumption that European hierarchy (little effort has been made to fit African or Asian traditions into the pattern) gave way to American democracy fails to recognize that both forms of authority and the types of consent appropriate to them are quite diverse. Max Weber distinguished three bases of authority—tradition, legal or bureaucratic framework, and charisma of the leader. Any of these (traditional, legal, charismatic) might be related to factors having to do with its exercise—whether authority was lay or clerical, centralized or decentralized, hierarchical or not. Quite complicated combinations have existed, as some of the illustrations cited above should suggest.

First, both the historical arguments positing a one-directional flow from hierarchy to freedom and revisionist discoveries of a contrary pattern of increased hierarchy fail to discriminate expressions of authority. Second, both the traditional and revisionist readings assume authority and consent to be mutually exclusive. However, the Anglo-American fear that authority always seeks to encroach on liberty, which underlies the historiography of Americanization, does injustice to the relation of consent and authority. They prove to have been interdependent. Religious groups seemed to have served a vital society-building role in providing through their authority a basis for order, community, justice, and culture. Consent to that authority effectively established the new society. Once established, that authority was indeed pressed to retain consent and forced over time to accommodate new consensual patterns. Yet at all times, the two required one another. Finally, the conception of Americanization in the revisionist formula is as simplistic as the notion of authority and as problematic as the purported movement from order to freedom. Quite simply it makes Anglo-Saxon Protestant evangelicalism the *telos* of American history and presumes that assimilation to that religio-cultural pattern is normative. While that perception was sufficiently vivid in both Anglo-Saxon and immigrant culture for it to be given some historical credence, we still need to be careful not to impose that reading where nonexistent. In short, we should be wary of simplistic statements about the nature of consent and about the direction of the historical process.

Third, because persons join freely and because they consent by their joining to that for which the institution stands, the voluntary associations of American religion have been defined by their purposes. That is especially striking in the nineteenth-century voluntary societies and evangelical denominations that tended to be single minded in their endeavor to stamp locality, nation, and world with a revivalist imprint. They were, as Robert Handy and others have shown, intent upon building Christian culture. Handy makes patent that changes in purpose—mainstream Protestants in the early nineteenth century sought a Christian culture as a "means"; the late nineteenth century accepted it as an "end"; in the twentieth century the ideal collapsed altogether—had dramatic impact upon religious institutions.[10] In a sense, mainstream Protestant bodies lost their primary reason for being. For good or ill, these denominations had over the years gathered unto themselves other purposes and hence have survived the loss of that overarching goal. Ironically, the recent growth of evangelical bodies demonstrates that purposiveness is highly functional and even that the purpose disavowed by mainstream Protestantism—Christianizing nation and world—remains highly efficacious as a recruitment device whatever its plausibility for world history.

The salience of purpose has made religious institutions highly brittle, unyielding, and schism-prone. Congregation, mission society, denomination, and cooperative agency could, like the railroads, build incredible steam for motion along a single set of rails. So they fired up groups of individuals, committing themselves like a machine to run a specific track and consenting to a common, overriding purpose. To reorient or divert them to another purpose threatened their consensual basis, particularly when the new issue was as divisive as antislavery (for the nineteenth century) or gay rights (for the twenty-first).

Fourth, because consent has to be continually reestablished around the purpose or purposes of the voluntary association, religious institutions demand considerable political skill in their leaders and politics in their common life. This point is particularly important because many in the churches cultivate the conceit that in policy formation, decision making, and leadership selection, religious institutions should not be political. They sometimes combine this conceit with the distinguishable notion that religious institutions should not be political and should refrain from lobbying, organizing, or persuading in civil politics. Occasionally denominational leaders active in one or both political senses nevertheless advance

---

10. Handy, *Christian America*.

this conceit, thereby cloaking their exercises of power. This deception (and self-deception) derives plausibility because religious political activity often combines several political cultures.

Each of the five kinds of institutional understandings under review in this essay actually prescribes a code of political behavior. Each represents a distinct type of political culture, with its own leadership styles, codes of acceptable interaction, and sanctions. Denominational political behavior can be that appropriate for a charismatic entity, a particular denominational tradition, an ethnic heritage, a voluntary association, a complex organization, or some combination thereof. The person proscribing politics in religious institutions may feel that only one of these political cultures is legitimate or may seek to return the movement to an earlier self-understanding. If successful, he doesn't rid the denomination of politics but only legislates or imposes one political culture.

As voluntary associations, then, American religious institutions must of necessity be political entities, at least internally. Without politics, institutions can neither maintain their organization nor sustain their direction. Voluntarism does not necessitate, however, that the politics exercised must be identical to that elsewhere prevailing in the contemporary voluntary culture—that to be found in other voluntary associations of the day. This was the point at issue in the trusteeism controversy in nineteenth-century Roman Catholicism. Would the church structure its political interactions according to emergent (largely Protestant) American patterns of association? Would it vest property in local boards of trustees like its Congregational or Baptist neighbors? To protect its ecclesial self-understanding and episcopal authority the church refused. So also the Old Order Amish and the Unification Church function with distinctive political cultures deemed essential to their continued existence and quite at odds with surrounding cultural patterns.

Finally, those groups that did accept the voluntary culture itself and *were welcomed* into it claimed the right to structure American society. So the in-group of seemingly competitive denominations and voluntary associations defined the boundaries, codes, rituals, symbols, and networks that created a nineteenth-century Protestant establishment. In recognizing the church-like role of "voluntaristic churches," Singleton proclaims it incorrect to term them denominations. "They assumed they were—and to a large extent they in fact were—coextensive with their society."[11] While his denial of denominational status to these Protestant groups does not

---

11. Singleton, *Religion*, xix.

The Denomination as Institution

seem fully persuasive, it serves to underscore his positive point, which students of voluntary associations have long made, beginning at least with Alexis de Tocqueville—that the threads that bound Americans in these small units also held the society together.

The social functions and effects outlined above may or may not have been fully intended—the degree to which the Protestant denominations through revivals and through the complex of voluntary societies sought dominion over American society was and remains in dispute—but the fact remains that voluntary religious institutions served to orient their membership to American society as a whole. In the early nineteenth century that orientation assumed the transparency of nation, culture, and society. These latter were but means to the kingdom. By the end of the nineteenth century the kingdom glowed within culture, and religious institutions reoriented themselves to cultural goals. In the middle third of the twentieth century those same mainline Protestant denominations that had sought the kingdom through voluntary means abandoned the goal of a Christian America. But the vision of a voluntary establishment lives on in conservative Protestantism, in Republican Party rhetoric, and in national programs of voluntary action. This passing of the mantle of voluntarism, change in goals, and secularization, epitomized by the YMCA, should not obscure the importance of voluntary religious institutions in nineteenth-century America and, for our purposes the more important point, the importance of voluntarism as a culture in American religion.

Religious Organization

While pluralism and voluntarism certainly have had defenders, they have also had critics. In the nineteenth century Roman Catholics, theologically sensitive representatives of Lutheran and Reformed traditions, anti-mission Baptists, Christians, and individuals like the Presbyterian (later Episcopalian) Calvin Colton and the Unitarian William Ellery Channing—strange bedfellows obviously—concurred in opposing the seductive and coercive features of voluntary culture. In this century their sentiments have been developed by religion scholars into a full-fledged social control theory of American history. Sociologists, political scientists, Tea Party Republicans and radicals on the left as well attack voluntary associations, foundations and the press for elitism and oligarchy. They and kindred religious critics sometimes indict religious institutions as well on two counts. First, as part of the voluntary culture, denominations and other voluntary bodies

PART TWO: Perspectives on Denominationalism

have created and must take responsibility for a society in which power is exercised by privately organized, "irresponsible" organizations and elites. Critics and interpreters of this private government do not depict religious hands at the controls, as did Calvin Colton in the nineteenth century when he termed the array of voluntary societies, with their interlocking boards, "Protestant Jesuitism." They decry instead the arbitrary and oppressive power of corporations, unions, and professional organizations. Such private power is deemed dangerous because it is politically unaccountable, beyond the controls of the democratic process, and not subservient to the protections granted individuals under the Constitution. Second, religious institutions prove to be susceptible to similar charges of elitism, bureaucracy, and popular disenfranchisement. Here too professionalism, managerial procedures, and corporate structures permit elites to establish dominion. One line of critique in organization studies and by religious activists attacks religious bureaucracy; draws contrasts between formal, traditional conceptions of religious authority on the one hand, and operative informal power on the other; and pits lay or local expectations of consensus against the reality of national expertise and elitism. This scholarship, sometimes with the allure of an exposé, reflects profound discomfort with the growth in denominational bureaucracy that has occurred in this century, as well as preferences for other models of religious organization.

At its best, organization studies, eschews the histrionics and conspiratorial visions of these often right-wing operatives, and provides a more balanced account of these changes that religious bodies have, in fact, undergone. These organization studies rest on two important developments, one societal, the other academic. The societal development stems from what Alfred D. Chandler termed "the managerial revolution," the reconstruction of American business from single units whose enterprise was "coordinated" by the invisible hand of the market to multiunit enterprises, administered by hierarchies of professional managers whose visible hand and rational-technical expertise coordinate those "market" functions. This entrepreneurial capitalism Chandler distinguished from the earlier financial and family forms of capitalism. The triumph of the manager had occurred by World War I but was anticipated by such nineteenth-century developments as railroad organization and the professionalization of important sectors of American society. In underscoring the enormity of the changes, Chandler remarked that "the American businessman of 1840 would find the environment of fifteenth-century Italy more familiar than that of his own nation seventy years later."[12] The import of business chang-

12. Chandler, *Visible Hand*, 455; John, "Elaborations, Revisions, Dissents."

es for American society as a whole has been captured in other phrases like "the organizational society" and the "organizational revolution." Robert Wiebe effectively charted the reshaping of American society as managerial patterns, the identity and linkage of persons through professions and organizations, large-scale hierarchical organization, and various forms of regulation spread from business into government and private sectors.

Academic theory development captured and reflect these societal changes. Indeed, it would be an interesting exercise in the sociology of knowledge to depict the various stages in organization studies as an evolving societal consciousness of the phases of the organizational revolution. From Max Weber's studies of bureaucracy and rationality to Robert Michels's iron law of oligarchy to Frederick W. Taylor's scientific management to Fritz J. Koethlisberger and William J. Dickson's emphasis on human relations and Chester I. Barnard's on cooperation; to Talcott Parsons's theory of social systems to theory-functional (Peter M. Blau) and decision making (James G. March and Herbert A. Simon), compliance (Amitai Etzioni), exchange (Peter M. Blau), open systems (Daniel Katz and Robert L. Kahn), and rational choice—the study of organizations has had both analytic and exemplificative value. The phases of organization studies have double value for us as well. They function as tools for the analysis of complex organizations (religious included), and they document the growing academic awareness of the organizational revolution. That is, they function both as secondary (interpretation) and primary (evidence). They analyze and document what Louis Galambos once termed "The Emerging Organizational Synthesis in Modern American History." He contended:

> Our history no longer stressed liberal-conservative political struggles leading to pulses of progressive reform; instead, the primary processes of change involved organization building, both public and private, and the creation of new and elaborate networks of formal hierarchical structures of authority that gradually came to dominate our economy, polity, and culture. America's rendezvous was not with the liberal's good society. It was with bureaucracy.[13]

The contrast that Galambos drew between progressive and organizational values is, on the level of historiography, most instructive. On another level, as a depiction of the actual Progressive platform and action, it is somewhat misleading. For it was precisely the Progressives, the apparent enemies of economic concentration and corruption, the historians of

---

13. Galambos, "Organizational Synthesis," 451.

the saga of liberty against privilege, who championed the use of scientific method, efficiency, expertise, order, organization, and professionalism—business methods—in governmental and voluntary associations. Ironically, then, the reformers who conceived history as the struggle between elites and the populace and who would be considered by history as anti-business, were the twentieth-century architects of the organizational society. This masking of their role has created the impression that the adoption of organizational culture outside the business sector derived from inadvertent, ill-advised, or unprincipled capitulation to corporate interests, an impression that colors some of the conspiratorial "discovery" of corporate style organization in religion.

The truth is that religious institutions were quite deliberately modernized by liberals (Social Gospel proponents), who as leaders of denominational or interdenominational agencies self-consciously sought to appropriate modes of administration, specialization, communication, and organization from business. Inspired by this "ideology of organization," they succeeded in refashioning denominational boards and agencies, created interdenominational organizations, and established various voluntary bodies and thereby institutionalized this gospel. The correlation of bureaucracy and liberalism continues to prevail, not because liberals somehow captured the apparatus, but because they and their forebears had run it from the get-go. The organizational gospel also institutionalized itself in religious research divisions and seminary sociology departments, which functioned like research-and-development divisions for religious "management." So organization studies, within or on behalf of denominations, assumed tasks once left to the Holy Spirit—determining where to plant and sow, how to do so more efficiently, how to increase yield, and when to enlarge the field. By methods deemed scientific, quantitative, and behavioristic this research spread and nurtured the seeds of organization. Eventually organizational research broke free from denominational control, sought greater academic neutrality and founded professional societies to confirm its independence. But until then, organizational research was dedicated more to establishing the principles of organization than to studying it. For religion as for American society, organization study serves as evidence of' the important changes for which it also provides interpretive theory.

A succession of distinguished research efforts exhibit the theoretical side of organization studies in religion.[14] These studies take the premise

---

14. See Richey, "Institutional Forms," 49.

that American religion can profitably be viewed through the conceptual lenses used for other complex organizations. The research has proceeded beyond the stage of proclaiming religious conformity with "iron laws" of association—inevitable institutionalization, minority rule, goal displacement, and goal succession. One theory, that of open systems, widely used in the late twentieth century, illustrates something of the value of organization studies for the analysis of American denominations and denominationalism. In this framework, religious organization is depicted "as a huge transformation system, whereby its personnel procure resources (input), do something with and to them (throughput), and exchange the products (output) with other persons and organizations in the environment." This model directs attention to the openness of systems to their environments; to the resources of ideas, people, materials, goals, and money requisite for survival or growth; to the processes of recruitment, nurture, socialization, and ordering by which the system operates; and to the structures through which the system coheres—including specialization, formalization, centralization, and authority configuration.

What are the principal findings about American religion by organization studies? The first and perhaps most important is, as we have indicated, implicit in its very existence and successful application. That is, contemporary religious institutions, however they may think of themselves theologically, spiritually and religiously are complex organizations implicated in an organizational society. Second, the theory has rather consistently exposed a relatively common failure on the part of American religions to acknowledge this complexity. Most penetratingly documented a half century ago by Paul Harrison in treating the American Baptists, this failure consisted in the Baptists' inability to comprehend functioning structures, processes, and leadership within formal polity. The theological or perspectival oversight (misperception) frustrated institutional oversight (accountability). Task-oriented agencies that were developed in the nineteenth century as voluntary endeavors on the society principle had stabilized themselves as bureaucratic power-centers. They performed critical duties, exercised unchecked power, and possessed considerable resources. The Baptists' congregational polity (in the late nineteenth century) did not recognize the legitimacy of these agencies and could therefore not hold them accountable. Harrison's insights prompted investigation of other polities—Protestant, Catholic and Jewish.

This work dramatically exposed the limited usefulness of the traditional (Christian) distinction of episcopal, presbyterial, and congregational

PART TWO: Perspectives on Denominationalism

governance for purposes of organizational analysis. Instead, most large-scale religious bodies (or at least those rooted in the Judeo-Christian tradition) typically possess dual, parallel structures. A pastoral structure derives from formal polity, though it has perhaps been adjusted (democratized) in important ways by the American experience (as has my denomination, United Methodism). An agency structure exists in uneasy (but varied and complex) tension with this pastoral structure. Its resources and staff, which may be concentrated at national, regional, or state levels (or all three), carry on much of the vital work of the institution. The relationships between the formal or pastoral and the agency or bureaucratic structures do differ. Differences reflect the importance of polity, tradition(s), ethos, the relative authority of regional and local bodies vis-à-vis national offices, the power exercised by key leaders, ethnic make-up, and historically-created factors (crises, schisms, trends). Yet, in one form or another, the gap or tension between authority and power analyzed by Harrison prevails. Whether the commonality will produce unity, as ecumenists once hoped and hypothesized, the comparable structural patterns within the diverse polities of Protestantism and in Judaism and Roman Catholicism are worth noting. Indeed, Lyle Schaller once suggested that religious organizations could be classified as congregational or connectional on a fiscal rather than theological or theoretical basis. He surmised that economically self-sufficient local bodies can and do function in a congregational (autonomous) mode. Those, on the other hand that require one or another kind of dependency (for technical, personnel, or monetary assistance or support) really function in a connectional mode.

A third finding relates to the emergence of the dual structure and complex organization of religious institutions. Incidentally, it also suggests limits to organization studies that do not take seriously enough the historical dimension—what denominational and voluntarism studies amply document. The significant growth, interconnection, and centralization of religious machinery occurred in the late nineteenth and early twentieth centuries. The tension between formal polities and the societies related to those polities also became acute at that time. To be sure, voluntary societies had been seen as anomalous and unaccountable earlier by Old School Presbyterians, by the Christian and anti-mission movements, and by groups within many religious bodies. Yet if discernment of the problem of unaccountable power was not new, the scale of' it certainly was. The borrowing of business methods of fund-raising and finance, enlargement and increased specialization of staffs, coordination of national machinery and tasks through departmentalization, and the increased complexity of communication and command—in short, the investment of time and money on administration—were to enhance religious mission and effectiveness. The openness to business culture in the late nineteenth and early twentieth centuries dramatically altered religious institutions.

Gibson Winter dramatized the enormity of this transformation by terming it "The Other Protestant Schism," attempting thereby to suggest an importance in the organizational revolution comparable to that of the Protestant Reformation. He challenged the secondary status accorded societies, boards, and agencies by proposing that missions be thought primary and denominations called "paramissions." And he invoked Roman Catholic orders as providing precedent and legitimacy for these structures.[15] While Winter intended by these proposals to argue for the normality of such structures in Christian history, they can also be used to underscore the fact and importance of the changes American religion underwent at the turn of the twentieth century. Organization study calls attention to the realities. It can, at times, need to be reminded, perhaps by denominational and voluntarism studies, of the slow emergence and evolution of the business-like structures within religious organizations.

Ideal Typology

Ideal types as originally utilized by Max Weber might be thought of as extended definitions, as hypothetical-theoretical constructs based on empirical research but elaborated for their capacity to portray and relate variables critical to given phenomena, for their value in executing comparisons, and for their capacity to depict the role of' the specific phenomena in overall societal transformation. Such tools permitted Weber to view religious leadership, membership, and structure in relation to the broad processes of change now loosely gathered under the rubric of secularization. The two religious institutional types advanced by Weber were the church and the sect, a dichotomy really focused particularly on the character of membership.

Ideal typologies, by nature, diverge from concrete instances of religious organization. Nevertheless, Weber's typology, like any, required revision as research sought to isolate other factors. Thus, it was perhaps inevitable that his typology was significantly altered as the sociology of religion matured into a discipline, developed new lines of inquiry, addressed

15. Winter, *Religious Identity*.

PART TWO: Perspectives on Denominationalism

itself to new societies, including the United States, and confronted changes in religious institutions. The addition of other types and multiplication of subcategories for sect have led some scholars to view the transformations in typology after Weber as so disastrous as to warrant a return to his foundations. For our purposes these critiques function to highlight how important the American scene has been in forcing reconceptualization of institutional types. Additional constructs, notably the denomination and the cult, were among a variety of elaborations introduced to make sense of' the American institutional pattern.

Ernst Troeltsch represents the stage after Weber. In *The Social Teaching of the Christian Churches* (1912, 1931), Troeltsch adapted Weber's typology for historical-theological purposes, a history of Christian social ethics. His addition to the typology, a third type of mysticism, was to be of 'less importance for sociology and for analysis of American religion than two other contributions. First, in Troeltsch's hands, the typology became more a historical generalization than an ideal construct. Second, he introduced the term *compromise* as a judgment to be applied to the relation between ideals and their institutional embodiment.

In *The Social Sources of Denominationalism* (1929), H. Richard Niebuhr furthered the transformation of the typology from an ideal into a historical and ethical construct (reification). Its inclusion among the religious studies and ethics classics and its subjection to revision and even criticism suggests its importance. The fact is that Niebuhr introduced the typology into American scholarship. His formulations influenced a generation of' scholars, many of them directly, and found their way into the basic works in American religious history and the sociology of religion. Surveying the American scene, Niebuhr added the denomination to the church and the sect and recognized it as the dominant institutional type. 'That contribution has seemed firm.

Further elements of his theory, less appreciated now by sociologists, should be seen as aspects of the theological reorientation captured by historical constructs like neo-orthodoxy, ecumenism, and "the second disestablishment."[16] Niebuhr viewed religious institutions and their relation to culture from within the church—a church, he thought, threatened by enemies without and within, a "church which has made compromises with the enemy in thought, in organization, and in discipline."[17] This "question of the church" had found expression in *Social Sources* as his-

16. Handy, *Christian America*.
17. Niebuhr et al., *Church*, 1.

torical generalizations, laws really. For a period they guided sociological research but now would be recognized as more illuminating of Niebuhr than of history. Placing religious institutions in a socioeconomic context, Niebuhr argued that the vital (Christian) religious spirit, ethic, and commitment emerged and took form in radical, lower-class, sectarian movements. These authentic expressions of the (Christian) religious impulse inevitably compromised themselves in their endeavor to conserve, embody, and transmit their vitality. That compromising transformation produced churches or denominations. The denomination or church came to terms with the dominant culture; and denominations further capitulated to class, caste, regional, national, and racial interests. To Niebuhr, denominations seemed to be about the most sinful creatures on the religious landscape-guilty of the sin of schism by their sanctification of division, guilty of a breech of brotherhood by their reinforcement of societal interests, and guilty of a betrayal of the Gospel by their exchange of its radical claims for a potage of middle-class culture.

Against the backdrop of the American experience, the notions that all religious movements originate among the dispossessed as sects, that sects inevitably metamorphose into denominations or churches, and that the process of' institutionalization should be conceived as compromise made sense to Niebuhr to many of his early readers. It did seem that in the American environment European sects (and churches, one should add) took denominational form, that their constituency typically became middle class, and that they institutionalized themselves in relation to the dominant trends and divisions of American society. American evidence generated Niebuhr's generic rules. (His later typology in Christ and Culture was less provincial. However, while indeed relevant to institutions its greater breadth docs not seem to help here.) For sociology, the American specificity of Niebuhr's scheme limits its value. Few would now concur with Niebuhr as did one sociologist in the 1930s that "Denominations are simply sects in an advanced stage of development and adjustment to each other and to the secular world."[18] That point, and indeed Niebuhr's whole argument, might well be seen less as a sociological theorem and more as a reading (albeit an ethically evaluative one) of the prevalence of the denominational form at a point of its vulnerability in the early twentieth century.

---

18. Becker, *Through Values to Social Interpretation*, 116; and Becker, in Wiese, *Systematic Sociology*, 626.

PART TWO: Perspectives on Denominationalism

While Niebuhr's subjection of ideal typology to historical and ethical constraints (and American ones at that) may seem in hindsight "unhelpful,"[19] he was among the many to recognize that the earlier typologies misread the American scene. The churches of Europe—Roman Catholic, Lutheran, Reformed, Anglican—often found themselves, initially at least, in adversarial quasi-sectarian relation to a Protestant American built on evangelical foundations. Their traditional place as world-embracing, universal, inclusive, objective institutions, meshed with the authority system of the state, integral with society and culture, enveloping the whole life of members, and effectively redeeming the individual and the world had been preempted by the collective of Anglo-Saxon denominations (black and white). And without an established 'Church' to define itself against, the sectarian spirit—world-denying, voluntaristic, rejecting of church, society, and state, exclusive, anti-sacerdotal, intolerant, totalistic, morally rigorous—diffused itself vis-à-vis the denominational establishment. All bodies, at least since the nineteenth century, have shared the essential sectarian requisite, voluntarism, whether they played an establishment or dissenting role in American society. The denomination has been seen as the American form of organization and its characteristics as strikingly American. William Swatos underscores the denominations' openness to and "at-homeness" in American society by terming them "the structural-functional forms that dominant religious traditions assume in a pluralistic society."[20] Hence, after Niebuhr, typologies and classificatory schemes oriented toward analysis of American institutions have featured the denomination.

Sociological efforts to comprehend the dynamics of American religious produced various classificatory/typological proposals, some quite elaborate. In the 1930s Howard Becker and other sociologists suggested a continuum of cult, sect, denomination, and church. The continuum represented a scale of adjustment to the world and stages in the life cycle of a religious impulse. A movement might emerge as a cult, take sectarian form, consolidate itself as denomination and settle eventually into churchly status vis-à-vis its society. Milton Yinger built an even more complex continuum—universal church, ecclesia, denomination, established sect, sect, cult—with subvarieties of churchly and sectarian types.[21] His criteria for definition and categorization measured group inclusion of members

19. Beckford, "Religious Organization," 116.
20. Swatos, *Into Denominationalism*, 222.
21. Yinger, *Scientific Study*.

of society, acceptance of "secular values and structures of society," and "organizational complexity, professionalization, and bureaucracy."

After Yinger, much of the creative work on typology has concerned itself not with a continuum but with the sect. Illustrative are the many publications of Bryan Wilson. Although writing in a British context and increasingly moving beyond a western orientation, Wilson has applied his theory to American institutions. In a succession of important works, he elaborated quite intricate subcategories of sects, e.g., conversionist, revolutionist, introversionist, manipulationist, thaurnaturgical, reformist, and utopian. His study of sectarianism, and particularly of permanent sects, renders highly problematic Niebuhr's notion that sects are ephemeral stages in the life cycle of religious movements that inevitably become denominations. Essential to the sect's nature and prospects is its relation to the world. Wilson discerned "world-denying, world-indifferent, and world-enhancing" responses.[22]

These and similar refinements of sect theory and of the typology as a whole have been partially prompted by the effervescence of the so-called new religions, many of them new only to Americans, and the growth of other major world religions, neither of which fit neatly into existing institutional theory. So once again the religious fertility of the American soil promises as rich a yield of theory as of phenomena. Not only the world and new religions but also the rapidly growing nondenominational churches, the large-budget and high-visibility media evangelists, and the coalescing Christian Right call for typologies that make sense of the American scene. Are the existing schemes that reflect the earlier cultural dominance of the once mainstream denominations and feature the denomination as *the* American institution passé? Already Swatos recast the category of denominationalism in the light of shifting patterns of religious institutionalization.[23] Whether others will heed his call to reject classificatory schemes and return to Weber for ideal constructs we have yet to see.

What is clear is that despite such critiques by some users and dismissals by other theorists, ideal typology continues to direct scholarly attention to religious institutions. Part of its continuing appeal has to do with discussions internal to the sociology of religion. But its value both within and without the discipline derives also from the capacity of the typology to focus upon critical issues in the interpretation of religion. In particular, this approach, really alone of those surveyed here, takes seriously the

22. Wilson, *Religion*, 111.
23. Swatos, "Beyond Denominationalism."

institutional consequences of religion's claims to otherness, the holy, and God. Institutionalization of religious experience, what Weber termed the routinization of charisma, has proved an ambiguous enterprise. Thomas O'Dea appropriately described these ambiguities as dilemmas and paradoxes.[24] Office, symbols, administrative order, ethos, and authority never prove adequate bearers of the meanings that give rise to them. Typologies recognize, whether in the evaluative overtones of Troeltsch and Niebuhr's "compromise" or in O'Dea's dilemmas, that the finite strains to hold that which is experienced and viewed as infinite.

Oriented to the relation between the sacred and the world, typologies do greater justice to movement's self-conceptions and perceived missions than other approaches. However, it is often the initial world views, particularly sectarian ones, that typologies portray in sharpest outline. It should be no surprise, perhaps, given the interest in origins and beginnings, that sect theory, rather than theory of denomination or church, has been most highly developed. Typologies also make clearer than other theories that the transition from initial to subsequent leadership, with all that entails, differs from subsequent change. Perhaps Weber's notion of routinization is to be preferred to the life-cycle pattern of subsequent theorists. At the very least, much of typology theory focuses on the critical moment in the life of institutions. While that may not be the last thing to say about a religious body, it is not an unimportant insight.

Ethnic Studies

"American religious denominations are ethnic groups," and America is a denominational society. So proclaimed Andrew Greeley in rejecting the notion that the denomination "is a compromise or halfway house between sect and church," in viewing it as "a unique and new social form of religion," and in portraying American pluralism in denominational terms.[25] Greeley's virtual equation of religious institutions and ethnicity represents an extreme. Yet it dramatically illustrates the dubious quality of the longstanding popular and academic expectation that ethnic particularism and religion disintegrate before the forces of modernity and secularization. As the titles of similar period observations, Michael Novak's *The Rise of the Unmeltable Ethnics* and Nathan Glazer and Daniel P. Moynihan's *Beyond the Melting Pot* indicate, the scholarly community awoke in the 1960s and

24. O'Dea, *Sociology*.
25. Greeley, *Denominational Society*, 71, 108.

1970s to what seemed at times like a worldwide resurgence of ethnicity. Presumptions about the inevitable and imminent demise of religion and ethnicity seemed, at least, premature. With the larger dimensions of ethnicity and even the relation of religion and ethnicity we cannot here concern ourselves. Suffice it to say that they are now the domain of a sizable scholarly community, whose productivity has been termed an explosion and that communicates with itself through numerous periodicals.

Two points that recur in this literature are of importance for understanding religious institutions. First, studies of immigration and ethnicity over the last several decades have revised our conceptions of the history and prospects of unity and diversity in American society and of the relation of group formation and institutionalization to American identity. Philip Gleason isolated four distinct answers to the fundamental question, what does it mean to be an American?—four models of how legitimacy is achieved. Two of these emphasize the unity essential to American well-being—Americanization, by stressing a requisite ideological minimum; Anglo-Saxon racialism, by demanding an exclusive form of American unity. The other two sanction diversity—the melting pot, by accepting diverse origins as productive of eventual cultural unity; and cultural pluralism, by envisioning a multiplicity of American identities.[26] Others proposed the slightly variant models of unity and diversity, assimilation and pluralism. It is of importance for our interpretation of institutions which of these proves most historically accurate. At a minimum, we need to be concerned with two interrelated questions. The first has to do with the relative unity or diversity in institutional patterns at any point in time and the degree to which either reflects ethnic factors. The second concerns the ethnic origins of our institutional patterns (whether relatively uniform or diverse).

To illustrate, historians have in the past assigned the salient features of American institutional life to the Puritan/evangelical heritage and monitored Roman Catholic, Lutheran, and Orthodox conformity as signs of Americanization (Anglo-conformity). However, recent studies of various supposedly ethnic churches, including Roman Catholicism) over the last quarter century have suggested that institutional patterns of leadership, promotion, piety, organization, and common life long thought to be distinctively American derived from the respective traditions or from the dynamics of immigration and relocation, not from borrowings from the

---

26. Gleason, "American Identity and Americanization," in Thernstrom, *Harvard Encyclopedia*; Gleason, *Speaking of Diversity*.

host society. Catholic forms of revivalism, to take a dramatic instance, can be seen as continuous with European parish missions and need not be read as signs of capitulation to Protestant practice. That may not make them less American, but it does suggest that the origins of American institutional life may be more ethnically diverse than has often been supposed. And the fact that institutional traits taken to be distinctively American may derive from French or German Catholicism rather than New England Puritanism further suggests that it would be quite easy to overstate the degree of conformity and to underestimate the vitality of ethnicity in current institutional practice. Hence voluntary action research and organizational studies (and to a lesser extent denominational histories) that, in consensus fashion, employ societal models of organization to explain religious institutions may lack the lenses to see configurations derived from ethnic experience.

First, then, studies of ethnicity suggest plural origins of institutional patterns and more subtle transactions between immigrant bodies and the host culture than other more assimilationist models would suggest. Second, and ironically, ethnicity bids to be *the single* most important determinant of religious institutionalization. Here the accent falls not so much on the plurality of institutional traditions as upon the commonality of the immigrant and ethnic experience itself. These two points are not mutually exclusive, but the distinction and the irony still hold. Like the voluntarist pluralists, the ethnic pluralists at times seem to offer a single explanation for religious institutions—ethnicity.

We referred at the outset to one such instance, Greeley's functionalist estimation that in America religious institutions play ethnic or quasi-ethnic roles, and that as *Gemeinschaft* groups they are a central feature of American society as a whole. With this functionalist approach, denominations not typically thought of as ethnic (Southern Baptists and Episcopalians, for instance) might be deemed ethnic to an extent. In such a reading the ethnicity that the SBC sustains is that of being southern, an identity either inherited or borrowed. Similarly, in the richly Elizabethan flavor and ethos of the Episcopal Church, its many converts from liturgically lower denominations acquire an English heritage and identity. And at least in the not too distant past a Scottish accent did wonders for clerical advancement among Presbyterians.

With a less functionalist approach but even more ambitiously and quite subtly, Timothy Smith offered a general theory of religious institutions and their history with ethnicity as the controlling category. As ethnicity appeared to be the key factor in American institutional life, so also religion appeared to be the major determinant of ethnicity. Migration, Smith argued, "was often a theologizing experience."[27] Migration disrupted relationships, shattered personal identity, and dismantled frameworks of meaning—what Peter Berger called "the sacred canopy." By necessity the immigrants became, according to Smith, creators both of new social structures and of their meaning. The product of this creativity was peoplehood—new group and personal identity. The process began, Smith argued, at least for the immigrants of European origin, in the juxtaposition of peoples through commerce, warfare, and urbanization within Europe and before emigration. It accelerated in America, in part, because individuals receptive to such new alignments and groups in the process of formation were migration prone. The role of religion in forging ethnic community and institutions was threefold. (Smith did point out that other types of ideology have played this role.)

First, religion marked out new boundaries of peoplehood drawing upon prior traditions of language, nationality, association, and belief but reworking them in a significant manner. Those of a given linguistic, cultural, and national background often constituted not one but several peoples. The Germans and Magyars, for instance, clustered into Lutheran, Reformed, Catholic, and Jewish communities. And eventually, in addition to bodies that represented themselves as faithful to such inherited traditions, various other ethnic possibilities presented themselves—new movements, groups that had altered significantly in interaction with the dominant culture, and new constellations perhaps across confessional lines. Hence individuals faced the problem of into which community to cross not just whether to cross a boundary into one community. Ethnicity derived from the elaboration of and choice between religiously defined communities.

Religious institutions, first congregations, then successive layers of structure built to service congregations, defined, consolidated, and symbolized those new boundaries. The common patterns to be found in religious institutions derive from the common burdens that congregations and denominations were forced to bear. To them fell the tasks of order, nurture, meaning, and interpretation that had been the responsibility of village elders, authorities (both civil and religious) at various levels, kinship groups, and culture. It is, then, to ethnicity that the distinctive attributes of American religious culture are to be ascribed. And conversely, ethnicity has been largely defined in religious terms. So Smith.

27. Smith, "Religion and Ethnicity," 1175.

Second, the anxiety, grief, guilt, and loneliness produced by migration and the strangeness of the new customs in the new land prompted deep inner cravings for meaning and certainty. Such inner turmoil often found expression and release in religious commitment. This served, on the one hand, to reinforce the institutional commitment individuals made. On the other hand, it produced patterns of institutional or collective religious behavior thought to be typically American. These included the intense piety itself; a moralism that drew clean lines between what was acceptable and what was not, the notion that the people were in covenant with God, a biblicism establishing a clear and acceptable basis of authority, and the pragmatic or progressive orientation to adjust to new situations.

The third contribution of religion to ethnicity, according to Smith, was the belief, framed by Jewish messianism or Christian millennialism, that the peoplehood defined and the institutions created served the larger purpose of the unity of humanity. This catholic and purposive orientation—long thought to be the characteristic mark of the Anglo-Saxon Protestant establishment and the missionary and denominational institutions it created—Smith also ascribed to ethnicity. The forms of this universalism varied. The Hasidim, the Moravians, the Eastern Orthodox, and the African American religions construed the hope for the human race in different fashion. They concurred in asserting a catholic meaning to their particularity.[28]

The close identification of religion with ethnicity posited by Smith and Greeley effectively illustrates this approach to institutionalization. Others have stressed the variety of factors formative of ethnic identity, various relations between ethnicity and religion and comparably wide divergence on how ethnicity ought to be defined (one counting came close to thirty distinct definitions). Harold Abramson proposed a threefold relation of religion and ethnicity: equation, with religion defining ethnicity in the manner suggested by Timothy Smith; centrifugal disengagement, with religion narrowing ethnic boundaries, perhaps through schisms; and centripetal convergence, with religion consolidating or enlarging ethnic borders, as perhaps in something like the triple melting pot popularized by my late Drew colleague, Will Herberg, in *Protestant, Catholic, Jew*.[29] There is, as Abramson and virtually all students of ethnic religion indicate, an ethnic dimension to religion and a religious dimension to ethnicity.

28. Ibid., 1155–85.

29. Abramson, "Assimilation and Pluralism"; and Abramson, "Religion," in Thernstrom, *Harvard Encyclopedia*.

But studies of ethnicity worry, in a fashion not unlike the immigrants they study, over the tugs of both particularity and unity, of pluralism and assimilation. As far as religious institutions are concerned, the question finally is one of degree. How much of institutional life derived from the heritages imported or the exigencies of migration itself and how much from interaction with and appropriation of patterns elaborated by earlier and now dominant immigrants? That will doubtless remain an open question.

An Evolutionary Theory

As we have traced the emergence of the several theories of religious institutions, we have remarked, where appropriate, on the evidential character of the theories themselves. In particular, we noted that denominational history seems to mark an important stage in the evolution of institutional consciousness. Voluntary action research seemed especially apropos for the period in which it first appeared, namely the nineteenth century. Organizational theory both evidences and interprets the dramatic changes of the late nineteenth and early twentieth centuries. We have also remarked on the different aspects of religious institutions that the theories bring into view. Here we would like to build on those two notes to suggest that the several theories do help us to understand what might best be termed the evolution of American institutional culture, and that they complement one another in important ways. Here, we take note of how the stages in this evolution draw on the several approaches to denominationalism. For a more straightforward historical account of the evolution see the chapter, "American Denominationalism: A Historical Overview" and note that we draw on the evolution in several other chapters to make sense of the changes in the life of specific denominations.

Alfred Chandler's observation about the radical dissimilarity between the business culture of different periods applies even more strikingly to religious institutions. Members of today's United Church of Christ would be more at home, we suggest, in contemporary United Methodism than in earlier phases of their own movement in mid-nineteenth-century Congregational or Christian churches, in eighteenth-century Massachusetts parishes, or in seventeenth-century Puritanism. The institutional configurations on every level differ markedly from period to period, a fact masked by the continuity of denominational identity, and more important, by the employment of the denominational language to cover successive and differing institutional realities. To be sure, language does define the religious system of a given body and the access to those meanings that denominational history provides is not insignificant.

Nevertheless, a religious institution existing at any given time seems to be shaped by three sometimes independent, often interactive dynamics: the institutional environment of the society as a whole, the level and character of its ethnic identity, and its orientation to both its own peculiar vision and the world. The latter two dynamics are recurrent possibilities, as the theories devoted to them (ethnic studies and typology) presume. That is to say, at any given point in American history, down to the present, either or both of those dynamics may be the primary determinants in institutional life. For instance, analysis of recent Hispanic developments in Roman Catholicism and Korean movements in Presbyterian, Methodist, and Baptist churches requires both typology and ethnic theory. However, it is not the case that the institutional configurations of Hispanic Catholicism or Korean Presbyterianism will appear through either ethnic or typological lenses to be identical to nineteenth-century versions of ethnic Catholicism or Presbyterianism. The successive phases of the organizational culture of American religion affect even quite particularistic movements. For that reason a few generalizations about major stages of American religious organization are in order.

Over the course of American history four distinctive configurations of religious community have emerged, assumed a certain prominence, even dominance, and then gradually found themselves not displaced, but subsumed in a successive communal form. A fifth pattern or stage seems to have emerged but its characteristics remain somewhat in flux. The institutional expression of each closely resembled styles of community found elsewhere in the society. The first, represented by both the confessionally congregational Puritans and the more accidentally congregational Anglicans, ordered and legitimated local community. This institutionalized localism appeared in the seventeenth century but continues in places down to the present. Its aspiration for uniformity took varying temporal-spatial forms in the different regions. In New England, religious institutionalization completed the town; fittingly the meetinghouse defined the center of the community. In the Chesapeake, the parish was as much event as place; Anglicans established churches at places of convenience and sustained their community through a variety of ritual events. In the middle colonies religious institutionalization marked off neighborhood, thus legitimating pluralism. In each case the congregation was primary. Civil support, colonial clerical gatherings, and European religious authority ideally served the local institution. Whether legally and politically "established" or not, these institutions sought religious monopoly in the community within which they resided and over which they presided. If they acknowledged the existence of other forms of locally-defined denominationalism—among Baptists especially—they did so grudgingly. This phase of denominationalism had not yet fully lived into the spirit of toleration. Access to this phase of institutional life through denominational history should be balanced by judicious use of perspectives drawn from typology.[30]

The second institutional stage appears most strikingly in mid-eighteenth-century Presbyterians and Lutherans (see the introduction and the case-study chapters). Ethnic voluntarism might name it best, for it betrayed that paradox identified by Timothy Smith of giving universal significance to ethnically limited endeavor. Modest paracongregational structure was elaborated, primarily clergy networks designed to support existing and new congregations among the target ethnic population. Denominational histories rather effectively retrieve this stage since, like most histories, they tend to feature beginnings, and since denominational machinery elaborated during this stage constitutes an essential component of their narrative. But ethnic studies provide a needed balance, for the paracongregational or denominational structures served the ethnic functions outlined by Smith.

The third and fourth institutional stages have figured prominently in our discussion and can be more quickly sketched. Early nineteenth-century Methodists exemplify the third stage: the era of expansive, purposive national missionary denominational order, reinforced by voluntary societies, and oriented toward inclusive evangelization and the establishment of religious civilization (see the chapters on Methodism in the case study section). Experimental and pragmatic attitudes toward institutional machinery went hand in hand with a (limited) openness to other evangelical denominations. The several Protestant (and evangelical) denominations deemed all activity and organization subservient to the common goal and tasks of building the kingdom of God. While the local and ethnic forms of community lived on in this new order, community now increasingly defined itself in national terms, a voluntary community of evangelical cells knit by purpose and catholic Protestant belief into federation and confederation. This was the heyday of denominationalism. Yet, ironically, this stage belongs to voluntary action research. For this voluntarism had "established" itself in a Christian America.

30. Swatos, *Into Denominationalism*.

In the fourth stage, denominational and ecumenical structures, increasingly centralized and bureaucratized, give shape to religious community. Within those structures, clergy define their own special community, a professional one like that now dominant in American society. Lacking the communal prominence of the local institutions of stage one, the ethnic universalism of stage two, and the national vision of stage three, twentieth-century denominations of the ecumenical variety at times peer nostalgically at the institutional formulae of earlier stages. They chafe as evangelical bodies (megachurches with human, financial, and digital resources exceeding those of many denominations), various online ministries, and new religious groups profit by combining corporate and media culture with past visions. What the future holds for any of these initiatives and the denominational bodies increasingly affected by such transformed modes of delivery and communication lies beyond the purview of this chapter. (See the next chapter for an attempt to portray a fifth stage.) What we can say is that organizational studies provide access to the various dimensions of the fourth phase and perhaps a fifth.

These four stages do not exhaust the saga of American religious institutions but only outline the path charted by those movements that claimed dominance. To the degree that such dominance prevailed, the above patterns helped define one of the three dynamics in American religious institutionalization: the institutional environment of the society as a whole. The other two dynamics, the forces of ethnicity and the powerful appeal of new visions, brought ever new communities into being. At times, the new communities seemed to replicate the four stages just described. But they also appropriated the styles of the day. And in many cases they invented or imported what they were thought to have pirated. The mainstream (represented by these four cycles) doubtless was more indebted to successful innovation at the margin, to new structures or procedures established by Catholics, black Protestants, or sectarian movements, than it has been willing to admit. Americans admired what worked. Hence the three dynamics interplayed to create new patterns of institutional life to fit the society of the day. To understand these complexities, we need all five of' the theories here analyzed. We would also profit from significant dialogue and engagement between them.

8

American Denominationalism

A Historical Overview

IN A 1972 MAPPING of religion, sociologist Andrew M. Greeley discerned denominationalism to be such a central, stable facet of American life that he entitled the volume *The Denominational Society*. The U.S. he thought was one of four denominationally defined societies (along with Canada, Holland, and Switzerland). While subsequent developments and more recent scholarship would contest the characterization as overstated, his usage of the rubrics denominational and denominationalism points both to the historic importance of this dimension of American religion but also to the multivalent character of the terms themselves. Employed both in academic and popular discourse, the words can be a shorthand for religious identity or affiliation (as, for instance, of military chaplains). The rubrics describe the diversity in American organizational religious life—the named or "denominated" faith communities. They point to major Protestant divisions and traditions, so mainline, evangelical, and historically black denominations. The terms sometimes refer to religions that coalesce around or organize themselves through regional or national assemblies, leadership or bureaucracy, that is, to Protestant-normed patterns of religious organization, uniting congregations within regional judicatories into national or global polities.

The collective term *denominationalism* can stand for the salience or societal clout of the collectivity of mainline Protestant bodies. Sociologists employ the single term, *denomination*, typologically, and so compare

PART TWO: Perspectives on Denominationalism

it with other "ideal types"—cults, sects, and churches. In several ways, then, denominationalism identifies a distinctive way of being religious. It indicates, for instance, that a faith, ethic, tradition, single-purpose cause or parachurch entity has developed into a multipurpose, multifunction belonging entity with some measure of centralization and corporate structure, with identifiable membership, and with affiliated congregations, leadership, and regional and national judicatories. Similarly, denominationalism can function as a theory or theology of the church, which discerns individual denominations as branches of the one vine (Christ). Alternatively, as an Internet search will uncover, denominationalism renders theological judgment, a denunciatory rubric for religious division, elitism, diversity, sectarianism, and schism. *Denominationalism* and *denominational* can mean many things.

LOCATION

The denomination is an invention of modernity. It emerged in Western societies as they searched for stratagems and policies, other than coercion and repression, for coping with the religious diversity and discord generated out of the sixteenth-century reformations and seventeenth-century religious wars. English contributions—explorations of tolerance or comprehension after the Restoration and particularly after the Glorious Revolution, the Acts of Toleration, the writings of John Locke and colleagues, and the path-making efforts of newly tolerated English Presbyterians, Congregationalists, Baptists, and Quakers (recognized as Dissenters or Nonconformists)—proved vitally formative of the North American denomination. *Denomination* named voluntary religious organizations (initially Christian) operative under conditions of religious pluralism, codes of civility, and some measure of toleration. The collective term *denominationalism* references the existence and coexistence of tolerated voluntary religious bodies; their uneasy competition with one another establishing a larger pattern; the production thereby of an organizational field with its own norms, expectations, and boundaries; and a set of beliefs or practices, perhaps inchoate and not fully articulated or displayed, that govern participation in the denominational order.

In their American context, both the denominational organizational field and individual denominations have evolved significantly over time, acting and reacting to other creatures of modernity, particularly with the political party, the free press, and free enterprise; with other voluntary organizations; and with all levels and all powers of civil government (executives, judiciaries, and legislatures). The relation and similarity of denomination to political party and to free enterprise have been especially marked and important. Sometimes recipient of practice and precept from business and politics, denominationalism also contributed to these other sectors. The malleability, porosity, and dynamic character of denominationalism owed in no small measure to denominations' highly successful missional efforts in American society, to pressures to stay current with communication idioms and systems, to the freedom they enjoyed to experiment and to their capture of intellectual, cultural and political elites.

Denominations' culturally adaptive and sensitive character—embracing slavery in the South but abolition in the North—have earned both plaudits and denunciation, a matter to be returned to below. Here it is important to underscore the culturally adaptive and elastic character of the larger organizational ecology and its similarity to other sectors of modernity. As individual newspapers and magazines compose the free press, individual businesses compose capitalist free enterprise, and individual parties compose representative democracy, so individual denominations compose the organizational ecology of denominationalism. These four creatures of modernity have tended to evolve together and to influence one another. That the denomination looks bureaucratic and has resembled the corporation for the last century should not be surprising. It has resembled the current business form of the day, and also the current form of the political party and of the press. And no less than these other systems, denominationalism functions with sets of practices, understandings, and norms—owned by no one denomination, not codified or even fully articulated; dynamic and evolving, subject to violation or repudiation. As free enterprise evidenced its operative policy in corporate practice and democratic politics in partisan behavior, so denominationalism defined itself through the activities of the several denominations, in how they interacted, from the boundaries they set, through their efforts to shaper American society. Denominationalism defined itself in practice.

Denominational Styles and Stages of Denominationalism

From the eighteenth to the twenty-first century, one can isolate five denominational styles, five (implicit) normative patterns for denominations to emulate or against which to react, and five textures of the larger

PART TWO: Perspectives on Denominationalism

ecology (denominationalism). Ethnic voluntarism or provincial voluntarism emerged in the revivalism or awakening of the eighteenth century, shaping the religious pluralism of the middle colonies. In the religious free-for-all of the early national period, popular evangelistic movements patterned purposive missionary association, seeking converts across the whole society. A churchly or confessional style appeared in the Civil War era, invigorated by both immigrant religiosity and nativism, taking both high church and primitivist expressions, and seeking deeper foundations for belief and polity (in Romanticism and other popular theory). In the late nineteenth and early twentieth centuries, Protestantism reinvented itself for world evangelism by adopting corporate and managerial processes and forms. A fifth style, still defining itself, emerged in the late twentieth century, as conservative/evangelical movements and historically Black denominations enlarged the mainstream, and newer and non-Christian movements began negotiating their place in American society as well.

The typology serves a variety of purposes. First, it indicates that denominationalism and the denomination reinvent themselves, change, evolve over time, and become something new. This dynamism should caution us against equating denominationalism with its mainstream, bureaucratized image. Second, each stage modeled a normative style, thereby drawing boundaries, sometimes explicitly, sometimes implicitly, determining which movements belonged and which did not. Over time, the denominational system increasingly enlarged itself, again inviting the query as to whether that is ongoing now. Third, at least in several stages the transformative impulses operated from the margins, importing a new dynamic into the religious picture, effectively enlarging the system by carving out new space for denominational formation and identity. Implicit in such renewal; and fourth, the typology draws attention to renewal impulses that underlay and guided each new stage. Further, the schema should suggest, though we can only hint at it here, that also shaping denominations were interactions with business, politics, communication systems and culture generally and that denominational patterns of leadership, organization, decision-making and 'business' looked very much like counterparts in the American social, economic and political orders. Nor can the treatment here probe yet a sixth possible value, namely that to some extent movements new to the American scene may recapitulate some, if not all of the stages. That said, it must also be conceded that the schema does not accurately describe individual denominations for any period. It "idealizes." It identifies a predominant denominational style. It accents the denominational profiles, purposes, dynamic principles most powerfully operative for a specific era. Specific denominations adjusted these goals and principles, given their own context, relative maturity, and confessional self-understanding.

Ethnic Voluntarism

The ethnic ferment of the middle colonies, under conditions of toleration, set the sage for the first stage or style of denominationalism in what has been termed the First Great Awakening. Various factors preconditioned colonial society's capacity to yield this new form of the church. First, the reality of religious diversity, of the splintering of the church, of various confessions enjoying some measure of coexistence made policy in fact if not in theory. In the middle colonies peoples of Dutch Reformed, Quaker, Scottish, Scotch-Irish and Irish Presbyterian, English Baptist, Anglican, transplanted New England Congregationalist *and* various (German-speaking) persuasions (Dunker, Lutheran, Reformed, Moravian, Schwenckfelder, Mennonite) lived side by side. African Americans, then seldom Christianized, and Jews also had their places. Second, as already noted were policies and/or practices of toleration or of land grants to groups seeking asylum that implicitly permitted religious practice. William Penn's policies were of immense importance, as of course, were English precepts.

The impetus and form for *ethnic* voluntarism lay in immigration and whatever measure of religious heritage the immigrants brought. The dynamism for ethnic *voluntarism* lay in Pietism, in the waves of revival that *imported* Pietism unleashed, and in religious reactions to Pietism which had their own community-formative power. Congregations and associations, quasi-independent because of the sheer distance to "proper" authority, accomplished through their problem-solving two related but distinguishable social transactions, establishing hyphenate new ethnic community and legitimating it religiously as German-American Moravians, Scottish-American Presbyterians, Dutch Reformed.

Most imported religion comes to American shores with little in the way of trained and credentialed leadership or of the capacity to create such (the Puritans being the notable exception). Middle colony immigrants, modeling a pattern, found themselves largely fending for themselves religiously. They drew on their (often lay) memories of church practice and structure, they pressed someone into leadership, they gathered in one another's homes, they wrote religious authorities in the homeland pleading for proper preachers, they put in place processes by which to recognize authority. When preachers came or a community selected one of their own to serve, they founded congregations. The newly installed preachers, perhaps with laity, reached out to leadership from congregations of the same apparent "persuasion" to initiate presbyteries, consistories, or their tradition's counterpart. And around these modest structures emerged immigrant community, ordering itself religiously while adhering to colonial authority and further pleading to some home country judicatory for additional ministers, for print resources and for adjudication of disputes that threatened community.

Religious community formation began in early stages of immigration and settlement but took off with the itinerant, revivalistic, conversionist, Pietist practices which surfaced in Dutch settlements under Theodore J. Frelinghuysen in the 1720s, continued among Presbyterians under William and Gilbert Tennent in the 1730s, appeared in quite diverse confessional forms thereafter, and spread across the colonies tracking the several decades of itinerations by George Whitefield. Pietism's tactics proved highly effective in stimulating both new religious identity and community and angry reactive responses, themselves community-strengthening, from existing and more confessionally oriented leaders. Formative but controversial were Pietism's emotional invitational preaching, expectations of conversion and a morally regenerate life thereafter, allowance for lay testimony, encouragement of prayer, Bible reading, and disciplining small groups (conventicles), itinerant preaching (beyond a community to which the minister might be called), focus in sermon and witness on sin and salvation, blunt criticisms of worldliness in other laity and of unfruitful and unconverted ministers, and willingness to experiment with new ways of training and credentialing leadership.

This repertoire, known thereafter as revivalism, proved to be of enduring value in forming (religious) community, in part because it authorized local or indigenous processes and leadership generation, in effect making declarations of religious independence from its confessional "Rome" (its European home base) and its alignment with more evangelical resource centers (Halle, in the case of Pietism). Spiritual struggles yielded conversion and revival, converted strangers became "brothers" and "sisters" (religious family), family established moral authority and discipline, congregations formed, and leaders reached out to kindred bodies to establish modest fellowship associations (denominational structures). Elective, voluntary, ethnic denominational identity emerged, as most of this Pietist community-formation occurred within lines of kinship, language, national origin, religious tradition, and race. These communities, however, understood their new identity not in sociological but in pneumatological and eschatological terms. An outpouring of the Holy Spirit had brought conversions, revivals and new life as God's redeemed.

Others, particularly in congregations formed earlier and on the then-normative- Protestant-confessional model, took great exception to what they deemed censorious criticism, emotionalism (enthusiasm), lax theology, irregular lay activity, and untrained/unauthorized ministries. These confessional communities filed disciplinary charges at headquarters (Edinburgh, Amsterdam), read the enthusiast Pietists out of synod or assembly, shored up these organizations, and so countered with measures of denominational formation that also followed lines of kinship, language, national origin, tradition, and race. Religious energy and division yielded ethnic identity and cohesion. So among Presbyterians, both the Awakening New Side and the more confessional Old Side offered versions of Celtic-American ethnicity, each organizing along received polity lines.

Denominations at this stage consisted of a few congregations loosely tied together by small, periodic leadership gatherings. These pastor-led associations concerned themselves with care of congregations, problem solving, leadership supply and credentials, hymnals and service books, catechism, and the like. Denominations did not elaborate a public theology, see themselves caring for the whole of colonial society, or seek to transform the social order. Ethnic, voluntaristic, provincial, and provisional, denominations remained largely dependent upon European resources (either Pietist or confessional) for preachers and materials. Insofar as perceptions of belonging within a denominational field (denominationalism) existed, they did so quite vaguely in a sense of alignment with or against the Awakening and/or within a confessional or Pietist realm.

Purposive Missionary Association

A second denominationalism derived its primary impulse from Pietistic revivalism as well, in what has been termed the Second Great Awakening, but conceived of purposes in relation to the new nation and invented mechanisms to missionize the entire society. A civic theology harnessed revivalistic energies to build a Christian America. The then mainline (Congregationalists, Presbyterians, Episcopalians) each regionally dominant supplied the vision of a Christian America and key institutions for

PART TWO: Perspectives on Denominationalism

enculturation (voluntary societies, colleges). More marginal and newer bodies (Baptists, Methodists, Christians) supplied the expansive, energetic evangelism that transgressed lines of language, ethnicity, and race, and that aspired to Christianize (convert) the whole society. The camp meeting epitomized its missionary dynamic.

Presbyterians and Congregationalists provided the leadership and the intellectual framework that guided denominations in evangelistic efforts, in establishing new societies, in founding colleges, in elaborating norms for community and family life, in creating a Christian culture. The new nation needed, they thought, a common moral framework for the good order that a republic required. To elaborate such, they drew heavily on Reformed theological traditions, on Puritan covenantal notions, on Scottish moral philosophy, and on the rubrics of republicanism. When integrated, this new paradigm assigned to the several denominations, themselves especially, the responsibility of creating and overseeing a Christian America. So they elaborated denominational purposes in providential and eschatological language; applied covenantal imagery to the nation; tied both civil and religious well-being to a society appropriately ordered; and oriented their efforts towards the building of a Christian America.

Notwithstanding Congregational and Presbyterian presumptions—and they graciously included Episcopalians as well—other movements, in fact, supplied both the human resources and the effective model for implementing such high policy and grand aims. The popular, even despised, evangelistic movements—Baptists, Methodists and Christians (Restorationists)—suffused denominationalism with its missionary energy.

Requiring only, as the Methodists put it, "a desire to flee the wrath to come," the popular denominations adapted Pietism's revivalistic repertoire to expansive, open, inclusive missionary purpose. The imperative of evangelism trumped social codes and lines of ethnicity, language, national origin, class, and even race and of ecclesial boundaries of parish, confession, and prior Christianization. These denominations raced settlers into western lands. Missionary impulse shaped these denominations with new, expansive, outwardly oriented, inclusive presumptions, procedures, and structures. To be sure, the new denominationalism and even its signature camp meeting could only breach but not eradicate or transcend the social barriers (class, ethnicity, region, language, race and slavery). Language- and race-specific denominations emerged—African Methodist and Baptist and German- and Scandinavian-speaking denominations. They too, often or in places, took on the new expansive, aggressive, competitive,

American Denominationalism

entrepreneurial, expressive, boosteristic style. Increasingly so did Presbyterians and Congregationalists.

The integration of Reformed vision with Methodistic missionary evangelism took several decades, requiring emulation from both sides, and creating consternation in some quarters, as we will see in the next section. When this integration matured, purposive missionary denominationalism harnessed the revivalistic energies of the popular movements under Reformed institutional and covenantal self-understandings towards the upbuilding of a Christian America. The missionary self-understanding demanded new mobile, entrepreneurial skills of leadership, new vernacular, popular idioms of speech, new experimental communication media, and new, more elastic organization. Denominational initiative, risk-taking, openness and borrowing combined mission and covenant into an incredible institution-building effort, much of which went into transforming the denominations from modest associational structures into engines for national ministerial deployment and governance, making them powerful democratizing and creative forces.

The three then-mainline denominations invested significantly in establishing voluntary societies focused on various urgent causes (distributing Bibles, forming Sunday schools, furthering various reforms), drew supporters and workers from various traditions, and worked nationally. Other denominations mounted their own voluntary-society endeavors. Denominational publishing houses serviced congregations and Sunday schools with lessons, newspapers, and magazines. Colleges, founded sometimes on more promise than prospect, trained denominational ministers and lay elites. And from the local level, women and men joined the denominational and interdenominational reform and mission societies to deal with the urban poor, seamen, prostitutes, slaves, and slavery. So denominations would Christianize the continent. Purposive, missionary association generated structure and procedure faster than formal theologies and ecclesiastical polities could adjust. The adjustment would yield other styles of denominationalism.

Confessional Denominationalism

A third stage or style, a confessional denominationalism, culminated in trans-Atlantic fellowships the Lambeth Conference (1867), World Presbyterian Alliance (1877), Methodist Ecumenical Conference (1881), International Congregational Council (1891), Baptist World Alliance (1905).

PART TWO: Perspectives on Denominationalism

Various impulses, some international, some American stimulated more pronounced awareness of doctrinal, liturgical, or polity identity and the generation of a style of denominationalism competitive with purposive denominationalism. The dynamism, cultural power, and seductive appeal of American revivalistic evangelicalism induced emulation and adaptation within some communions which traditionally defined their identity in other ways, notably Reformed, Lutheran, and Anglican churches (as well as Catholicism and Judaism).

Within some of these confessional Protestant churches, augmented by immigration or by fresh theological currents, accustomed to established status abroad and threatened by marginality here, leaders emerged who drew on their respective traditions to critique camp-meeting style revivalism, the "new measures" thereof advanced by Charles Grandison Finney, expansive voluntarism generally, and associated denominational practices. Especially articulate and important were the Mercersburg theologians, Philip Schaff and John W. Nevin, who in various works parodied revivalism as the anxious bench and a "methodistical" scheme. Signature elements of purposive missionary denominationalism they deemed alien to their German Reformed tradition and its converting ordinances—catechism and the sacraments. Similarly, Charles Philip Krauth spoke for confessional Lutheranism and John Henry Hobart and Calvin Colton for proper Anglicanism, in each instance moving their denomination or a newly formed one (Missouri Synod) onto proper confessional foundations. These spokespersons appealed to their respective doctrinal heritage but drew variously on currents of Romanticism that also valued tradition, confessions, sacraments, mystery, catechism, and other hallmarks of ecclesial identity.

A second stimulus to confessionalism derived from the contest over slavery within evangelical denominations. Presbyterians divided in 1837 and Methodists and Baptists in the early 1840s, in each instance, various factors driving the schism, but slavery or anti-slavery at least in the background (for Presbyterians) and in the foreground (for Methodists and Baptists). Once divided, the rival churches rationalized their causes and explained their purposes theologically, confessionally, Biblically. In fights over turf—Methodists and Presbyterians reunited only in the mid-twentieth century, Baptists never have—each defended its polity proclaiming first principles, appealing to founder, reverting to tradition.

A third and related impulse towards churchly or confessional orientation focused on the voluntary associations a hallmark of purposive, missionary organization and, in part, on their dedication to the antislavery cause. Among Presbyterians, Old School theologians like Charles Hodge saw such institutions as ecclesially anomalous. Organized interdenominationally, overseen by interlocking boards of donors, accountable only to themselves they trafficked on churchly matters (Bibles, Sunday schools, tracts, missions) and within churchly contexts that ought to be the denomination's domain. They undertook ventures and pursued ends absent ecclesial warrant. On what basis and by what authority, did they do the church's business? Motivating the Old School and driving the 1837 division were associated concerns—over a missional concordat struck with the Congregationalists earlier in the century, Finney's "new measures," discipline cases, anti-slavery. Post-division, the Old School, restructured itself denominationally so as to bring under ecclesial authority the functions and tasks that had been launched by the interdenominational voluntary societies. Missions, Sunday school, tract, temperance and various other societies became intradenominational operations. Other movements echoed the Presbyterian brief against voluntary or missionary societies and sought to bring such ventures under church control, a pattern to be widely emulated. Similarly, antimission Baptists and Restorationists denounced voluntary societies as unbiblical, articulating a kind of nonconfessional confessionalism. Of long-term significance were the kindred efforts and primitivist ideas of Landmark Baptists, which leapt back to the New Testament and repudiated intervening centuries of Christian tradition, to warrant ecclesiologies of localism and close communion.

Corporate Organization

The fourth style of denominationalism drew on both prior stages to achieve accountability over but to affirm and increase the effectiveness of the powerful voluntary, purposive missionary societies that evangelical Protestantism had created. During the Civil War, religious community mobilization, by women and men, to supply, support, nurse and minister had demonstrated the extraordinary delivery capacities of focused, popularly based, vertically integrated, nationally managed organization. Like northern business, denominations had experienced first hand in the war effort the pay-off of top-down control and corporate organization. In part emulating the business community, in part capitalizing on its own experience, mainstream Protestantism undertook, in the late nineteenth and early twentieth centuries, significant structural reforms. Whether basically

PART TWO: Perspectives on Denominationalism

connectional or congregational in polity, denominations sought to bring under judicatory control the complex of voluntary societies—men's and women's by which they had done their business. Thereby denominations established a *corporate, board and agency system,* in effect a "managerial revolution."

This revolution—no conspiracy but broadly supported by clergy and laymen alike (the women quite another story)—aimed at checking the free enterprise, the parallel, competitive, self-guided, trustee-accountable societies that ran denominational programs. More positively, the revolution sought to increase the effectiveness of the array of enterprises being undertaken on the denomination's behalf, to achieve some coordination of their several efforts, and to bring the coordinated efforts under denominational authority. The problem? With self-perpetuating boards, distinct collections or appeals for funds across the denomination, prerogatives over programs, their own staff, separate publishing endeavors, and a network of auxiliary societies from national level, to the regions, down to congregations—all under an executive secretary—denominational societies functioned beyond denominational control.

By legislative action, as northern Methodists voted in 1872, or by more gradual initiatives, as did northern Baptists, denominations reorganized themselves internally, provided denominational oversight to heretofore voluntary societies and created a corporate board structure. Denominational boards governed these agencies. Elaborate procedures coordinated programs, finance, communication and publication. The churches experimented with new modes of collaboration between agencies and local churches, especially in areas of program and finance. And denominations structured themselves along these board/agency lines top-to-bottom, prescribing an organizational grammar. Every level of the church, from congregation, to state, to regional, to national, structured itself with the same bodies, with the same names, with the same duties. The changes created national power centers, essentially bureaucratic in nature. Gradually the churches began staffing agencies with professionals; increasing their numbers dramatically; requiring higher degrees of specialization and expertise; and exploring new schemes of systematic finance.

The mainstream denomination (described below under "The Denomination") came into being and as a collective system effectively dominated American society and culture until the mid twentieth century. In world missions, through new ecumenical orders (world, national, state and local councils of churches), by legislating temperance, in war efforts,

American Denominationalism

by control of the airwaves, despite internal doctrinal squabbles, through media coverage, and sending members into every political office, mainstream denominations ran the show. Their several-fold authority systems, internal complexity, bureaucratic program structure, professionalized leadership aligned them with American society generally, especially with business and government. By mid century, their professional elites collaborated with African Americans in leading the society and the denominations themselves to overcome segregation and racism. They began to accommodate women and minorities in the ministry. Mainstream Protestantism had weathered theological crises early in the century and seemed to be poised for continued societal leadership. Instead, as indicated, mainstream Protestantism found itself upstaged by conservative and evangelical movements, badly divided itself, facing a much more pluralistic society and effectively disestablished.

Post-Christian Denominationalism?

A fifth stage of denominationalism, might be variously dated, pinned on the 1965 Immigration Act which opened the door to Asians and Middle Easterners, to Vatican II and the election of JFK, to the Civil Rights movement and Martin Luther King Jr.'s "I have a dream" speech, to urban and Vietnam crises, or to Ronald Reagan and the ascendancy of conservative evangelicalism. Characterizing this new style proves more difficult because standing within it, we do not yet see its contours or its determinative set of understandings and practices. The received shape, described below (under "The Denomination"), evidences its determinative formation within mainstream Protestantism. However, interactions between and among mainline, historically Black and conservative-evangelical denominations in both subtle and forthright fashion and at various levels effectively exchange societal roles, operational styles, program features, communication systems, outreach mechanisms, organizational purposes. Unclear at this juncture is whether these interactions, catalogued as myriad strains below (under "Status"), are producing a new form of or the demise of denominationalism. Even less clear is whether the increased pluralism in American society and the salience of non-Protestant and non-Christian religions augur even more dramatic reconstitution of denominationalism as implied by the questions posed above (below "An End to Denominationalism").

Not yet apparent, then, is the operative theory for a fifth style and whether Protestant, Judeo-Christian, or pluralistic. More evident are

165

efforts across religious traditions to experiment with contemporary cultural forms, delivery systems, and communication networks, some undertaken by denominational agencies; others through parachurch, independent, or mega-church entities; some by congregations themselves. Members, congregations and judicatories preach, teach, and worship in digital, streaming, and electronic modes; program with franchised products; credential leadership through modular training events; focus financial and human resources with grant making and consultants; network and associate through new information systems; adopt niche strategies to recruit, reach specific cohorts (age, ethnic, lifestyle), form congregations and small groups therein; build new international and interconfessional linkages. Experiments with technique and technology stress existing associations, traditional expectations of leadership, professional elites and professionalism. Culture war divisions, internal debates over immigration, war, terror, the global economy, jostling between and among religious communities further pressure denominational systems. In places, religious life charts a nondenominational course, elsewhere a hyperdenominationalism results. Will institutional ferment produce a religiously plural American denominationalism or denominationalism stratified globally or a Protestant denominationalism adjusted to minority status in North American society?

The Denomination

The modern denomination, at least as typified by mainstream Protestantism, exhibits internal features which lend themselves to sometimes varying, sometimes multiple characterization and to differing overall impressions. In fact, denominations function with complex or multiple authority systems, each part of which proves capable of pulling in its own distinct direction, pressing for interests intrinsic to its domain, so presenting itself externally, and vying to image the denomination overall. A religious authority system—theologically warranted, biblically based, confessionally labeled, or constitutionally protected—shapes a denomination's discipline, operations, ethos, practice, decision making, and self-understanding. This system denominations sometime proclaim in their names—the African Methodist Episcopal Church, the Associate Reformed Presbyterian Church, the Evangelical Congregational Christian Conference. The names locate a significant, perhaps primary, source of authority—in the congregation, in presbyteries, in bishops (the episcopacy).

And the religious authority systems have yielded distinctive political structures or polities—episcopal, presbyterial, congregational—authority vested in bishops, in an array of church courts or legislatures (presbytery, synod, assembly) or in the congregation(s). In actuality, denominations within each of these distinctive polity types borrow aspects of the other two. Congregations, especially large or wealthy congregations, call many shots in episcopal or presbyterial polities. Most denominations have some representative or popular assembly. And in ecumenical understandings, every church has, it is argued, some bishop-like function or authority, some gathering, institution, office or process through which it exercises *episkopé* [set macron over final e] (the ministry of spiritual ordering and oversight).

Sometimes that leading or teaching function is effectively undertaken by a second system, an administrative, agency or board apparatus. Often mimicked at every level in the denomination with offices, commissions, or committees, this system implements much of the program, publishing, mission, social action, employee care (pensions, insurance) and financing (stewardship and expenditure) for the denomination. Theoretically accountable to the religious authority system, boards and agencies often function like corporations, their general secretaries operating as CECs, their staff effectively charting denominational policy, and their initiatives only redirected by bishops, conferences or conventions with great effort.

Such campaigns disclose yet a third internal system: that of congregations and regional or middle judicatories. The latter, variously termed (association, presbytery, conference, diocese, region, synod), functions administratively between congregations and the national or international structures and authority. At this level, persons join or affiliate; decisions are made to ordain, hire, and dismiss clergy; problem solving goes on; educational, training, and outreach programs are mounted; denominational style, ethos and identity are negotiated. Bishops, presidents, clerks, district superintendents, and their staff interact with pastors and congregations in quite complex ways, behaving in effect like the latter's regional service centers. Personnel services at this level once included discipline of members as well as ministers but now sustain only the latter. Here charges of clergy misconduct get dealt with either through denominational judicial procedures or by judicatory appearance in civil or criminal proceedings (or both). Findings can sometimes be appealed to other levels (one denomination, The United Methodist Church, has a separate Judicial Council), but much denominational judicial, disciplinary and personnel

PART TWO: Perspectives on Denominationalism

activity focuses on the regional judicatory. Congregations and judicatories have minds of their own with regard to nurture, outreach, program and worship, sometimes resourcing themselves with branded items from denominational agencies and publishing houses, sometimes turning to para-church or independent suppliers.

Congregations and regional judicatories nevertheless generate a fourth system, that of a representative, delegated or popular national, continental or even global assembly. Sometimes meeting annually, sometimes more periodically, sometimes permitting messengers from each and every congregation, sometimes confined to representative delegates, most frequently unicameral, these assemblies function as congresses. Such legislative prerogatives belong constitutionally there for some denominations and the assembly appropriately initiates constitutional change, votes on offices, authorizes new hymnals or doctrinal statements, sets missional policy, speaks on public issues and the like. However, even in nonconnectional or congregational denominations, the national assembly becomes the most visible, public, media-covered event, and its members or groups thereof take the opportunity to pass resolutions, press for change, or speak on moral matters. This system then provides for some measure of lay and congregational consent to or roles in denominational decision making, property holding, and financial administration. Closely related and perhaps emerging as yet another internal system are the caucuses, struggle groups, and organized campaigns—the ecclesial counterparts to political action groups, think tanks, and legislative caucuses. These come in every flavor and color, largely mimicking their sociopolitical equivalent. Pro-life and pro-choice, against and for the ordination of homosexuals, Asian, African American, Hispanic, Native American, committed to evangelism or social action, the caucuses organize, publicize, raise funds, and legislate at every level in denominational life.

Caucuses, regional judicatories, and national assemblies draw leadership from yet another denominational system, that of the church's professionals and in particular the clergy. Ministers, priests and rabbis lack state authorizing or professionally controlled associations by which all mainline, all Protestant, all Christian or clergy are credentialed or advance their professional interests. However, at least in some instances, the regional or national assembly has functioned as a denominationally-specific professional society, despite the presence therein of laity. The latter serve there on a representative capacity, sometimes for a single session, while the clergy enjoy on-going membership, lodge their identity and retain professional standing therein. Regional judicatories function thereby like professional organizations and/or the state bar. They set standards, review credentials, admit to practice, guard prerogative, press for better compensation, contract for health care, maintain pensions, oversee professional ethics. In some instances, judicatories delegate such function to clergy-only or clergy-dominated boards, committees, ordination bodies, or executive sessions, thereby masking the way ordinary denominational processes serve ministerial interest, prerogative and purpose.

Other professionals and specialists within denominations—religious educators, missionaries, deacons and deaconesses, musicians, urban ministers, college and military chaplains, evangelists, information officers, fiscal officers, large-church pastors, agency administrators, even judicatory staff—have to create their own professional organizations, have done so typically in more loosely structured and less regularly attended annual gatherings, and may seek their professional recognition through some other denominational connection, perhaps in relation to a national board or agency. Seminaries compete with denominational agencies, parachurch organizations, megachurch training programs, and various institutes in resourcing and promoting the professions. And by such representative advocacy as by its work, the professional system(s) make their own competitive effort to guide, direct, indeed, to be the church. Denominations are indeed complex systems.

Perspectives

As humanly imagined and constructed, such societal artifacts as the denomination and denominationalism should, in principle, be readily interpreted through any of the humane and social scientific academic disciplines. In recent years, sociology, particularly sociology of religion, has probed the denomination most extensively and with the greatest array of theory. Most familiarly, ideal typology locates the denomination on a spectrum—church, denomination, sect (perhaps in several categories), cult (sometimes) and mysticism (in some versions). These orderings of religious life differ in relation to the society or state, basis of membership, social ethic, foundations of authority, leadership. Sociology also examines denominations in studies of societal composition and evolution, secularization, pluralism, and religious preference (rational choice).

History, not sociology, however, offers the oldest perspective on denominations—indeed, one coeval with the phenomenon. Chronicling and

PART TWO: Perspectives on Denominationalism

publishing its own story constitutes one signal that a religious movement understands itself as a denomination. And early efforts to depict American religion did so by narrating the histories of the several denominations, an encyclopedic practice that continues. The most important of such efforts, guided by German-born theologian and historian Philip Schaff, founder of the American Society of Church History (1888), undertook to survey American religion by studying individual denominations (or denominational families) in the thirteen-volume American Church History Series (1893–97). Histories of individual denominations, for much of the twentieth century left almost exclusively to insiders and amateurs, have resurfaced as sophisticated period or region-specific case studies.

Among newer perspectives, the field of organizational studies and some examinations of voluntarism, voluntary associations, not-for-profits, and nongovernmental organizations include denominations in their purview. Bringing these several perspectives together and adding anthropology is the emergent field of congregational studies. Once more neglected even than the denomination, the congregation now is studied—close-up, carefully, creatively—as the context, shaper, instrument and expression of American religiosity. Congregational studies can, and often do, offer fresh views from the bottom-up of the denomination, its leadership, its polity, its ethos, its culture, its effectiveness. And congregational studies, when it looks across the panorama of American religion, can measure the overall health of the denominational system and assess the degree to which newer and non-Christian religious impulses take on congregational form (de facto congregationalism), a probable indicator of their assuming denominational shape as well.

Christian theology and ethics, whose intellectual domains include ecclesiology and institutional social policy, with notable exceptions have rather neglected the denomination and denominationalism.[1] And when theology has taken up the topic, it has tended to render judgment and offer criticism. In the early and mid-twentieth century, such assessments derived from ecumenical and neo-orthodox perspectives. Denominationalism emblemed Christian division and disunity, the ethical failure of the church to be the church made one in Christ. And as porous, culturally sensitive institutions that accommodated, occasionally championed, some of the worst of human practices (slavery, war, segregation, class prejudice, worker exploitation, and more recently sexism and homophobia), denominations compromised the gospel with the world, a theological scandal.

1. Gustafson, *Treasure*.

American Denominationalism

The individual who most forcefully synthesized these ecumenical and neo-orthodox judgments, H. Richard Niebuhr, did so as among the first to analyze the collective phenomenon of American denominationalism. Taking up one after another of the denominations or denominational families, he found each to have established and shaped itself around social impulses of class, caste, nationality, region, ethnicity, and language. These socially partial origins and denominations' difficulty in surmounting them earned the scathing Niebuhr's reproach and his work and views still typify perceptions of denominationalism.

> The evil of denominationalism lies in the conditions which makes the rise of sects Desirable and necessary: in the failure of the churches to transcend the social conditions which fashion them into caste-organizations, to sublimate their loyalties to standards and institutions only remotely relevant if not contrary to the Christian ideal, to resist the temptation of making their own self-preservation and extension the primary object of their endeavor.

He went on to assert, "the denominations represent the accommodation of religion to the caste system. They are emblems, therefore, of the victory of the world over the church, of the secularization of Christianity, of the church's sanction of that divisiveness which the church's gospel condemns."[2]

Niebuhr's usage of *church*, *denomination*, and *sect* made popular, indeed fashionable and evaluative, the typological categories advanced by social scientists like Ernst Troeltsch and proposed the categories of denomination and denominationalism as most apt for understanding American society. Niebuhr wrote at the highpoint of mainline Protestant ascendancy in national affairs, perhaps in world affairs—symbolized by legalized prohibition, collaboration in the war effort, formation of the Federal Council[3] of Churches and comparable leadership in establishing world organizations. But Niebuhr also wrote at a point when Protestantism's middle-class profile; prior embrace of World War II; limited sensitivity to urban, poor, immigrant and working classes; and highly racialized character were becoming ever more evident. Niebuhr consequently accented denominational conformity to society and culture and compromise of an egalitarian, inclusive, world-denying Christian ethic. Niebuhr revisited the denomination's relation to society in various sub-

2. Niebuhr, *Social Sources*, 21, 25.
3. Niebuhr, *Christ and Culture*.

PART TWO: Perspectives on Denominationalism

sequent works, in one of which he set forth a fivefold typology aimed at characterizing the longer saga Christianity's relation to the state, the social order, and culture. One of his categories, that of the "Christ of Culture," revises in less denunciatory style, the judgment he earlier levied on the denomination. His other categories, applicable in some moments to denominational life and activity in America suggest a more complex story. "Christ the Transformer of Culture" accents denominational contribution to American economic, political, and social life. And his other categories honor the diverse strategies that religious movements have imported or assumed as they negotiated their place in American society: "Christ against Culture," "Christ above Culture," "Christ and Culture in Paradox."

Status

The multivalence of denominationalism and complexity of the denomination make their status in American society partly a definitional issue. However, a variety of developments suggest, if not its decline, certainly the destabilizing of the central societal role to which Greeley pointed, as one can discern from the Pew Forum on Religion & Public Life. *U.S. Religious Landscape Survey* and from the several works by commentators on the American religious institutional scene like Robert Wuthnow and Nancy Ammerman.

- The growing North American religious pluralism may require other categories than *denominationalism* to recognize the salience and unique patterns of local and translocal institutionalization of non-Protestant Christians, Jews, Buddhists, Muslims, Hindus, followers of Native American and New Age faiths, and various types of the unaffiliated.

- Protestantism breaks into three traditions—mainline, evangelical, and historically Black—each denominationally divided but together slipping to only 51 percent of reported membership, a trajectory indicating probable future Protestant minority status.

- Membership in mainline Protestant denominations has eroded (and aged) over the last half century; and the salience, prestige, and power of mainline denominational leadership is now contested, often bested (especially as symbolized in access to the White House).

- Conservative, evangelical, and fundamentalist bodies and their leadership have experienced corresponding growth, vigor, visibility, and political prowess: their collective membership exceeds that of the mainline and constitutes over a quarter of the overall American population.

- Membership growth in Latin America, the Caribbean, Africa, and Asia and stagnation or decline in North America threatens long-standing patterns of assembly, governance, ethos, worship, and morality (on homosexuality especially).
- Denominational ethos, values, commitment, and cohesion now contend with the facts of switching, of adults shopping for a religious home after moves or childbearing, and of membership raised in other traditions or denominations: a quarter of adults are no longer a part of the religion that nurtured them; this pattern reaches 44 percent if switching among Protestant bodies is traced.
- Marriages across religious, confessional, and denominational lines (37%), persons retaining a sense of being Methodist or Presbyterian but no actual membership, disaffiliation in younger age cohorts, and adherents experimenting with various individualistic, face-to-face or media spiritualities and meditative practices also attest the weakening of denominational identity and allegiance.
- Protestant denominations contend with similar patterns of congregational independence or diffidence, reflected in selection of nonstandard educational materials or hymnals, in diversion of collections to local or nondenominational projects, in resistance to denominational programs and in the removal of denominational signage.
- Competing for congregational business and competing with denominational agencies are an array of independent and/or parachurch publishing houses, curricula suppliers, music licensers, bookstore chains, program franchisers, consultants and training outfits.
- Megachurches, some independent or nondenominational, some remaining denominationally affiliated (often loosely) now boast resources comparable to small denominations, with sophisticated broadcast, Internet, and digital presence and the capacity to meet needs heretofore supplied by denominations (such as training, literature, expertise, missions, new-church planting).
- Coalitions of megacongregations or their church plantings coalesce into denomination-like entities or function more loosely as quasi-denominations, offering training events and inspiration gatherings for wannabe clergy.

PART TWO: Perspectives on Denominationalism

- Single-purpose, lobbying, humanitarian and mission organizations and more occasional movements, gatherings, and events claim the interest, involvement, commitment, and resources once channeled through congregational structures and through denominations and denominational programs. (Such organizations include Focus on the Family, World Vision, Promise Keepers, the Institute on Religion and Democracy, Habitat for Humanity).

- Similar single-purpose, struggle, ideological or caucus groups within denominations, especially within mainline denominations, turn assemblies and conferences into contentious culture-war gatherings, tend to align into broad progressive or conservative camps, and effect connections to similar camps in other denominations and/or through religious-political-action or coalition-forming entities like the Institute of Religion and Democracy.

- Older interdenominational organizations—state, National and World Council of Churches—once harmonizing the leadership of the mainline, function within the ambit of culture wars, tending to retain the allegiance of the more progressive and to function as foil for the more conservative denominational leaders.

- Marginal membership attachment, congregational independence, culture-war sentiments, and societal prejudices engender indifference, suspicion, and sometimes hostility towards the centers and symbols of denominational identity—the regional and national headquarters and leadership, sometimes resulting in tax-resistance or other forms of revolt.

- Media ministries and newer virtual alliances and political action efforts that trade on religious sensibilities enlarge the marketplace within which religious expression and affiliation occur and induce consumption or invite appropriation of multiple beliefs, value systems, and ethical practices.

- Such public or digital visualizations of North America and of the world heighten awareness of American religious diversity, test tolerance levels, stimulate post-9/11 fears, and erode faith in or adherence to putative societal norms within which Protestant denominationalism has functioned (e.g., a Christian culture, public or civil religion, Judeo-Christian tradition[s]).

- And because denominational loyalty is tested on so many fronts, denominational leaders, ordination committees, and seminaries find themselves forced to accent confessional particularities, resulting in the strange phenomena of hyperdenominationalism contending with postdenominationalism.

AN END TO DENOMINATIONALISM?

Given the corrosive forces eroding the dominance, indeed the salience, of Protestant denominations, particularly of those that might be termed mainline or oldline, their societal, cultural, or political disestablishment, and widespread disenchantment with bureaucratic or centralized governance, should we conclude that America is no longer a denominational society? Or even that the end of denominationalism looms, as a chorus of doomsayers prophesies? Such judgments may feel appropriate to Protestant leaders anguishing over numerical decline, or to those outside mainstream denominations who experience megachurches, parachurch organizations, media ministries, or virtual spirituality to be the effective religious modality for the twenty-first century. Crisis imagery alarms and motivates for once-insiders or outsiders.

The historian, however, can ask whether the crisis interpretive mood obscures the longer saga of and overlooks earlier declarations of the doom of denomination and denominationalism. Denominationalism—the larger cultural or organizational field or family—has itself differed over time, as already noted. Adequate definitions of *denomination* and *denominationalism* can no longer be equated with mainline Protestantism or with bureaucratic-corporate forms and need to recognize changing modalities of denominational structure and governance over the course of American denominational experience and leave open the possibility that some of the newer and non-Christian movements will participate in the reshaping of denominationalism.

Indeed, the above catalogue of social strains prompts the query whether denominationalism is, in fact, undergoing reconstitution, the denominational system is broadening beyond even evangelical and historically Black churches and Judaism, and immigrant, non-Christian and newer religious impulses are organizing themselves in what might be termed a denominational pattern (the once Protestant-normed pattern of American religious organization functioning as a denominational organizational field)? Will newer movements embrace a denominational identity or label (what sociologists term "institutional isomorphism") to claim space in the religious marketplace, to safeguard their integrity in public institutions (schools, courts, places of employment), and to seek roles reserved for those religiously identified (places in military or hospital chaplaincy, for instance)? Will they coalesce as voluntary communities in patterns of de-facto congregationalism? Will they seek nonprofit status, advertise in newspapers or in Yellow Pages, and establish trustees and lay leadership cadres, committees, or boards? Will one or more of the leaders function in such congregational communities in minister-like capacities? Will the congregations gradually come to emulate their neighboring churches with 'Sunday' schools and an array of other community-building or outreach functions?

To support such multipurpose activities, will leaders and congregations collaborate with counterparts to build some translocal forms of denominational organization? And will such denominationalizing impulses be welcomed, recognized or even accommodated to by existing denominations and by American society as they did for Roman Catholicism and Judaism in the mid-twentieth century and seem to be so doing for evangelical and historically Black denominations now? Will the many studies, institutes, conferences and institutes now exploring religious diversity function as signals and means of accommodation as did Vatican II, JFK's presidency, the discovery of a Judeo-Christian tradition, and my former and late colleague, Will Herberg's landmark declaration of a wider denominationalism (in *Protestant, Catholic, Jew*)?

PART THREE

Case Studies in American Denominationalism

9

The Social Sources of Denominationalism

Methodism

The great iron wheel in the system is itinerancy, and truly it grinds some of us most tremendously; the brazen wheel, attached and kept in motion by the former, is the local ministry; the silver wheel, the class leaders; the golden wheel, the doctrine and discipline of the church, in full and successful operation. Now, sir, it is evident that the entire movement depends upon keeping the great iron wheel of itinerancy constantly and rapidly rolling round. But, to be more specific, and to make an application of this figure to American Methodism. Let us carefully note the admirable and astounding movements of this wonderful machine. You will perceive there are "wheels within wheels." First, there is the great outer wheel of episcopacy, which accomplishes its entire revolution once in four years. To this there are attached twenty-eight smaller wheels, styled annual conferences, moving around once a year; to these are attached one hundred wheels, designated presiding elders, moving twelve hundred other wheels, termed quarterly conferences, every three months; to these are attached four thousand wheels, styled traveling preachers, moving round once a month, and communicating motion to thirty thousand wheels, called class leaders, moving round once a week, and who, in turn, being attached to between seven and eight hundred thousand wheels,

PART THREE: Case Studies in American Denominationalism

> called members, give a sufficient impulse to whirl them round everyday. O, sir, what a machine is this! This is the machine of Archimedes only dreamed; this is the machine destined, under God, to move the world, to turn it upside down.[1]

THE GENIUS OF THE Methodist organization has often been remarked. George Cookman in the above passage employed the vision of Ezekiel as a figure to suggest the heavenly design of its operation. Abel Stevens, seeing the danger of barbarism in the spread of population beyond the reaches of religious influence, conceived of Methodism as a "religious system, energetic, migratory, 'itinerant,' extempore, like the population itself," necessary for and "providentially designed" for the United States.[2] This theme expanded and secularized received scholarly affirmation by William Warren Sweet in his works on Methodism and American religion. Methodist organization has been celebrated; it has also had its detractors—prophetic voices from within, some of whom exited in the name of republicanism or antislavery, and critics from without. One such critic, the Baptist J. R. Graves, organized his reflections under Cookman's image of *The Great Iron Wheel*. Its machine-like characteristics impressed Graves as "a crushing military *despotism*," "the very system of the Jesuits of Rome," "Antichrist," "spiritual tyranny," "clerical despotism," a threat to free institutions.[3]

It is not the purpose of this chapter to review or resolve the debates over the character, efficiency, methods, leadership, and impact of Methodist organization that have raged from the earliest days of British Methodism. Rather, the purpose of this chapter is to pursue a point implicit in the fact and substance of the discussion about Methodist polity. The thesis expressed in the title is that the distinctive form of the church that we know as the American denomination and designate as "denominationalism" is deeply indebted to Methodism. The principle of organization in Methodism has become the principle of denominationalism. And Methodism was the religious movement which first fully, effectively and nationally exemplified that principle. Methodism, to borrow (with alteration) H. Richard Niebuhr's phrase, was a significant social source of denominationalism. This thesis will have to be qualified in a number of important respects, Methodism's borrowings acknowledged, the role of other denominations and religious movements admitted and the place of denominationalism in

---

1. Cookman, *Speeches*, 135–37.
2. Stevens, *History*, 1:25–28.
3. Graves, *Great Iron Wheel*, 157, 162, 169.

larger societal and intellectual transformations noted. The qualifications should serve to suggest the complexity of the history of denominationalism and to raise questions about the ethical and sociological reductionism that has allowed to stand as explanation of denominationalism. The thesis when appropriately qualified should suggest that the form (as well as the idea) of denominationalism is rooted in vital religiosity. Denominationalism as a form of the church is not simply the resultant of the several divisive compromises of the Christian gospel.

H. Richard Niebuhr's *The Social Sources of Denominationalism* is generally acknowledged as the classic statement on American denominationalism. Some of what is said here is directed against Niebuhr's treatment of denominationalism. However, this chapter concerns itself with issues that are really implicit in Niebuhr's analysis and does not put his basic arguments under review. Niebuhr's theologically informed sociology, despite the title, does not seem to address itself to denominationalism as a form of the church. Rather he seemed to be concerned with the divisions in Protestantism and the factors of caste and class that explain their origin and perpetuation. He assumed the Weber-Troeltsch church/sect typology and the sect-to-church (denomination) movement. He sought to bring into view the less-than-ideal dynamics which are productive of the ideal types. This work, widely admired by historians, is more useful for its explanation of specific denominations and their social sources than for the perspective provided on denominationalism per se.[4]

Denominationalism as a Problem

A contemporary of the maturity of American denominationalism and with Philip Schaff, one of its best analysts, Robert Baird, celebrated its basic principle. The voluntary principle, he suggested, evoked Americans' "energy, self-reliance, and enterprise in the cause of religion."[5] More than adequate to the challenge posed by disestablishment and an expanding population, it betrayed the real genius of free enterprise, the American (Anglo-Saxon) peoples, and American religion, and bespoke the will (hence voluntarism) of Americans to make religious freedom work for the kingdom of God. That it produced separate denominations was not disturbing because the denominations—at least the evangelical denominations—were unified in a common mission.

4. Niebuhr, *Social Sources*.
5. Baird, *Religion in America*, 124; Schaff, *America*.

PART THREE: Case Studies in American Denominationalism

Baird's treatment epitomizes a basic strength, but perhaps also a weakness, in analyses of denominationalism. Baird looked through the denominations and denominationalism to more fundamental realities—evangelicalism, mission, voluntarism, religious freedom. Many of the most penetrating discussions of American religious institutions have shared this trait; they have looked through or around denominationalism to what appeared most basic. Hence the best treatments of religious structures are to be found in works on evangelicalism, missions, voluntarism, religious freedom, toleration, religious pluralism, separation of church and state, and religion and the nation. There is of course no want of studies of particular denominations and are ample numbers of works treating the denominations together. But Americans have been strangely reluctant to look directly at what is celebrated frequently in passing: the denominational form of the church. This reluctance must be attributable, at least in part, to a Christian conscience uneasy about divisions in the body of Christ. This uneasiness, expressed most eloquently in Niebuhr's *Social Sources*, has occasioned the search for unitive realities and unwillingness to speak about what is experienced on a day-to-day basis. Denominationalism has been left to the sociologists, whose ideal types (suggestive as they are) do not exhaust what historians and members of denominations ought to know about the phenomenon.

Denominationalism as a Form of the Church

The denomination and denominationalism, dynamic religious structures and processes, have altered considerably in the several centuries during which the term *denomination* was being employed to designate religious movements. For that reason it is important to specify that *denominationalism* will be used for the pattern of inter-institutional and intra-institutional structures, processes and relations that existed among mainstream American Protestants in the 19th century. That delimitation, while arbitrary, provides the term with specific social meaning and is necessary for discussion of the origins and character of denominationalism.

It must be acknowledged at the outset that to unravel the thread of denominationalism is to separate it from the fabric into which it was woven and thereby to remove it from that to which it belongs and which gives it shape, purpose, and significance. To affirm this is to acknowledge the value of the treatments of denominationalism under the rubrics mentioned above. Denominationalism is a form of the church possible in a society characterized by toleration or at least the spirit of tolerance, laws and customs supportive of religious liberty and de-facto (if not legal) disestablishment. Denominationalism, then, has to be understood in relation to the sagas of religious liberty, the democratic state, and bourgeois society. Quite clearly, Baptists, Quakers, and other Dissenting groups in their advocacy of and embodiment of religious freedom were social sources of denominationalism.[6] So too the struggles in this direction within other religious groups in several colonies were part of the social origins of denominationalism. The development and appropriation of the voluntary form of the church proved an essential ingredient, perhaps a precondition of denominationalism.

Histories conceived under the several rubrics related to freedom, therefore, describe important dimensions of the beginnings of denominationalism. They point to denominationalism's place within the larger story of Western voluntarism, societal differentiation, organizational specialization, and secularization. The denomination belongs within the array of associations—the free and often competitive institutions (essential to bourgeois, democratic society)—upon which Alexis de Tocqueville, William Ellery Channing, Ralph Waldo Emerson, and others commented. Association seemed the principle of democracy and of American society. Association in political life and association in civil (and religious) life were mutually reinforcing.[7]

Denominationalism, then, is to be seen as a form of the church adjusted to the realities of American society. It clearly is an adjustment to the realities of religious pluralism and voluntarism that characterized American society. The most important descriptions of denominationalism have been sketched against this background. Among the most perceptive remains Sidney Mead's depiction. It is worth quoting at some length:

> The denomination is the organizational form which the free churches have accepted and assumed. It evolved in the United States during the complex and peculiar period between the Revolution and the Civil War.
>
> The denomination, unlike the traditional forms of the church, is not primarily confessional, and it is certainly not territorial. Rather it is purposive . . . A church as church has no legal existence in the United States . . . Neither is the denomination a sect in a traditional sense and certainly not in

---

6. McLoughlin, *New England Dissent*; Stokes, *Church and State*.
7. See Tocqueville, *Democracy*, 2:123–28.

> the most common sense of a dissenting body in relationship to an established church. It is, rather, a voluntary association of like-hearted and like-minded individuals, who are united on the basis of common beliefs for the purpose of accomplishing tangible and defined objectives. One of the primary objectives is the propagation of its point of view.[8]

Mead elaborated the meaning of this purposive form of the church by noting a number of traits characteristic of denominations. They are 1) sectarian, primitivistic, and antihistorical; 2) voluntaristic, self-promotional, and activistic; 3) missionary; 4) revivalistic and therefore oversimplifying, Arminian, pragmatic, emotional, egalitarian and anti-intellectual; 5) anti-rational (anti-Enlightenment); and 6) competitive.[9]

Second to its purposiveness is another feature of denominationalism to which Winthrop Hudson as well as Mead drew attention. Denominationalism is predicated upon an understanding of the church as pluralistic yet united and in a sense ecumenical. "Denominationalism," Hudson suggested, "is the opposite of sectarianism."

> The word "denomination" implies that the group referred to is but one member of a larger group, called or denominated by a particular name. The basic contention of the denominational theory of the church is that the true church is not to be identified in any exclusive sense with any particular ecclesiastical institution. The outward forms of worship and organization are at best but differing attempts to give visible expression to the life of the church in the life of the world. No denomination claims to represent the whole church of Christ. No denomination claims that all other churches are false churches. No denomination claims that all members of society should incorporate within its own membership. No denomination claims that the whole of society and the state should submit to its ecclesiastical regulations. Yet all denominations recognize their responsibility for the whole of society and they expect to cooperate in freedom and mutual respect with other denominations in discharging that responsibility.[10]

Never adequately articulated but implicit in the self-understanding of denominations was the recognition that there was a unity of the church which transcended the observable disunity. The disunity, an inevitable

---

8. Mead, *Lively Experiment*, 103–4.

9. Ibid., 108–33.

10. Hudson, "Denominationalism," 32.

result of human diversity, did not undermine unity on essentials, on fundamentals. It did not mean that individual denominations were schisms (as Niebuhr's analysis would suggest). It did mean that unity was not to be achieved through coercion. And it meant, most importantly, that the true church and its unity were not to be fully manifested in human institutions.[11] Denominationalism was a witness to the true church by its pointing beyond the divisions in human structuring of the church to the shared unity.

The denomination in the view of Mead and Hudson is a purposive structure and conception of the church implicitly unitive or ecumenical in character. A third feature of denominationalism related its purposive character to this wider vision. The denomination was instrumental to the Protestant endeavor to Christianize society—to Christianize the new Republic and eventually also the world. The several Protestant (and specifically evangelical Protestant) denominations collaborated in endeavoring to build a Christian commonwealth in preparation for the coming of Christ's kingdom. In some instances this common task motivated and expressed itself in cooperative endeavor. The various voluntary societies—Bible tract, Sunday school, reform societies—were the most obvious reflections of the common end. As frequently, the common end was sought through competition—competition among the denominations and competition of denominations with the voluntary societies. The competitiveness has sometimes obscured the common end. But commentators on American religion from Robert Baird to H. Richard Niebuhr, James Maclear, Elwyn Smith, Martin Marty, Robert Handy, George Marsden, Mark Noll, and others have described the common efforts to erect a Christian (evangelical Protestant) society (The British sociologist David A. Martin at one point presented a similar portrayal of the denomination. Martin did not, however, relate the pragmatism or instrumentalism of the denomination to the end which legitimized the pragmatism, namely the building of the kingdom. Since the end of the kingdom was what kept the tendencies to relativism, politicization divisiveness and other human exploitations of religion in bounds, this omission is significant. To no small degree, it would seem to me, do the cynicism about the compromises of the denomination found in sociological literature derive from this oversight. To no small degree also do present difficulties in the denominations derive from their loss of the higher purpose and larger unity which once defined them and made them more than bureaucracies.)[12]

11. Ibid., 39–47.
12. Martin, "Denomination."

PART THREE: Case Studies in American Denominationalism

As Baird recognized in dividing American religion into evangelical and nonevangelical denominations, and as more recent commentators have recognized in analyzing the building of a Christian empire (society, establishment, kingdom), this unitive end of the denominations permitted and elicited degrees of participation. Religious, ethnic, racial, and regional factors affected the level of participation. Roman Catholics, Jews, and Unitarians were by definition and hostility excluded. Lutheran and certain Reformed bodies allowed ethnic and theological factors to regulate the degree of their participation. Episcopalians, Presbyterians, Methodists, and Baptists struggled over the implications of participation for tradition, theology, and polity. Black denominations, while animated by the passions of the Christianization of society, were by racial exigencies and racial prejudice excluded from full participation. Mormons, millenarian groups, and utopians defined their Christian societies over against the dominant society. Slavery and sectionalism finally wrought divisions within denominations and in the nation as a whole in the labor for a Christian empire. But when the spectrum of participation in the cause of building a Christian America is recognized, the fact remains that the dominant or normative conception of the denomination was this instrumental one. The denominations (evangelical) singly and collectively were means, that is, instruments, for the Christianization of society and the building of the kingdom of God.

H. Richard Niebuhr in *The Kingdom of God in America* recognized the dynamism, unity, and force in American religion. In emendation of his stance in *The Social Sources of Denominationalism* he analyzed the ideal of the kingdom of God on earth, showing it to have been a central preoccupation of American religious movements. But he continued to view the denominations as the halting places, the forms for preserving, the institutionalizations of these dynamic processes. Denominationalism marked the end of the dynamic movements in the church. It was the end in the sense that in attempting to conserve and preserve, leaders created institutions which killed the spirit of the movements. It was an end in the sense that the denomination became an end in itself, thus displacing with a static structure the dynamic ideal of the kingdom of God.[13]

Niebuhr's conception is at variance with the view just set forth of the denominations as purposive voluntary associations, possessed of a vision of their place in a wider Christian unity and instrumental to the kingdom of God and to the Christianization of society. Niebuhr was probably right

---

13. Niebuhr, *Kingdom of God*, ix–xiv, 11–12, 44, 164–84, and esp. 177–78.

in viewing the denominations as eventually becoming ends in themselves. The question is whether they were intrinsically the death of Christian vitality; or more to the point, perhaps, whether they are by definition static, conservative, lifeless. Much depends upon the attitude held toward institutions and upon at what point in the life of the several movements they are to be defined as denominations (only in their mature late nineteenth or early twentieth century form or in their more dynamic phases). And also open to question and/or modification is the inevitability of the sect-to-denomination process which Niebuhr posited.

These broad theoretical and historical questions cannot be addressed directly here. What can be investigated is the appropriateness of the view here set forth to the development of one denomination, The Methodist Episcopal Church (a major contributing stream to successor denominations, The Methodist Church and The United Methodist Church). What can also be shown is how the vitality of institutional development within Methodism served as a model for the denomination-building process in other religious movements. Implicitly, then, Niebuhr is answered by showing Methodism in its dynamic phases to have been a social source of denominationalism.

Methodism as a Social Source of Denominationalism

The evangelical denomination in early nineteenth-century America was, as we have suggested here and in other chapters, a purposive voluntary association, possessed of a vision of its place in a wider Christian unity and structured as an instrument for bringing in the kingdom of God and Christianizing society. The denomination was then a missionary structure and by intention national in its aspirations. Where were its origins, its fabricators, its early manifestations? They were, as the second section of this chapter and as the Introduction indicated, imbedded in the American and European experience, in the thrust of various religious movements, in the fact of pluralism, and in the conditions of religious freedom and disestablishment. To single out one religious movement as a social source of denominationalism is only to suggest a prevalence within it of influences from other religious movements and of trends affecting various facets of American and European society. To argue that Methodism was a social source of denominationalism is only to suggest that Methodism was representative, an early embodiment, an available model.

PART THREE: Case Studies in American Denominationalism

Methodism's role as exemplar of the purposive, ecumenical, and instrumental church structure derived from the genius of John Wesley; from the ambiguous status of early Methodism; from the new meaning conferred on Methodist structures and activities by its transference to the American environment where its Anglican context and ecclesiology were largely lost; and from its very successes. These factors and certain strategic and ethnic ones were to make it, rather than Moravianism, a similar embodiment of the denominational principles and also a forceful mediator of Pietism's practical (purposive), ecumenical, and reforming (instrumental) impulses, the effective transmitter of denominational form of the church.

What was Methodism's genius? It was largely the genius of Wesley. By upbringing, education, inclination, and theology John Wesley was, as Frank Baker has argued, a High Church Anglican, an early bigot for the Church of England, whose later comprehensiveness represented an appropriation of that other spirit of the Anglican Church.[14] Wesley's experientially and theologically derived eclecticism, his maturation as a folk theologian,[15] or catholic theologian[16] did not dissolve Wesley's dedication to the church or his resolve to maintain the evolving Methodist connection within it. By principle and prejudice averse to falling in with the Dissenters, Wesley through the force of his own indomitable will and a richly textured evangelical Anglicanism kept his connexion in a formally and legally anomalous position. Methodism was not a new church; nor was it to be during Wesley's lifetime one of the denominations within Noconformity. Poised between theologically and legally constituted systems of ecclesiastical authority, the Methodist structures could, like the Pietist structures that preceded them, be governed by their purposes. Methodism was purposive, a leaven within the Anglican Church, a movement to spread Scriptural holiness across the land. "The chief design of His [God's] providence in sending us out is, undoubtedly, to quicken our brethren."[17] "We look upon the Methodists," Wesley affirmed, "not as any particular party . . . but as living witnesses, in and to every party, of that Christianity which we preach." So Wesley charged his people:

> Ye are a new phenomenon in the earth—a body of people who, being of no sect or party, are friends to all parties, and endeavour

14. Baker, *John Wesley*.
15. Outler, *John Wesley*, vii–viii.
16. Williams, *John Wesley's Theology*, 13–22.
17. Wesley, "Reasons against a Separation from the Church of England," I.12, in *Works*, 9:336.

to forward all in heart-religion, in the knowledge and love of God and man. Ye yourselves were at first called in the Church of England; and though ye have and will have a thousand temptations to leave it, and set up for yourselves, regard them not; be Church-of-England men still; do not cast away the peculiar glory which God hath put upon you, and frustrate the design of Providence, the very end for which God raised you up.[18]

Affirming Methodists to be distinguished only in their commitment to "the common principles of Christianity" (not by opinions, emphasized phrases or parts of religion or "actions, customs or usages, of an indifferent nature"),[19] Wesley asserted,

> By these marks, by these fruits of a living faith, do we labour to distinguish ourselves from the unbelieving world, from all those whose minds or lives are not according to the Gospel of Christ. But from real Christians, of whatsoever denomination they be, we earnestly desire not to be distinguished at all, not from any who sincerely follow after what my Father which is in heaven, the same is my brother, and sister, and mother." And I beseech you, brethren, by the mercies of God, that we be in no wise divided among ourselves. Is they heart right, as my heart is with thine? I ask no farther questions. If it be, give me they hand.[20]

Methodism was a purposive religious society, a people, dedicated to the spread of scriptural holiness as a way of life and it was, at least by its own intentions, unitive in character. Its structures and disciplines were instrumental to these ends. Wesley was candid on this point.

> What is the end of all ecclesiastical order? Is it not to bring souls from the power of Satan to God, and to build them up in His fear and love? Order, then, is so far valuable as it answers these ends; and if it answers them not, it is nothing worth.[21]

Wesley's understanding of the development of Methodism betrays this instrumental or pragmatic view of order. Methodists, he insisted,

> had not the least expectation, at first, of any thing like what has since followed . . . no previous design or plan at all; but every

---

18. Ibid., III.1, in *Works*, 9:327. Wesley, Sermon 121, "Prophets and Priests," §18, in *Works*, 4:82–83.
19. Wesley, "The Character of a Methodist," Pref. & §3, *Works*, 9:32, 34.
20. Ibid., §18, *Works*, 9:42.
21. Wesley, "Letter to 'John Smith'" (25 June 1746), §10, in *Works*, 25:206.

> thing arose just as the occasion offered. They saw or felt some impending or pressing evil, or some good end necessary to be pursued. And many times they fell unawares on the very thing which secured the good, or removed the evil. At other times, they consulted on the most probable means, following only common sense and Scripture: Though they generally found, in looking back, something in Christian antiquity likewise, very nearly parallel thereto.[22]

The pragmatism kept Wesley in the Church as the context for his 'catholic' evangelicalism but also drove the missional initiatives towards what would be separation for the Americans during his lifetime and for the British thereafter. In his *Journal* he mused over the issues:

> One of the most important points considered at this Conference was that of leaving the church. The sum of a long conversation was (1) that in a course of fifty years we had neither premeditatedly nor willingly varied from it in one article, either of doctrine or discipline; (2) that we were not yet conscious of varying from it in any point of doctrine; (3) that we have in a course of years, out of necessity not choice, slowly and warily varied in some points of discipline by preaching in the fields, by extemporary prayer, by employing lay preachers, by forming and regulating societies, and by holding yearly Conferences. But we did none of these things till we were convinced we could no longer omit them but at the peril of our souls.[23]

Also reflective of Wesley's instrumental view of order or structure was his willingness to borrow what seemed to work—classes, bands, lovefeasts, covenant services, watchnights. The efforts to save souls produced a remarkable freedom over the structuring of the religious life.

Expediency, "inspired practical improvisation," common sense, pragmatism, eclective borrowing, the ability to recognize the general applicability of a successful local experiment, the willingness to be tutored or corrected by experience and the Holy Spirit Wesley made the Methodist way.[24] His experimental approach to structure, appropriate to the experiential mood of the eighteenth century, evidenced itself throughout the

---

22. Wesley, *A Plain Account of the People Called Methodists*, Pref., §2, *Works*, 9:254.

23. *Journal* entry, 6 August 1788: *Works*, 24:104.

24. Frank Baker, "The People Called Methodists," in Davies and Rupp, *Methodist Church in Great Britain*, 1:211–55, 213; and John Lawson, "The People Called Methodists—2. Our Discipline," in ibid., 181–209, 183; and Wesley, *A Plain Account of the People Called Methodists*, in *Works*, 9:254–80.

development and records of Methodism. Wesley structured Methodism instrumentally to its evangelical and unitive purposes. The bands, classes, and societies; itinerancy, circuits and conferences; rules, directions, minutes, sermons, *Notes upon the New Testament*; the preachers and leaders—the social network that composed the Methodist connexion—was, as Wesley declared in the "Large Minutes," "to reform the nation and to spread scriptural holiness over the land."[25]

The Wesleys, John and especially Charles, sought to keep the British Methodist movement within the Church of England and to prevent it from separating into a distinct denomination or church. Yet in its national aspirations and missionary style, in that its structures were instrumental to its unitive purposes, Methodism embodied what was to become the denominational principle. Of course, British Methodism's denominationalism was in the very real sense suspended. Wesley's churchmanship kept the connexion from perceiving itself and being perceived as a new form of the church, the denomination. However, as my former colleague Richard Heitzenrater has shown, despite Wesley's rhetorical commitment to remaining within the Church of England, his many initiatives in providing missional infrastructure to the movement oriented Methodism towards separation and independence.[26]

By Wesley's death, when the connexion was in the process of becoming independent, the organizational and missional principles constitutive of the denomination would be appropriated by the Dissenting denominations in England and by other Protestant denominations in America. The common early nineteenth-century commitment to evangelization and appropriation of missionary structures have obscured the development of denominationalism and Methodism's contribution thereunto. It appears that Methodism's denominationalism consisted in its break with the Church of England and reconstitution as an independent body. The survival after the founder's death, accompanied by the agonies over authority, ordination, licensing, and sacraments make this reading plausible and in one sense accurate. However, British Methodism could not be fully a denomination until the structural principles it embodied were allowed to become fully determinative of the connexion. This could happen when British Methodists gave up on efforts to remain part of the Church of England. But the break alone, and legal standing under appropriate English laws, would have made Methodism a denomination in name only.

25. "Large Minutes," Q. 3, in Wesley, *Works* (Jackson), 8:299.
26. Heitzenrater, *Wesley*.

PART THREE: Case Studies in American Denominationalism

Wesley had already given it its denominational style and substance, the inner missional structuring that would characterize nineteenth-century denominationalism.

By the same token the Dissenting denominations may appear to have been denominations for the duration of the eighteenth century. They bore that name and standing under the Toleration Acts. Were they not denominations? By the criteria established here—purposive, unitive, instrumental, national, missionary organization—they were, in fact, not. Until midcentury the primary institutions in Dissent were Dissenting (rather than missionally denominational) and the Presbyterians, Congregationalists, and General and Particular Baptists were names, denominations, given to ministers and congregations loosely bound by history, belief, and practice. The primary self-identification, even at points for Baptists as we note in another chapter, was that of Dissenter. Internal structuring of Congregationalism gathered momentum in response to the growth of rational and heterodox currents in Dissent in the 1730s. It was not until evangelicalism impacted itself upon both Congregationalists and Particular and General Baptists in the final third of the century, that they developed structures or recast structures—ministerial associations and academies initially—for purposes of self-propagation and mission. Their maturity as denominations was as evangelical denominations, purposive in character, whose unitive and missionary intentions manifested themselves in the work of the founders of the modern missionary movement: William Carey and company.

Whether Baptists, Congregationalists, and Anglicans borrowed missionary, purposive denominational form from Methodism is difficult to show. What can be said is that the evangelicalism that through the agency of Wesley informed the organization of Methodism came by the end of the eighteenth century to inform Baptists and Congregationalists as well. The Presbyterian interest languished until revivified by Scottish missions in the South. The Unitarians who emerged out of Presbyterian, Congregationalist, Baptist, and Anglican ranks began the process of organization in the 1790s. In their own way—hardly evangelical—they developed structures for growth and elaborated a theology in its own terms unitive which together provided them the denominationalism necessary for the stabilization of their cause.[27]

27. Watts, *Dissenters*, 1; Haykin, and Stewart, *Advent of Evangelicalism*; Wolfe, *Evangelical Faith*; Noll et al., *Evangelicalism*; Noll, *Rise of Evangelicalism*; Lincoln, *English Dissent*; Bebbington, *Dominance of Evangelicalism*.

The Social Sources of Denominationalism

Methodism's contribution to denominationalism proved ironical. Wesley's efforts prevented it from falling in with the Dissenters and becoming a Dissenting denomination. Yet the principles in the Methodist movement—what, among other factors, assured its growth and what fellow Methodist but Calvinist, George Whitefield and company, lacked—were to become the essentials in Dissenting denominationalism. While critical of the Methodists for the bulk of the century, the Dissenters came eventually to emulate them. A movement which at all costs avoided becoming a denomination was, despite its best efforts, to be the quintessential one, not in the details of its polity or ecclesiology but in the principles which, in fact, underlay them. Methodism, which has probably not received its proper recognition as a preliminary phase of the missionary movement, has also lacked credit for its contribution to denominationalism. Priority has been given to those who possessed the name—denomination—rather than to the movement within which the denominational principles were elaborated.

Denominationalism and American Methodism

The Methodist contribution to American denominationalism is not totally unacknowledged. Martin Marty in *Righteous Empire* comes close to crediting Methodists with the most basic change "in the administrative side of Christian church life in fourteen hundred years."[28] William Warren Sweet argued that Methodists were the first to organize independently and nationally. Sweet affirmed: "The first American religious body to form a national organization was the Methodists and their priority in this respect is due to the fact that their national organization was largely worked out for them by Mr. Wesley."[29] The overall importance and influence of Methodism has driven some to speak of the nineteenth century as the "Methodist Age" or to credit Methodists along with other popular denominations in the democratization of American Christianity.[30] The "stirrings" towards denominationalism within the Wesleyan movement noticed by Marty, the example of Methodist organization nationally cited by Sweet, and the Methodist mediation of revivalistic, Arminian, practical, emotional, lay

---

28. Marty, *Righteous Empire*, 67–72.
29. Sweet, *Story*, 280; Sweet, *Methodism in American History*, 100.
30. Hatch, *Democratization of American Christianity*; Schneider, *Way of the Cross*; Heyman, *Southern Cross*; Wigger, *Taking Heaven*; Lyerly, *Methodism*; Andrews, *Religion and the Revolution*; Hudson, "Methodist Age."

PART THREE: Case Studies in American Denominationalism

Christianity analyzed by Hudson suggests a large but diffuse Methodist contribution to denominationalism (of which the stirrings, organization, and religiosity are expressions) that Methodism witnessed to most effectively in America. Methodists embodied the principle that the church or denomination (church order, church structure, polity, the church as a visible reality) must be purposive, instrumental, missionary, and though in aspiration national yet recognizant of sharing that aspiration with other denominations. The principle implied that the church order did not emanate from God or by divine constitution or by scriptural dictate. It was a human creation. Of course, humanity created order in response to the guidance of the Holy Spirit, but nevertheless by an ordering of the church achieved in the present and designed to suit its activity. This denominational principle required de facto surrender of claims to be *the one, true* church—to be the church continuous with the early church or to be the only church exemplificative of the New Testament. Methodism by the accidents of its creation and implantation in America witnessed to this principle.

Methodism witnessed to this principle less ambiguously: indeed, much clearer in America than it had in England where it functioned as *ecclesiola in ecclesia*, sought to reform not leave the Church of England, and did not in Wesley's lifetime surrender the claims to be part of "the church." In America, especially after Independence, ongoing disestablishments, the agony of the transfer of Wesley's authority, and the establishment of an independent Methodist Episcopal Church, the movement became clearly what one critic quoting Coke called a "new plan." Indeed, the critics perhaps best saw Methodism's strange role. From the Episcopalian John Kewley in the early nineteenth century to the Landmark Baptist J. R. Graves in the latter part of the century, opponents denounced Methodism as "merely a human device." Kewley repeatedly called Methodism a "new plan."[31] Graves put it crassly:

> Were you asked if the economy of the Christian Church is of divine origin and appointment, you, in common with every other Christian, would answer, most emphatically, YES . . . Why, sir, in what light would a Protestant Christian be regarded in our day, who held and taught that the Christian Church was merely a human institution—a man-invented society or organization,

---

31. Kewley, *Validity of Methodist Episcopacy*, 4; For discussion of the range of anti-Methodist ideas see Lawrence O. Kline, "Anti-Methodist Publications (American)," in Harmon, *Encyclopedia*, 115–99; and Frank Baker, "Anti-Methodist Publications (British)," ibid., 119–22.

like the institutions of Odd Fellowship or Masonry, and like them, subject to all the modifications of man's ever fluctuating and capricious fancy! Would not Christendom unite in a holy crusade against the sentiment? . . .

Now, Methodism, considered as a church or society, is purely and clearly of *human origin* and device, and of a *very recent date*—indeed, it cannot boast of as an illustrious a founder as Masonry, nor of as high antiquity, by some thousands of years. Solomon is claimed (I do not pretend to say it,) as the inventor of Masonry, and the cause of its organization, the building of the Temple; while John Wesley, *when an unconverted* man, is the boasted founder of Methodism, and the cause of *its* being organized into a Church was the *Revolutionary war!!*.[32]

Methodists could and would defend their episcopacy, church order, and theology, invoking providence and the Spirit. Not being the only imitators of the primitive church, experiencing their growth before American eyes, and making their pragmatic changes in Wesley's structures, Methodists were not in a good position to claim to be the unchanged church of the New Testament. They did, in the main, remain loyal to Wesley. But Wesley himself had charged them to chart their own purposive course: "They are now at full liberty simply to follow the Scriptures and the Primitive Church. And we judge it best that they should stand fast in that liberty where with God has so strangely made them free."[33] That freedom American Methodists had exercised and continued to exercise. From what Frederick Norwood calls its "lay beginnings,"[34] through the labors of Wesley's missionaries; through the early phases of organization by Rankin, Asbury and others; through the gradual elaboration of conference structures; through the trials of the Revolution; through Wesley's ordinations, abridged Articles of Religion, revised *Sunday Service,* and appointment of Coke and Asbury as joint superintendents, "Methodists stumbled their way from society to church."[35]

With John Wesley's blessing and provision of basic documents, The Methodist Episcopal Church in a Christmas Conference of 1784 constituted itself a distinct denomination. And considerable formation lay ahead. The process of building denominational infrastructure had just

---

32. Graves, *Great Iron Wheel*, 34–35.

33. Wesley, "Letter to 'Our Brethren in America'" (10 September 1784), *Letters* (Telford), 7:239.

34. Norwood, *American Methodism*, 61–69.

35. Ibid., 101.

PART THREE: Case Studies in American Denominationalism

begun. The definition of *episcopacy*, refinement of the conference system, development of a delegated general conference, nurturing of the traveling ministry and class system, establishment through the *Discipline* of definite shape to the denomination, creation of a Methodist Book Concern and periodicals, and the testing of the denomination in early internal and external controversies made of Methodism a church order by intention national and governed by its purpose. However, in certain respects 1784 changed little, as the small American Methodist movement already had shaped itself and defined its ethos in Wesley's energetic, missionary, evangelistic, purposive style and had already accustomed itself in the Wesley mode to working alongside other religious communions. Colonial Methodism had already become a missionary order. Independence in 1784 made that ecclesial principle into a denomination.

To be sure, there were limits to Methodism's purposive or functional character. These were clearly indicated in the circle-the-wagons response to the republican revolt led by James O'Kelly and his brief for ministerial rights, the defensiveness evidenced on a variety of polity issues, the retreat from anti-slavery, the authoritarianism of Asbury, and the conservatism so pronounced in the six restrictive rules of 1808. But to note some inertias and inabilities to respond freely to new opportunities and challenges is only to say that the Methodists were not fully conscious of the significance of their own novelty nor capable of living fully into its promise. The Methodist witness to the new purposive, missionary form of denominationalism attracted adherence and emulation. In particular the United Brethren under Phillip William Otterbein and the Evangelical Association under Jacob Albright adopted and adapted Methodist structures and procedures for Reformed and Lutheran German constituencies and translated Pietist ideals, including that of being *ecclesiola in ecclesia*, for the American environment. In time other denominations would join these three in making their structures instrumental to the spreading of scriptural holiness over the land.

Denominationalism

Though Presbyterians, Congregationalists, Baptists, and Disciples of Christ reached that stage following different paths and by adapting and altering their own traditions, nevertheless in so doing they were replicating the Methodist pattern. As denominationalism reached maturity in the early decades of the nineteenth century, it did so as the joint testimony of distinct peoples and traditions that the Christianization of American society was to be their individual and common endeavor. That mission, as Robert Handy has so carefully shown in *A Christian America*, was the purpose of the denominations. Denominations were and denominationalism was purposive. To be sure there were social sources for each and all. But transcending the theological and ecclesiastical differences and the social, class, and racial distinctions was a common endeavor. The denominations were instruments of the kingdom of God. Denominations were not, then, as Niebuhr argued, the end of the kingdom. They were, under the conditions of disestablishment and religious freedom, its beginning. They were not, in their earliest phases, ends but means. That they later became ends in themselves—as Niebuhr quite rightly asserts they did—was a sign that denominations as well as the quest for the kingdom has lost the original vision.

10

History as a Bearer of Denominational Identity

Methodism as a Case Study

So it was that Methodism, with a system more mobile than that of any other church, with a message more democratic and inclusive, and with a ministry that was part and parcel of the life of the frontier, came over the mountains with the great rush of emigration, and took over the spiritual command of the commonwealths which men were hewing from the wilderness—a command which it maintains to this day.[1]

WELL INTO THE TWENTIETH century, Methodists held several propositions about themselves and their role in society. The propositions, still implicit in the above, are: 1) Methodism was/is a child of providence. 2) Providence especially fitted Methodism and the Methodist connection for American society. 3) Methodist response to and stewardship of that providential calling had benefitted both church and nation, blessing the church with great numbers and the nation with troops of true believers in the American system. 4) The purposes and ultimately the health—spiritual and physical—of Methodism are bound up in this linked mission of nation and church. Methodism's nineteenth-century historians, as we

---

1. Luccock and Hutchinson, *Story of Methodism*, 270.

shall see, gave these propositions expressive form and M. L. Scudder particularly striking renditions of these four notions.[2]

Thereby, Methodists conflated the kingdom of God with the nation, construed denominational purposes in terms of those of a Christian America, and in making the church subservient to Christian nationalism, intimately tied the former's health to the latter's. So the propositional or ideational evidence suggests. To reiterate, this chapter works on the propositional level, that is, with what Methodists affirmed about themselves. Those affirmations are derived from Methodist histories. This chapter, then, will endeavor to show how historians initially conceived Methodism's propositions, how they altered those propositions into the above form as nation and church changed, and how they struggled to make sense of the Methodist saga when the propositions no longer made sense. For reasons of control, the focus falls upon the Methodist Episcopal Church (MEC), its successor the Methodist Church (MC), and its successor the United Methodist Church (UMC). For the most part, the generalizations apply, but with important variations, to the experience of the Methodist Protestant Church; the Methodist Episcopal Church, South; the United Brethren in Christ; and the Evangelical Association as well as to members of the Wesleyan family of denominations not contributory to United Methodism.

Important and further implications follow, namely, that the demise of Christian America, the event that Robert Handy called "the second disestablishment,"[3] shattered this mission that the church had taken as its own, that no comparable purpose of such energizing dimensions has arisen to take its place, and that the present malaise of mainline denominations in general and Methodism in particular roots in this loss of purpose. This analysis locates mainline Protestantism's problem not in present agendas so much as in a faulty earlier purpose. The wedding of denomination to nation, however stimulating it proved to denominational growth, built a fundamental flaw into denominational foundations. When the promises of the First Amendment and the realities of pluralism exposed the fault line in Christian America, Methodists and perhaps also other mainline denominations suffered structural damage.

These propositions about denominational identity were widely shared. The Methodist pattern then is but an instance of a common story.

---

2. Scudder, *American Methodism*, 270, 363 on (1), 521 on (2), 524 on (3), and 569 on (4).

3. Handy, *Christian America*, 159–84.

PART THREE: Case Studies in American Denominationalism

So also their use in denominational history—the ideological use of history was not unique. The premium Methodists put on a historical fabrication of identity allows us to use them as a case study, an illustration of how in the quest for a Christian America, Methodists (and other Protestants) wrought fundamental changes in their purpose and perhaps in their character.

Why History?

At a late twentieth-century General Conference of the United Methodist Church, individuals and groups concerned to redirect the denomination and to return it to full health chose a curious vehicle for renewal. They recast the history of Methodism. They rewrote the "doctrinal history" in the *Discipline* so as to accent those aspects of Methodism which, if re-emphasized, would rejuvenate the church.[4] The strategy was an obvious and well-tried maneuver for Methodists.

From the earliest *Disciplines* down to the most recent, Methodists have begun these formal, official self-presentations with a history of the movement. The first word that Methodists have wanted to say about themselves was an historical one. For the most part, these historical statements functioned to state and hence transmit the received Methodist identity. For long periods they would be carried over intact from one *Discipline* to another. But at points of significant change, as for instance in the 1939 and 1968 unions and in 1988, Methodists struggled to reshape the history to warrant the change.

That orientation to historical self-understanding—a preoccupation derived from Wesley's practice and precept—reflected itself at a variety of points in the life of Methodism. Narrative self-presentations both stimulated and derived sustenance from the common Pietist passion for recounting individual and corporate religious experience. It "authorized" the production of endless histories of the movement, from competent surveys of the whole denomination to quite amateurish local and conference narratives. It expressed itself in myriad studies of Methodist "worthies," the bearers of the Methodist standard. It found expression in the papers and magazines, particularly the *Christian Advocates*, which reserved disproportionate space for the stories of Methodism. And it led them to require and feature history, particularly the history of the movement, in the preparation of Methodist ministers. Beginning in 1816, candidates for

4. *Discipline*/UMC (1988), 40–60.

History as a Bearer of Denominational Identity

the ministry in the MEC and successor churches followed a prescribed course of study, a reading list initially elaborated and supervised on the regional "annual-conference" level, which eventually operated as a kind of national college. Methodist History was a prominent part of this course of study from the beginning. L. Dale Patterson has carefully identified the literature of the course and the years each item was used.[5] History served to express and even to shape Methodist identity and to transmit denominational culture.

This chapter will explore shifts in Methodist identity and culture as they are reflected in Methodist histories and proceed then to reflect about history as bearer and transmitter of denominational identity. The historians treated (in chronological order) are Jesse Lee, Nathan Bangs, Abel Stevens, Matthew Simpson, James M. Buckley, the team of Halford E. Luccock and Paul Hutchinson, William Warren Sweet, and Frederick Norwood—each of whom, in some sense, spoke authoritatively for and about the movement. With the exception of Jesse Lee and James M. Buckley, whose histories claimed preeminence on other grounds, the individuals given attention here figured prominently in the MEC course of study, constituting an important formative influence on successive generations of Methodist ministers. In most cases, the individual histories enjoyed a long life on the course. Abel Stevens's *History of the Methodist Episcopal Church* appeared on the course in 1864, 1868, 1880, 1896, 1890 and then again in 1932; his compressed version, *A Compendious History of American Methodism*, remained on from 1872 to 1908, with only a curious gap of 1900, when another of his works took its place. Lee wrote the first Methodist history and in many ways set the terms for the genre. Buckley's effort appeared in the prestigious American Society of Church History Series.

Providence

In 1784, the newly organized Methodist Episcopal Church provided itself a constitution or quasi-constitution, adapting one elaborated by the British Methodists under John Wesley, a document known as *The Large Minutes*. The first American *Discipline*, that of 1785, followed the question-and-answer format of the British *Minutes* and its sequence of questions.[6] The 1787 revision of the first *Discipline* put a new order to the questions and a historical frame on the constitution. The first asked, "What was the Rise of

---

5. Patterson, "Ministerial Mind."
6. Tigert, *Constitutional History*, 532–602.

PART THREE: Case Studies in American Denominationalism

Methodism so called in Europe?" the second, "What was the Rise of Methodism, so called in America?" the third "What may we reasonably believe to be God's design in raising up the Preachers called Methodists?" The answers briefly sketched the founding acts and founding impulses of the movement. The third answer deserves citation. It has been recited down to the present as a statement of Methodist purpose. It retained the substance of Wesley's answer but now nuanced to fit the new land. God's design was

> To reform the Continent, and spread scriptural Holiness over these Lands. As a Proof hereof, we have seen in the Course of fifteen Years a great and glorious Work of God, from New York through the Jersies, Pennsylvania, Delaware, Maryland, Virginia, North and South Carolina, even to Georgia.[7]

These early Methodists had a vivid sense of America. Even as a small band of itinerants, they had traveled its roads, forded its waters, crossed its mountains and penetrated its wilderness. This litany of states evoked their direct experience with the outpouring of God's Spirit upon the American landscape. The first proposition—that Methodism was providentially given and directed—expressed their very being. They found it axiomatic. Methodism was providential. The other propositions they would have found strange and discordant.

Jesse Lee shared the Christmas Conference's vision of Methodism as an impulse of providence. Indeed, we may fittingly view his *Short History of the Methodists*[8] as a fleshed out version of this initial providential reading of the Methodist saga. Jesse Lee missed the 1784 constitutional gathering known as the Christmas Conference, missed it because he was some five hundred miles distant when he received the summoning word and nursed some grudges for being so belatedly informed.[9] He began travelling with Bishop Francis Asbury immediately thereafter, came to exercise considerable influence in the Methodist leadership, blazed the way for Methodist into New England, and served as chaplain to Congress. Lee missed election to the episcopacy by a narrow margin. And, of course, he could serve Methodism in only one place at a time. However with due allowance for his frailty and finitude, we can say that otherwise Lee left his imprint on early Methodism. Sweet termed him "the most popular of all the early Methodist preachers."[10] He both made and wrote Methodist

---

7. *Discipline*/MEC (1787), 3–4.
8. Lee, *Short History*.
9. Thrift, *Memoirs of Jesse Lee*, 67ff.
10. Sweet, *Methodism*, 176.

History as a Bearer of Denominational Identity

history, as would be the case for Methodist historians throughout the nineteenth century. His *Short History* was the first serious effort to sketch the contours of the movement. Lee's construction of the movement did not, however, please all. The General Conference actually rejected the volume; Asbury thought it inadequate on his own role.[11] Certainly part of the reason for controversy derived from the very personal vision that Lee provided.

Lee told the Methodist story as he saw it. He had seen enough of the whole that we get from him a remarkably well rounded account. Subsequent historians have consistently drawn upon him for the documents that he reproduced, the events for which he provides the most complete eyewitness account, the very vividness of his portrayal. The revivals that he experienced and led; the conferences he attended and whose legislation he could then report first hand; the penetration of "enemy" Puritan territory that he led; the general explosion of the movement over the new nation, that his extensive travels documented; the advent of the camp meetings which he witnessed—these personal involvements in the development of Methodism give shape and vigor to his narrative. Doubtless that very personal, idiosyncratic perspective offended his colleagues who could not help but feel that Lee had implicitly claimed for his own what belonged to them all. And yet in another sense, this very personal vision did stand for them, in the way that the historical preface to the *Discipline* stood for them, for their conception of their history, history as immediate and perceivable instances of God at work. For that is how providence functioned for Lee. He offered no grand theory of providence at work. Nor did he explicitly claim the Methodist connectional system to be providential. Rather, he pointed concretely and specifically to the presence of God among the Methodists. For instance, of a 1788 Baltimore conference Lee reported:

> During the time of the conference, we were highly favoured of the Lord, and souls were awakened and converted. On Sunday, the 14th of September at 3 o'clock in the afternoon, Mr. Asbury preached in Mr. Otterbein's church; and the people were generally solemn and much affected; he then asked another preacher to pray and conclude: and whilst he was praying, an awful power was felt among the people. Some of them cried out aloud . . . and in a little time there was such a noise among them, that many of the Christian people were measurably frightened, and as there

---

11. Bangs, *History*, 2:322-23; Asbury, *Journals*, 2:640-41; and Leroy Lee, *Jesse Lee*, 466.

PART THREE: Case Studies in American Denominationalism

> was no opportunity for them to escape at the door, many of them went out at the windows, hastening to their homes. The noise had alarmed hundreds of people who were not at the meeting, and they came running to see what was the matter, till the house was crowded, and surrounded with a wondering multitude. In a short time some of the mourners lost the use of their limbs, and lay helpless on the floor, or in the arms of their friends. It was not long before some of them were converted ... This day of the Lord's power will never be forgotten by many who were present.[12]

Lee claimed Methodism to be providential by showing providence at work.

In similar fashion, he showed Methodism's attachment to the United States. He did not, most certainly did not, wrap the nation around the church. Indeed, with most early Methodists, Lee evidenced the pattern of affection-but-alienation that R. Laurence Moore shows to be so prototypically American—a kind of sectarian distancing of self and movement from nation and society at the same time that full loyalty is proclaimed and efforts are even made to convert and transform the society.[13] Lee did make unmistakable his own and American Methodism's patriotism. He criticized, for instance, the "head preachers ... all from Europe," some of whom "were imprudent too freely against the proceedings of the Americans" during the Revolution.[14] And he presented the Methodists' own march to independence from Wesley and the British connection as an appropriate development. But Lee did not providentially connect church and nation. Lee thought providence to be rather specifically focused on the work of salvation. Connections of general providence and the fate of nations therein did not interest him.

Providential Design

By 1792, according to Bangs, Methodism had brought "about one-twentieth part of the entire population" under its influence, some 198,000 attenders out of a population of four million. Such growth, "in the short space of thirty-six years," and despite the advantages enjoyed by other denominations, required explanation. Bangs found himself forced "to the conclusion that their prosperity must be attributed to the blessing of God

---

12. Lee, *Short History*, 139–40.
13. Moore, *Religious Outsiders*.
14. Lee, *Short History*, 60.

upon their labors." He continued, "We therefore say again, that its forward course can be accounted for only by supposing the sanction of the most high God upon their labors."[15] At the end of the fourth volume, having brought the church down to 1840, Bangs rendered the same judgment—that the "success and influence of Methodism" had "one true original cause, namely, the divine agency."[16] Concern with Methodist numerical success led Bangs from the providential character of Methodism towards a second proposition—the providential connection of church and nation.

Like Lee, Bangs was an actor in that which he interpreted. He also made his mark on New England Methodism, particularly as Methodism's foremost spokesperson for Arminianism and against Calvinism. "Nathan Bangs: Apologist for American Methodism" one interpreter called him.[17] That he was and more. Bangs labored effectively not only to speak on Methodism's behalf to its "cultured critics" and the religious establishment, but also to remake Methodism so that it might claim its place in the American religious establishment. Bangs played that reshaping role from his office as book agent, effectively the executive secretary and the teaching office of the church. What he wrought might be termed the revolution of the 1820s, the wholesale restructuring of Methodism—creating missionary, Sunday school, and tract societies; launching and editing a major weekly, *The Christian Advocate*, and a journal of theological opinion, *The Methodist Magazine*; establishing educational institutions; and founding the course of study, Methodism's four-year national reading course in preparation for ministry.[18] Bangs sought to make the church an effective force in national life.

When sketching the hand of providence in this Methodism on which he also had laid a hand, Bangs could not be content with simple and discrete providential instances, though he like Lee eagerly pronounced events both large and small to be of divine agency. No, Bangs saw that the divine agency extended also to Methodism as a system and its operation. And Bangs also recognized a providential connection between church and nation. To that end, he chose to begin the saga of American Methodism not with Wesley but with Columbus and proceeded to an examination of "the civil and religious state of the people at the time Methodism was

---

15. Bangs, *History*, 1:356–52.
16. Ibid., 4:436.
17. Hermann, "Nathan Bangs."
18. Pilkington, *Methodist Publishing House*, 169–219.

PART THREE: Case Studies in American Denominationalism

introduced."[19] This was a self-consciously interpretive gesture on the part of a man with quite keen historical skills. Bangs prefaced his four-volume work, for instance, with a discussion of his sources. Among them, he acknowledged Bancroft's *History of the Colonization of the United States* for his initial discussion. He defended his decision to make "Bishop Asbury the principal hero of the narrative." And he indicated his respect for and dependence upon Jesse Lee's earlier history.[20] Bangs saw "benignant Providence" in the peopling of the land, the development of civil and religious liberties, the respect accorded Scripture and the Sabbath, the widespread profession of Christianity, the influence of revivals, the atmosphere of toleration—in short, the creation of a situation "highly favorable" to Methodist "evangelical labors."[21] Methodism's introduction into the land also showed providential design.[22]

At various points, his providential treatment of America was evocative of the Christian republicanism now recognized to be so significant in both national and mainstream Protestant life.[23] And yet Bangs did not really offer a providential reading of the nation as such; he did not provide a public theology. Bangs took interest in providence and Methodism, not providence and America. Or perhaps we should say, he was interested in the public roles that providence exercised through Methodism. For instance, in measuring the impact of camp meetings and the revivals at the turn of the nineteenth century, Bangs spent some five pages on the "most happy and conservative influence upon our national character," "the conservative influence which vital, experimental, and practical Christianity exerts upon individual character, upon social and civil communities, and of course upon states and empires."[24] Though Methodism exercised a politically and socially constructive influence, Bangs insisted that it was purely religious in its intent and operation:

> The influence therefore, which she has exerted upon the civil destinies of the republic, has been altogether of an indirect and collateral character, growing out of that moral and religious

---

19. Bangs, *History*, 1:11.
20. Ibid., 1:6, 7.
21. Ibid., 1:22, 26, 30.
22. Ibid., 1:46.
23. See chapters 1 and 4.
24. Bangs, History, 2:146–48.

History as a Bearer of Denominational Identity

stamp with which she strives to mark and distinguish all her children.[25]

Bangs could be quite effusive about the political consequences of such indirection. For instance, he thought the national operation of Methodism functioned to cement the union together and to counter the politically divisive force of state governments.

> In addition to the direct influence which Christian principles were thus brought to exert on the heart and life, the itinerating mode of preaching had a tendency in the natural order of cause and effect, to cement the hearts of our citizens together in one great brotherhood . . . What more calculated to soften these asperities [state and sectional rivalries], and to allay petty jealousies and animosities, than a Church bound together by one system of doctrine, under the government of the same discipline, accustomed to the same usages, and a ministry possessing a homogeneousness of character, aiming at one and the same end—the salvation of their fellow-men by means of the same gospel, preached and enforced by the same method—and these ministers continually interchanging from north to south, from east to west, everywhere striving to bring all men under the influence of the same 'bond of perfectness'? Did not these things tend to bind the great American family together by producing a sameness of character, feelings, and views?"[26]

Bangs noted that the church in its General Conference recognized that "a general itinerating superintendency [episcopacy] would "prevent local interests and jealousies from springing up, and tend most effectually to preserve that homogeneousness of character and reciprocity of brotherly feeling by which Methodism had been and should be ever distinguished" (3:54–55).

(This is a point which Donald Mathews once elaborated into a general theory concerning the second Awakening and C. C. Goen into a theory of the cause of the Civil War.[27] But such notes were quite occasional. Bangs focused upon Methodism. It was the providential character of Methodism, not the providential character of the nation, that interested him. Incidentally, providence worked through Methodism and Methodists for the good of the nation. However, church not state remained providence's aim.

---

25. Ibid., 2:150.
26. Ibid., 2:148–49.
27. Ibid., 3:54–55; Mathews, 'Second Great Awakening"; Goen, Broken Churches.

PART THREE: Case Studies in American Denominationalism

Providential Connection

Bangs had tentatively connected church and nation. Abel Stevens drew the providential connection of church and nation firmly. Firmness was characteristic of Stevens, who held a series of important editorships in the tumultuous middle decades of the nineteenth century, *Zion's Herald*, the New England Methodist paper, then *The National Magazine*, and finally *The Christian Advocate*. Through those immensely influential posts, he spoke a moderating, even conservative word to the church, prizing its unity at the cost, some thought, of its witness.

Stevens entitled the first chapter in his *Compendious History*, "Methodism—Its Special Adaptations to the New World."[28] In what follows, we make most frequent reference to this condensed version (608 pages) of Stevens' various Methodist histories. This version appeared on the Course of Study for the quadrennia of 1872 to 1908 with the sole exception of 1900. That year his *Supplementary History of American Methodism*, which had just appeared, took its place. The course also featured Stevens's four-volume *History of The Methodist Episcopal Church* in 1864, 1868, 1880, 1896, 1900, and again interestingly in 1932. His work covering the whole Wesleyan tradition, *History of the Religious Movement of the Eighteenth Century Called Methodism*, enjoyed the longest, most sustained tenure on the course, continuously from 1860 to 1928, with the sole exception of 1884. The combined 92 year reign, 1860 to 1932, attests the great influence enjoyed by Stevens.

The chapter and the volume begins with a striking, but imaginary event of 1757. That year, John Wesley, "inventor" of Methodism, and James Watt, inventor of the steam engine, found themselves at Glasgow University. Stevens imagined a chance meeting of these two in the university quadrangle, the inventors of the two machines for the conquest of the new world. "Watts and Wesley might well then have struck hands and bid each other godspeed at Glasgow in 1757: they were co-workers for the destinies of the new world." Watts had produced the engine for the conquest of the new world physically, Wesley that for the conquest of the new world morally.

> Methodism, with its "lay ministry," and "itinerancy," could alone afford the ministrations of religion to the overflowing populations; it was to lay the moral foundations of many of the great states of the West.

28. Stevens, *Compendious History*, 17.

> A religious system, energetic, migratory, "itinerant," extempore, like the population itself, must arise: or demoralization, if not barbarism, must overflow the continent.
>
> Methodism entered the great arena at the emergent moment . . . It was to become at last the dominant popular faith of the country, with its standard planted in every city, town, and almost every village of the land.
>
> Methodism thus seems to have been providentially designed more for the new world than for the old. The coincidence of its history with that of the United States does indeed seem providential.[29]

Stevens liked the symbolism of the imaginary meeting of Watts and Wesley. He began his four-volume *History* with the same scene but with a different chapter title. His *Religious Movement* gave only incidental attention to American developments and so did not lend itself to this vignette. Stevens achieved the same point there, the providential fitting of Methodism for America, with different staging and assertion.[30] Between and among these affirmations, Stevens sketched the contours of the Methodism system, a machine the elements of which seemed providentially suited to this American mission. Providence had indeed blessed America with Methodism and Methodism with America. Stevens saw in this new order that vision that Augustine had sought, "the city of God."[31]

Though enunciating the third of the Methodist axioms, Stevens like his predecessors stopped short of a full-fledged public theology. Indeed, his affirmations about America touched land as much as state, the new world as much as the new republic. Watt and the steam engine, Wesley and the Methodist engine, imaged a providential ordering of America as a whole—land, culture, peoples, society, economy. Providence extended its rule over America preeminently through Methodism.

A CONJOINT MISSION

Matthew Simpson focused Methodist attention more sharply on the American state and so articulated the fourth Methodist axiom. This was a fitting service for a man whose life was dedicated to politics, in church and in state. College professor and president, like Bangs and Stevens an editor

---

29. Ibid., 18, 19, 22–23, 24.
30. Stevens, *Religious Movement*, 2:434–37.
31. Stevens, *Compendious History*, 176.

PART THREE: Case Studies in American Denominationalism

(*Western Christian Advocate*), delegate to General Conferences, then in 1852 a bishop, Simpson employed pen, platform, and power on behalf of antislavery and union. Confidant to Lincoln, Simpson used his access to Washington inner circles to gain appointments for Methodists and control over Methodist Episcopal Church, South buildings in territory that fell to Union troops. When Lincoln fell, Simpson preached funeral sermons in Washington and at graveside.[32] Simpson's history, unlike that of Stevens, reflected Methodism's Civil War experience, an involvement which had wedded the Methodist Episcopal Church to the nation. (An even more striking public theology, wedding church and nation, can be seen in Jesse T. Peck's *The History of The Great Republic, Considered from a Christian Standpoint*.[33])

Simpson's *A Hundred Years of Methodism* appeared in observance of the American centennial. It did not displace Stevens on the Course of Study but was put on a different segment of the Course, the reading list for local preachers. It first appeared there in 1876 and remained for three more quadrennia, following the General Conferences of 1876, 1880, 1884, and 1888. Appropriately, for the time and certainly for the man, Simpson began with a survey of national accomplishments, the contributions of America to the world. Then he flashed back to Wesley and British Methodism. It was American origins, however, not these "foreign" ones that stamped American Methodism. "The rise of Methodism," he insisted, "was coeval with the Revolutionary spirit." Both during the Revolution and thereafter Methodism suffered because of its British connection.

> It is somewhat singular that nearly all the troubles and secessions in Methodism have arisen from trying to introduce English ideas and plans into our American Church, or, in other words, from trying to condense our immense continent into the area of a little island. Every agitation has begun by extolling British usages and depreciating American.
>
> In every instance, however, the Church has adhered to American ideas, and has resolutely refused to change her policy at such dictation.[34]

An *American* Methodist church, that was Simpson's topic. It was this dynamic and rapidly growing church, the success story of American Methodism, that Simpson sought to explain. Like his predecessors,

32. Crooks, *Matthew Simpson*, 397–403.
33. Peck, *History of The Great Republic*, 2, 693, 707.
34. Simpson, *Hundred Years*, 41, 68.

Simpson gloried in statistics, in growth. He found "reasons of the remarkable increase of the Methodist Church" in three superior features of its life, "the superiority of its doctrines, the efficiency of its organization ... the piety, earnestness, and activity of its ministers and members." Such claims had led his predecessors almost inevitably and immediately to invocation of providence. So M. L. Scudder as we noted initially or C. C. Goss in his *Statistical History of the First Century of American Methodism*: "The moral influence of Methodism is at least commensurate with its numerical strength. In no department of Christian effort are Methodists behind their sister denominations." Such affirmations abound in this period.[35]

However, Simpson made much less of providence than predecessor historians. When he did speak of it, the nation rather than the church came into focus. Of the war and emancipation, for instance, he said:

> We can now ... see the guidance of an all-wise Providence, which overruled the counsels of men in the midst of all these commotions. It was the Divine will that slavery should be destroyed. With determined purpose, step by step, the South moved forward in the separation, first, of the Christian Churches, and then in the attempted division of the States, to that fearful war which resulted in the emancipation of the slaves. No instance in history more clearly shows how God has made "the wrath of men to praise him, and the remainder of wrath" he has restrained.[36]

Here was Mead's "nation with the soul of a church" or perhaps even a church whose soul was the nation. Simpson held all four Methodist propositions. However, the accent fell on the last, the providential linked mission of church and state. In the spirit of the centennial, Simpson spoke with confidence of this conjoint mission, mindful to be sure of the great cost with which it had been vindicated, but even so, especially so, with a providential, even millennial confidence.[37]

WHITHER PROVIDENCE?

James M. Buckley struck no such ebullient note. Rather he concluded his assessment and essayed twentieth century prospects in *A History of the Methodists in the United States*[38] by pondering the question, "Has Method-

---

35. Goss, *Statistical History*, 15; Scudder, note 2.
36. Simpson, Hundred Years, 345 156–57.
37. Ibid., 209.
38. Buckley, *History*.

ism lost to a dangerous degree its original vital impulse?" and by invoking John Wesley's worry that "the people called Methodists" might become "a dead sect, having the form of religion without the power." Buckley obviously shared Wesley's worry:

> The founders of Methodism had no enterprises that were not distinctly subordinate to the conversion of men and their spiritual training. Now its enterprises are many and complex, often pervaded by a distinctly secular element, which contends constantly with the spiritual.[39]

American Jeremiahs have typically prophesied doom to achieve revival and reform.[40] Buckley proved no exception. He called for the renewal of the Methodist spirit and identified the requisite resources. And yet his rendering of Methodism's history, if carefully read, suggested grounds for pessimism. In Buckley's account, providence had seemingly loosed her grasp on church and on nation.

This judgment about Buckley and providence is extremely ironical, for in some ways Buckley was more self-conscious about providence than his predecessors. That concern he shared with the general editor of the important series in which his volume figured, the American Church History Series (ASCH). The editor was Philip Schaff, who argued strenuously that it was the church historian's office and responsibility to discern the activity of God in human affairs. Schaff was a major, perhaps the major, figure in the emergence of the discipline of church history. The inclusion of Buckley's volume in his series gave it great prominence. It was certainly frequently reprinted or republished, twelve times according to Kenneth E. Rowe's *Methodist Union Catalog*. First published in 1896, Buckley's history went through six editions as a part of the ASCH series, the 6th appearing in 1907. Another version was reprinted in a 3rd edition in 1909. The first edition enjoyed yet a later reprinting in 1973. It is because of the importance of this series and of Buckley's inclusion in it, that we include Buckley in this study. His work apparently did not appear on the Course of Study.[41]

Philip Schaff designed the series to display the professional prowess of The American Society of Church History. For the Methodist volume he chose its preeminent spokesperson. Buckley played a major and a conservative role in its national affairs. He was delegate to General Conferences

---

39. Ibid., 685–86.
40. Bercovitch, *American Jeremiad*.
41. Rowe, *Methodist Union Catalog*, 2:209–10.

from 1872 to 1912. He edited the official and national paper of the denomination, *The Christian Advocate*, from 1880 to 1912. On several important matters, most notably women's role in the church, he stood steadfast and effectively against change. The past and history seemed, at times, to be his forte.

At two important places in his *History*, Buckley stopped to consider the relation of the human and the divine. He devoted Chapter VIII to the work of the Spirit in early Methodists, specifically considering Benjamin Abbott, John Dickins, Caleb B. Pedicord, Thomas Ware, and Jesse Lee and the responses they elicited. Noting that Methodists construed the highly demonstrative behavior evident in conversions and revivals "to be direct results of the power of the Holy Spirit, and manifest proofs of His presence and approval of the work." Buckley inventoried other explanations—naturalistic and particularly psychological explanations—of the phenomena. He conceded that "Various factors were involved in producing the effects of Methodist preaching and methods," but that among them "was the might of the Holy Spirit." And the effects when carefully essayed and correlated with Scripture, Buckley affirmed, establish "the divine origin of the movement as conclusive as that furnished when holy men of old spake not of themselves, but as they were moved by the Holy Ghost." So Buckley wrenched a providential meaning out of Methodism.[42]

Buckley returned to the theme of providence at the end of his narrative, to worry again over Methodism's prospects. For the most part, however, Buckley remained uninterested in the providences underlying Methodist development and content to explain Methodism in naturalistic fashion. Quite a few of the stray exceptions—statements that God's hand can be found in Methodist affairs—occur in passages that he cited.[43] Buckley offered us, then, a curious irony. He insisted vehemently on the importance of providence but proved curiously unwilling or unable to point to its presence and activity. Providence had assumed doctrinal rather than historiographical force for him.

One could hardly assert that his reluctance to advance providential claims for Methodism typified the turn-of-the-century movement. Methodists generally continued the triumphalism so clearly evidenced in Scudder and Simpson.[44] Nor was he typical in his neglect of similar triumphal claims for the nation. Historians after him would entertain the four propo-

---

42. Buckley, *History*, 217, 220–21.
43. Ibid., 170–71, 173, 176–77, 179, 203, 205, 248.
44. Wheeler, *One Thousand Questions*, especially questions 1 and 66 (pp. 1, 16).

PART THREE: Case Studies in American Denominationalism

sitions and search for appropriate meaning thereof. Nevertheless, Buckley had taken Methodism around an important turn. He had effectively given up the affirmation that lent plausibility to the four propositions—that providence could be seen at work in Methodism.

This was a fitting posture to be taken in a volume that would stand cover-to-cover with histories of other American denominations. Buckley may well have felt constrained by the series. He certainly forewarned the reader that he could not, in good conscience, advance providential claims: "It is not within the province of the historian of his own communion, and in part of his own time, to pronounce judgment upon the motives of those professing 'like precious faith.'"[45] At most, historians should aspire to present the developments so fairly that the reader would draw that conclusion.

The reader intent on drawing the four propositional conclusions would have received help from Buckley only on the first. He did present Methodism as "the lengthened shadow" of Wesley and construe Wesley as "The Man of Providence." [46] As we have seen, a limited providential meaning for Methodism can be detected. The other claims apparently did not interest him. He chose, in fact, an interesting place to begin the Methodist story, one wholly out of keeping with the other three propositions. He started with Henry VIII and the English Reformation. From such national and denominational humility interesting consequences flowed. They flowed gradually.

Humpty Dumpty

In spirit and assertions, Halford Luccock and Paul Hutchinson's *The Story of Methodism* resembled Simpson, not Buckley. They chatted with the reader about Methodism; provided upbeat, celebrative, and personal estimates of its power and significance; and claimed providential guidance for the movement with a frequency that recalls Lee or Bangs. Yet, their very easiness with the providential claims is striking, perhaps worrisome. Do Buckley's critical premises haunt their breezy confidence? Do their assertions betray superficiality or conviction? Illustrative, perhaps, is this statement concerning the crowds who heard Wesley: "Clearly the hand of God was in this, for here were myriads—the word is Wesley's own—of people who never darkened a church door brought to hear a word that was again proving its ancient power." (19). Or again, "Whether he realized

45. Buckley, *History*, xviii.
46. Ibid., 1–2, 40–72.

History as a Bearer of Denominational Identity

it not, John Wesley returned to his great task in England at the moment when the movement of world forces had marked that 'tight little island' for a spiritual shaking. ... England was ringed round with revival. It was time something burst loose."

Of the sending of missionaries to America: "It was a prophetic moment at which Boardman and Pilmoor sailed." And, "Methodism did not spring to life in America without long years of preparation. There is always a background for spiritual marvels, even when it is least apparent."

Of the church-organizing events of 1784:

> The ordinations of Methodism are entirely outside the mechanical realm. They derive their authority from the fact that their originator, John Wesley, was a man whose ministry was evidently approved of God. And if ever the time comes when the ordaining ministry of Methodism is not thus approved, it will be time to scrap the whole thing, and start again from another life with self-authenticating powers.

Similarly breezy is the comparison they make between the shadows of two men on horseback: Napoleon Bonaparte on Europe, and Francis Asbury on America: "It is still easy to trace in the affairs of the United States the influence of this single man, Francis Asbury—Methodism's man on horseback. God send us such another!"[47]

Halford E. Luccock held pastorates, served as editorial secretary of the Board of Foreign Missions (1918–24), taught in several theological schools, including a long stint as professor of preaching at Yale (1928–53). A prolific writer, from 1924 until his death he contributed to *The Christian Century*. The *Century*'s managing editor from 1924 to 1947 and its editor from 1947 to 1956 was Paul Hutchinson. Hutchinson shared Luccock's literary and missionary activities and concerns. He too was prolific. Their common journalistic bent is evident in this popular account of Methodism. Their predecessors, even Lee, attempted to be scholarly according to the expectations of the day. Luccock and Hutchinson made no such effort. The volume footnoted only where cited material was protected by copyright. Luccock and Hutchinson's *The Story of Methodism* appeared on the Course of Study from 1932 through 1956. For all of those quadrennia except 1944, it was collateral reading. In 1944, it was required for admission of persons to ministerial candidacy on probation or as historically and still then termed, "on trial."

---

47. Luccock and Hutchinson, *Story of Methodism*, 19, 73, 142, 172, 158, 232.

PART THREE: Case Studies in American Denominationalism

Evident also is the premise they shared that the twentieth would be *The Christian Century*. They confidently traced the parallel development of nation and church. One early chapter, titled "A Tale of Two Villages," examined two English towns "which gave to the English-speaking world the most transforming spiritual forces of the seventeenth and eighteenth centuries." Scrooby launched the Pilgrims; Epworth was home to Wesley. "From the first, in truth if not in actual chronicle, the Mayflower set sail to plant a new world. From the second, John Wesley went out to save an old one."[48]

Once they had Methodism firmly planted on these shores, they returned to the parallels of church and nation. In "Methodism in the New Republic," for instance, they implicitly compared Asbury and Washington and explicitly compared James O'Kelly and Patrick Henry (213–17). They dwelt on Methodism's popular, even democratic, character and celebrated its pioneer and frontier spirit (217–300). The genius of the movement, in fact, is its spirit of adventure, its willingness to experiment, its pragmatism. They did not invoke Frederick Jackson Turner explicitly but found their own term for the frontier spirit, Methodism's "irregularity" (333–34, 494–95). The camp meeting typified Methodism's irregularity (264). They found that spirit of adventure also in missions, to which they devoted considerable attention, making their volume in some respects a study of world Methodism. But again and again, they returned to Methodism and the nation. In the late nineteenth century, nation and church were paralleled on seven particulars: the application of polity, spirit and organization to new conditions; elaboration of national organization; extensive building; the closing of the frontier; an increase in democracy, foreign affairs, and Negro education (440–42). They also paralleled the international perspectives of nation and church in the period after the First World War (486–87). And of course, they took great interest in the causes that riveted the church's attention on the nation—the civil war, reconstruction, temperance, the social gospel and world war.

Such challenges evoked the Methodist spirit, of adventure, of irregularity. Luccock and Hutchinson end the volume on that positive note, hopeful that Methodism will in the future draw upon that experimental spirit and reach out to the world (494–95). That note concluded a thoughtful discussion of problems—modern developments, post–World War I developments—that tested Methodism. They listed ecumenism, peace, technological-industrial matters, race. They also examined the great

---

48. Luccock and Hutchinson, *Story of Methodism*, 28, 34.

campaign that sought to address such challenges by transforming wartime religious mobilization into peacetime enterprise. This Centenary financial campaign Methodism initially pegged at one hundred million dollars. Luccock and Hutchinson entered their skepticism about the campaign, deftly but clearly. Their comments bear citation, for they point to the overreaching that Handy analyzes as constitutive of Protestantism's "second disestablishment."[49]

> That the Centenary was not all permanent advance will be admitted. There was, it is probable, too much use of war psychology . . . Moreover the Centenary did, by certain of its promotional methods, tend to make shoddy thinkers believe that the task of building the kingdom of God is simply a task of perfecting a high-pressure organization of churches and ministers for the raising of certain definitely ascertainable sums of money. In these, and perhaps some other ways, an atmosphere of false excitement and achievement was created, which could not be kept up. Gradually this promotional fever evaporated. With its passing there were left certain problems of adjustment which have perplexed many leaders, and many whom the church had commissioned for work in various difficult fields. The solution of these problems is a matter of time and hard thinking. When the readjustments are completed, the permanent benefit which has grown out of the Centenary will be clear.[50]

The hard thinking that followed—neo-orthodoxy it has been called—saw ironies where liberals had claimed providences, perceived an immoral nation where the Centenary had glimpsed the kingdom, recognized cultural enslavement in visions of a *Christian Century*. In Luccock and Hutchinson we find the now liberal Protestant establishment facing the implausibility of its premises. Methodism's four propositions come to rest on "irregularity" not providence, a sandy "human" foundation where Methodists had once found rock.

Professional Not Providential Estimates

Luccock and Hutchinson wrote a historical idiom that Lee and Bangs would have understood. William Warren Sweet and Frederick Norwood simply did not. The "second disestablishment," pluralization of American

---

49. Handy, *Christian America*, 161–64.
50. Luccock and Hutchinson, *Story of Methodism*, 487–88.

religion, secularization of the academy, and ascendency of religious studies as a way of doing history have rendered the privileged, providential reading of American history impolitic and implausible. So for Methodists, the four propositions no longer guide historical analysis. Or perhaps it would be more accurate to say, those dogmas have now recast themselves as historical generalizations.

Sweet found difficulty in claiming Methodism providential, but in the second chapter of *Methodism in American History* he treated "The Message of Wesley to His Time." That, once "providential," fit of movement and age could be diagnosed. "Methodism arose out of two great urges: the first was the religious experience of John Wesley; the second was the vast spiritual destitution of eighteenth-century England." So the first proposition found objective form.

The second proposition, the relation of Methodism to American society consumed Sweet. However, he found the relation to hinge not on providence but on Frederick Jackson Turner's frontier thesis.

> The greatest accomplishment of America has been the conquest of the continent . . . the most significant single factor in the history of the United States has been the Western movement of population, and the churches which devised the best methods for following the population as it pushed westward were the ones destined to become the great American churches (143).[51]

A series of chapter titles charted that destiny:

> Organizes for a Great Task
> Invades New England
> Crosses the Alleghenies
> The Circuit Rider Keeps Pace with the Westward March
> Shares in the Missionary Enterprise
> Begins her Educational Task.

Conquest defines destiny. Methodism charted its destiny in the nineteenth century in conquest of the frontier, the conquest really of America, the missionary impulse to take the continent.

Stewardship of its missionary calling constituted the reason for Methodism's success, its rapid growth to become the largest Protestant denomination. Sweet rendered that third proposition also in objective or human rather than providential terms. Why did Methodism succeed? Sweet insisted that the Methodist Episcopal Church "possessed, or developed,

---

51. Sweet, *Methodism*, 27, 143.

the best technique for following and ministering to a moving and restless population" (143). What were factors in that technique? itinerancy, a centralized appointive power, circuits, short appointments, few repreached sermons, "zealous, energetic ministry," lay leadership, Arminian theology, a populist episcopacy, ample religious literature, and an "emphasis upon singing."[52]

Sweet's version of the fourth proposition followed readily. Sweet conceived of Methodism as the prototypical American church. He understood Methodism in terms of American society, and American society in terms of Methodism: "As the title of this book implies, the history of American Methodism is here considered as a phase of American history, and it is assumed that it can best be understood in relation to the history of the American people."[53] (Sweet employed this, in a more generalized form, as his organizing principle in *Religion in the Development of American Culture, 1765–1840*, a general history that gave Methodism a formative role in American society. But a church enmeshed in its society might well find itself caught in society's web, captive to American developments. Wealth was one.

> But such changes as were taking place in American Methodism were inevitable, for the church could not stand apart from the social, educational, and economic changes which were taking place in the nation. In the very nature of the case Methodists were bound to become economically prosperous.

And "the most serious problem faced by American Methodism as a whole at this time was its rapidly increasing wealth." [54]

In this and a variety of ways, Sweet transformed Methodist belief about itself into historical axioms. As such they could be tested by his graduate students at the University of Chicago. Sweet's intentions were laudable and widely shared by church historians. Church history would be a historical science, a species of history, a respectable university discipline. Sweet wanted American historians as colleagues. As president of the American Society of Church History and mentor to several generations of church historians, Sweet played a major role in secularizing and professionalizing the discipline. He gave such a reading to Methodist history. Sweet's *Methodism in American History* (1933 orig.) appeared on the

---

52. Ibid., 143–53.
53. Ibid., 8.
54. Ibid., 336.

PART THREE: Case Studies in American Denominationalism

Course of Study for the quadrennia beginning 1932, 1936, 1940, and 1944; for the first three as a requirement for admission on trial and for the last as collateral reading

Sweet taught at the University of Chicago from 1927 to 1946. For two years thereafter, from 1946 to 1948, he plied his craft at Garrett Theological Seminary. Soon after his departure, in 1952 to be precise, Frederick Norwood assumed that Garrett position, which he held until his retirement. Norwood achieved what Sweet intended, the execution of a Methodist history fully respectful of "secular" historical canons. From its appearance, his *Story of American Methodism*[55] enjoyed preeminence as the text of choice in the course required of United Methodist seminarians. Had these theologs known about and gone searching for the Methodist propositions, they would have found them, but in such a subtle and historiographically nuanced form as to be scarcely recognizable. Norwood dealt self-consciously and explicitly with these motifs that have been so important to Methodists. He did so in responsible interpretive fashion. A few citations provide some sense of his handling of Methodism's propositions:

> 1) Methodism began as a revival, and its history has been marked repeatedly by continuing revivals. From this point of view the denominational story is part of a constant theme in the history of Christianity in all times and places—continuing reformation. Inevitably, it seems, the church must go through such a process, as strong institutions languish and traditions ossify. The history of Methodism consistently demonstrates this theme.

> 2) American Methodists, and to a lesser extent United Brethren and Evangelicals, were caught up in the heady surge of the westward movement. A couple of generations of historical scholars have attempted to disparage the hoary Turner thesis on the westward movement as the determinative factor in American History. But all they have been able to accomplish is to qualify it as one factor playing a part with others. For Methodism this surge west determined at least the size and influence of the growing institution, and to some extent its quality and spirit.

> 3) [The Wesleyan or Methodist working theology] was so successfully peddled that it became a characteristic mark of American Christians of all kinds. The question remains to be discussed, whether this development was peculiarly Methodist or just plain American. Even Calvinism . . . was deeply affected.

---

55. Norwood, *Story of American Methodism*.

Methodism became in many ways the most American of the churches. Not only in its inception but throughout its development it was most in tune with the American song.

4) Does this mean that America was Methodized or that Methodism was Americanized? Probably some of both. ... [Methodism's various developments] all point to a close and continuing love affair, for better or worse, between the Methodist Church and the United States. Who was the dominant partner?

The process of Americanizing and Methodizing brought on a tension which might be judged as the overriding theme of Methodist history in America.[56]

Here Methodism's four propositions found scholarly expression.

Why Methodism?

It would be uncharitable to lay at the feet of Sweet and Norwood a transformation that most church historians, including the present writer, presume and one that the whole denomination effected. The "second disestablishment," in fact, enveloped all mainline denominations. It would be more appropriate to see Sweet and Norwood as mirrors, as their predecessors were mirrors, reflecting the church's self-understanding back to church members. We should underscore, however, the importance of this historical reflection, this historical estimate of Methodist identity. As we noted above, Methodists have consistently turned to history when called upon to say who they were, to state purposes, to define themselves. History looms first in the *Discipline*. History defines the denomination. And these secular versions of the Methodist propositions now render United Methodism's understanding of itself and its belief. In the 1988 *Discipline's* "Historical Statement"[57] Methodism's propositions survive, as in Sweet and Norwood, only as historical axioms. Methodists continue to turn to their history for self-understanding. They find a narrative from which providence has departed. In this sense the making of church history into a historical rather than theological science has interesting consequences for the church. For it means that theological claims that once came readily to Methodist lips now simply are not heard.

"What may we reasonably believe to be God's design in raising up the Preachers called Methodists?" Many now do not find that Wesleyan

56. Norwood, *American Methodism*, 15–17.
57. *Discipline* /UMC (1988) 7–15.

PART THREE: Case Studies in American Denominationalism

purpose appropriately rendered by the four propositions and a vision of a Christian America. Certainly those propositions and vision no longer shape Methodist histories or the *Discipline*. That particular constellation is not, however, the only appropriate statement of the Wesleyan purpose. Early Methodists and their first historian, Jesse Lee, claimed providence but did not find it expressed in nationalism or a national ideology. It may be time for Methodists once again to recognize that they may be about reforming the continent and spreading scriptural holiness over these lands without domesticating that purpose into a vision of a Christian America.

11

Culture Wars and Denominational Loyalties

The Methodist Version

CONVENTIONAL WISDOM TODAY HOLDS

- that denominational loyalty, at least among mainline denominations,[1] has weakened, decidedly;
- that the once-prominent "establishment" denominations[2] as institutions are fading;
- that individuals, congregations and regional judicatories are staging "Boston Tea Parties" protesting decisions, priorities, inefficiencies, waste, monetary claims and the onerous, oppressive burden of the bureaucratic board and agency structure which seems to be the cohesive principle in denominations today;
- that caucuses and struggle groups have balkanized denominations, turning conventions, assemblies and conferences into contentious and demoralizing rather than unifying and galvanizing experiences;
- that many of these struggle groups and caucuses align themselves into two broad coalitions, liberal and conservative;

---

1. Coalter, Mulder and Weeks, *Reforming Tradition*.
2. Hutchison, *Between the Times*.

- that these coalitions transcend denominational, indeed religious, boundaries;
- and that liberal and conservative[3] or liberal and evangelical[4] identities (variously named) threaten now to divide, perhaps even destroy, denominations.[5]

The range of such problems, including especially the divisions within denominations, spell, some would suggest, the end to denominationalism.[6] At the very least they portend, as a United Methodist bishop and a seminary president both prophesied in the aftermath of the last General Conference, the clean division of such mainline denominations into new conservative and liberal entities and the end to United Methodism as we know it.

Denominationalism as Division?

This chapter endeavors to show division not to constitute a new threat at all but to have haunted denominations and denominationalism rather continuously throughout American history. Indeed, were theology rather than history and sociology to be the thrust of this essay, one might affirm with H. Richard Niebuhr that division is the essence of denominationalism:

> For the denominations, churches, sects, are sociological groups whose principle of differentiation is to be sought in their conformity to the order of social classes and castes . . . They are emblems, therefore, of the victory of the world over the church, of the secularization of Christianity, of the church's sanction of that divisiveness which the church's gospel condemns.[7]

Niebuhr had earlier affirmed, "The evil of denominationalism lies in the conditions which makes the rise of sects desirable and necessary: in the failure of the churches to transcend the social conditions which fashion them into caste-organizations, to sublimate their loyalties to standards and institutions only remotely relevant if not contrary to the Christian

---

3. Wuthnow, *Restructuring*; and Wuthnow, Struggle.
4. Hunter, *American Evangelicalism*; Warner, *New Wine*.
5. Hunter, *Culture Wars*; Roozen, McKinney, and Carroll in *Varieties of Religious Presence*.
6. Wuthnow, *Restructuring*; especially Wuthnow, *Struggle*, 72–94; Roof and McKinney, *American Mainline Religion*.
7. Niebuhr, *Social Sources of Denominationalism*, 25.

Culture Wars and Denominational Loyalties

ideal, to resist the temptation of making their own self-preservation and extension the primary object of their endeavor."[8]

Even on historical grounds, one might view division to be a characteristic of denominations. Divisions and/or near divisions constitute the story of virtually any denomination or denominational family, a fact readily discernible in the annual *Yearbook of American & Canadian Churches* or any other effort at the full mapping of American religion. And the larger pattern of denominations or denominationalism evidences periods of intense fracturing and fragmenting—periods when existing bodies experience internal strain, when some denominations do split and when new denominations emerge, often with commentary on the prior denominational order as constitutive of their purpose and self-understanding.

The "great awakenings" of the eighteenth and early nineteenth centuries represent such periods of fracturing and fragmenting. So also do the slavery and sectional crisis of the middle nineteenth century and the late nineteenth; as well as the early twentieth-century time of centralizing, professionalizing, corporate restructuring, and cultural realignment. The latter period, with its great Pentecostal effervescence, has sometimes been portrayed as one of cultural crisis, as though the new denominations sprang ex nihilo. Recent scholarship suggests that Pentecostalism has stronger ties to Methodist and other existing traditions than has sometimes been supposed, and that those as well as the Holiness and Fundamentalist movements ought to be seen as developments from, if not divisions out of, earlier denominational stock. At any rate, the Holiness, Pentecostal, and Fundamentalist eras represent times, if not a time, of serious denominational sifting and shifting. And, so, too, does this period from the 1970s to the present. Division within the denominational house may be, to borrow an image from Robert Handy but employ it differently, the religious counterpart to economic depression.[9]

Certainly all denominational divisions do not occur in these periods of fracturing and fragmenting. Some movements, as this chapter will indicate with respect to the Methodists, have shown a genius for dividing every decade. And yet we should not lose sight of these larger patterns in the history of denominational division. Individual denominational divisions have coincided sufficiently with these larger processes of restructuring for one to suspect that denominationalism, in effect, renews and reconstitutes itself (that is, reshapes the denominational form) through

8. Niebuhr, *Social Sources of Denominationalism*, 21.
9. Handy, "American Religious Depression," 3–16.

PART THREE: Case Studies in American Denominationalism

divisions and severe tension. The Presbyterians perhaps best represent in their saga the larger pattern of tension, division, and reunion. They took their rise amid the Puritan crisis within and without the Church of England, divided new side and old in the First Awakening, suffered significant loses from the Cumberlands and to the Christian (Disciple) movements in the Second Awakening, split New School and Old over issues that would ultimately divide the nation, and narrowly escaped a major division during the fundamentalist controversy. Current turmoil within Presbyterianism, paralleled across mainstream Protestantism, suggests that once again individual denominations and the larger pattern of denominationalism is in a period of transformation.

Constitutive Division: The Methodist Story

Division is not only part of the fabric of denominationalism, it is also woven into the life of individual denominations. Such a history of division is well illustrated, perhaps fittingly illustrated, by the Methodists. Methodism began, of course, as a reform movement within the Church of England, pledged in deference to, if not always agreement with, the Wesleys—John and particularly Charles—who insisted that Methodism did not and would not separate from the Church. To that pledge British Methodism remained committed through and beyond John's life. And yet, as Richard Heitzenrater has demonstrated, even under Wesley, Methodism increasingly structured and conducted itself in ways that pointed towards separation.[10]

The inertial pressures toward separation from the Church of England that the Wesleys resisted were, if anything, more intense in the colonies. Methodists immigrating from Ireland or England and persons here who developed Methodist or Methodist-like sympathies found it more difficult to structure Methodist life within an Anglican parish, for that system was not everywhere established and even where established not always well led or maintained. The parish system deteriorated dramatically during the Revolution when Anglicans—clergy and laity—fled to Canada or to Britain (as did preachers whom Wesley had sent over, Francis Asbury excepted).

The first division occurred during this period, even before Methodism officially separated from the Church of England in 1784. The

---

10. Heitzenrater, *Wesley*, 207-8, 218-19, 232-33, 237, 256, 269, 284, 293-96, 304-5.

Culture Wars and Denominational Loyalties

movement split badly. In 1779, during wartime hostilities, the regularly called conference, meeting in Fluvanna County, Virginia, proceeded to establish American Methodism as a church through autonomous act and presbyterial ordinations. The intention of this body of preachers, quickly to be deemed schismatic, was seemingly quite laudable—to provide sacraments for their people. They asked,

> Q. 14. What are our reasons for taking up the administration of the ordinances [sacraments] among us?
>
> A. Because the Episcopal Establishment is now dissolved and therefore in almost all our circuits the members are without the ordinances, we believe it to be our duty.
>
> Q. 19. What forms of ordination shall be observed, to authorize any preacher to administer?
>
> A. By that of a Presbytery.
>
> Q. 20. How shall the Presbytery be appointed?
>
> A. By a majority of the preachers.
>
> Q. 22. What power is vested in the Presbytery by this choice?
>
> A. 1st. To administer the ordinances themselves. 2nd. To authorize any other preacher or preachers approved of by them, by the form of laying on of hands and of prayer.[11]

This declaration of independence had been anticipated and countered by an "irregular" conference held the prior month in Delaware to accommodate Francis Asbury, then in hiding, and clearly convened to contravene the anticipated separation. The 'official' minutes glossed Asbury's motive: "Quest. 8. *Why was the Delaware conference held?* Ans. For the convenience of the preachers in the northern stations, that we all might have an opportunity of meeting in conference; it being unadvisable for brother Asbury and brother Ruff, with some others, to attend in Virginia; it is considered also as preparatory to the conference in Virginia."[12] This 'Asbury' conference, almost exactly the same size as the later "regular" body, put for itself a question that parried the action of the body authorizing ordinations and the sacraments: "Quest. 10. *Shall we guard against a separation from the church, directly or indirectly?* Ans. By all Means.[13]

11. *Western Christian Advocate*, 18–19.
12. *Minutes*/MEC/1779 (1813), 19.
13. Ibid., 19.

And the following year, this Chesapeake group queried:

> Quest. 12. *Shall we continue in close connexion with the church, and press our people to a closer communion with her?*
>
> Ans. Yes
>
> Quest. 20. *Does this whole conference disapprove the step our brethren have taken in Virginia?*
>
> Ans. Yes.
>
> Quest. 21. *Do we look upon them no longer as Methodists in connexion with Mr. Wesley and us till they come back?*
>
> Ans. Agreed.[14]

This latter group, which insisted on awaiting John Wesley's provision for ecclesial order, eventually won out and the schism was healed.

Continuous Divisions?

I have dwelt at more length on this particular separation than I can on subsequent ones to make two points 1) that American Methodism was already dividing internally before it officially "divided" itself from the Anglicans and established itself as a distinct denomination and 2) that the formal separation in 1784 actually involved a threefold disengagement— a) from the Church of England, b) from the North American Anglicans among whom the Methodists had labored, who were then also being reconstituted as an independent church and among whom were kindred spirits, chief of them, perhaps, Devereux Jarrett, who were deeply offended by the Methodist departure, and c) eventually from Mr. Wesley and British Wesleyanism. The latter also was to be an occasion for offence, for in their first *Discipline*, the Americans pledged:

> During the Life of the Rev. Mr. Wesley, we acknowledge ourselves his Sons in the Gospel, ready in Matters belonging to Church-Government, to obey his Commands. And we do engage after his Death, to do every Thing that we judge consistent with the Cause of Religion in *America* and the political Interests of these States, to preserve and promote our Union with the Methodists in *Europe*.[15]

14. Ibid., 25–26.

15. MEC, *Minutes... Composing a Form of Discipline* (1785), Q. 2 (p. 3). Convenient access to the first Discipline can be had in Tigert, *Constitutional History*, 534.

Culture Wars and Denominational Loyalties

This pledge and unity, too, American Methodists found impossible to honor when Wesley sought to exercise church government. In 1787 Wesley ordered the convening of a general conference and the election of specific persons as bishops. The Americans resisted these commands and stripped the above pledge from the *Discipline*. So American Methodism began in a complex division, though one it has consistently celebrated, rather than bemoaned.

To 1787 is often traced yet another division, namely the beginnings of the African Methodist Episcopal Church, traditionally associated with Richard Allen's walkout from St. George's church. Full separation took a number of other provocations. In 1816 several African-American churches formed in similar reaction to Methodism's racial policies covenanted to establish the denomination. From these small beginnings and those of the African Union Church and the African Methodist Episcopal Zion Church much of Methodism's significant black membership was drained off.[16]

These losses were gradual and the actual break between black and white Methodists more gradual and more gradually recognized on both sides than we have sometime been led to believe. These were divisions caused by white racism and unfortunately rather ignored because of racism. By contrast another division, largely among whites, registered itself immediately and traumatically. It came in 1792, when Methodists from the Virginia-North Carolina area, followed James O'Kelly, an erratic but prominent leader, in demanding "democratic" rights for preachers, protesting monarchical behavior by the bishops, especially Asbury, and witnessing against slavery. The break came over a proposal made to the General Conference of that year that would have given preachers a right of appeal over their appointment, a popular initiative that seemed destined to pass.[17] When the legislation failed, O'Kelly's supporters, later called "Republican Methodists," walked out.

Their departure, from the vantage of the late twentieth century, looks like a minor one, primarily because the "Republicans" proved stronger in protest than they did in subsequent organization and evangelizing. Their "schism" was not minimized in the 1790s. Then it seemed a major "culture war," a battle over the soul of the movement, a question as to whether Methodism would be a Wesleyan or an American cause, a denomination

---

16. Melton, *Will to Choose*; George, *Segregated Sabbaths*; Allen, *Life Experience*; and Will B. Gravely, "African Methodisms and the Rise of Black Denominationalism," in Richey & Rowe, *Rethinking Methodist History*, 111-24.

17. For a first-hand treatment, see Lee, *Short History*, 178-80.

PART THREE: Case Studies in American Denominationalism

shaped primarily by the culture, practices, beliefs, style, and ethos of the inherited Wesleyanism or of the republicanism of the new nation. The latter had tremendous appeal and seemed to capture essential elements of what both the New Testament and Pietism envisioned for the Christian life. Republican Christianity, as O'Kelly articulated it, offered a vision of equality, fraternity, justice, and human rights. And it made sense to persons, particularly the preachers, who experienced any arbitrariness on the part of the appointive authorities, the bishops. A new church for a new nation, a democratic church for a democratic nation, so urged O'Kelly. Was the choice, as he presented it, between Wesleyanism and Americanism? To move beyond that dilemma and contain the schism took a decade of concerted effort on the part of Asbury and his supporters.

In appreciating the significance of this division and several of the subsequent Methodist schisms, we might well keep in mind the close divisions in the presidential contests within the Southern Baptist Convention in those years when moderates still mounted resistance to its conservative drift. A number of those votes were extremely close, suggesting a SBC that was deeply divided. Such proportions do not register, however, in the much smaller numbers of churches and clergy now formally affiliated with the moderate southern Baptist organizations. The depth and extent of a fault line and the size of the parties divided thereby do not then always correspond with, nor are they accurately measured by, the size of a party that departs. This was clearly the case for the Republican Methodists and would prove to be the case in the subsequent nineteenth century divisions. Similar, major "cultural" and social issues surfaced—in virtually every decade of the nineteenth century—to split Methodism again and again.

Divisions: Minor and Major

To be sure, not all the cleavages within the Methodist family can be traced to a decisive moment and a legislative contest or produced such serious trauma. The separate organization of the German movements, the United Brethren and Evangelical Association, reflect their distinct origins in the broader evangelical movement and the specific leaven of Reformed, Mennonite, and Lutheran pietism. Still the first conference of the former in 1789 and its formal organization in 1800, and the first conference of the latter in 1803 and its formal organization in 1807, represented failures (on both sides) to carry through on the looser comity they had enjoyed with the Methodists. Unification was revisited in the next decade and repeatedly thereafter until the two movements, united in 1946, joined with the Methodist Church in 1968. Early Methodism experimented with intercultural, bilingual community but found differences along language lines difficult to bridge.

Three protests of the early nineteenth century had regional or local effect. William Hammett, ordained by Wesley, settled eventually in Charleston. He built a strong following, resisted the authority of Asbury and Coke, and led a schism of Primitive Methodists (there and in North Carolina) that began around 1792 and largely dissipated after his death in 1803. At the northern reaches of the movement, a group of "Reformed Methodists," led by Pliny Brett who had itinerated from 1805 to 1812, sought church government and local authority more akin to that appreciated in New England. They protested episcopacy, emphasized the attainability of entire sanctification, and repudiated war and slavery. Formally organized in 1814 at a convention in Vermont, they drew several thousand adherents across New England, New York, and Canada. By the Civil War, most of the Reformed movement had affiliated with the Methodist Protestants.

In the second decade of the century, the African Methodist Episcopal (1816) and the African Union (1813) churches organized, as we noted. Their centers were and remained in Philadelphia and Wilmington respectively. The organization of the African Methodist Episcopal Zion Church in 1820 was closely related with a separation among white Methodists also in New York led by Samuel Stillwell, a trustee at the flagship John Street Church, and his nephew, William Stillwell, a preacher then in charge of two of the African-American congregations. At issue in both divisions was ownership of church property and control over ministry. The Stillwellites grew to some 2,000 members in the New York, New Jersey, and Connecticut areas, continuing until the younger Stillwell's death in 1851. Another separate Methodist body, also with the name "Primitive Methodists," developed around the figure of Lorenzo Dow, the export of American-style camp meeting revivalism to Britain after 1805, and import-of-the-export as a distinct denomination, beginning in 1829. The Primitives developed strength in Pennsylvania and especially in Canada.[18]

The democratic themes associated with these several movements came to focus in the reform efforts of the 1820s—to permit election of the episcopal lieutenants or surrogates known as presiding elders, to allow some conference role and representation to the two-thirds of the

18. Semple, *Lord's Dominion*.

Methodist ministry functioning as local rather than itinerant preachers, and to permit laity a say in the governing annual and general conferences. Here, as with the Republican Methodists, a set of legislative proposals gave focus to concerns, practices, and styles that went far deeper and presented the church again with the question as to how its internal life would draw on the best aspects of democratic society. Here, too, the reformers initially carried the day. They passed (decisively 61 to 25) legislation at the 1820 General Conference providing for election of presiding elders, a proposal surfaced early in Methodist history and repeatedly urged up to the present, but vehemently resisted by the bishops, by William McKendree in his opening episcopal address to that conference and by bishop-elect Joshua Soule, the architect of Methodist constitutional order. Soule pronounced the change unconstitutional and insisted that he could not "superintend under the rules this day made." Soule's resignation prompted the conference to suspend the new legislation.

A decade of intense, bitter, recriminating politics followed. New media emerged to carry the campaign to the populace. Popular conventions met to broaden the reform agenda. Bishops and conferences suppressed dissent and excommunicated dissenters. The reform movement found support from some of the strongest of Methodist leaders and its following at the heart of the Methodist movement, namely in the upper south and middle states. In 1830 a new denomination, the Methodist Protestant Church, came into being to consolidate the reforms. And here too the rather modest size of the new denomination scarcely registers the deep division and cultural war through which Methodism had passed.

Slavery, Region, Race

Each division produced not only losses—of persons, of richness and diversity, of leadership, of principle—but also countermeasures that sometimes paralleled, sometimes negated the points of the reformers. Losses and reactive countermeasures certainly attended the divisions of the 1840s and 1850s, the exiting of abolitionists to form the Wesleyan Methodist Church in 1842, the split of the Methodist Episcopals North and South in 1844, and the emergence of the Free Methodists in the late 1850s (formally organizing in 1860). In each of these divisions, high principle on one side produced compensating efforts on the other. The MEC, particularly in New England and the "burned-over district," became more receptive to abolition in the face of competition from the Wesleyans. The MECS

Culture Wars and Denominational Loyalties

intensified its mission to the slaves in the wake of the division of 1844. And New York Methodists contended with the witness of reformers who criticized elite control of the annual conference, the use of pew rents, slippage in the church's teaching on sanctification, and irresolution on slavery. "Freedom" emblemed their several pronged attack on Methodism's bourgeoisification and compromise with society's practices and their call for a return to primitive Methodism.[19]

The division of 1844 produced differing ecclesiologies and notions of the relation of church to the civil order, north and south, and both churches have, at times, read the division as though it primarily concerned notions of the power of general conference, the authority of bishops, the limits of social witness. Underneath these theological and polity concerns, of course, lurked slavery and the differing sectional attitudes thereunto. Sectional division of the churches produced intense moral warfare, principled posturing, undergirded by fears and hopes about slavery. The several church splits anticipated and aggravated, if they did not "cause," the growing division of the nation.[20] 1844, creating a Methodist Episcopal Church and a Methodist Episcopal Church, South, left scars that continue to this day and fault lines that now vibrate over abortion and homosexuality rather than slavery. If these current issues constitute banners in a larger and deeper culture war, so might we also portray the contest between slave and free civilizations of the 1840s and 1850s.

The 1860s saw massive population shifts among Black Methodists and one major new African-American denomination, the Colored Methodist Episcopal Church. The latter, formalized in 1870, represented the culmination of MECS efforts to minister to slaves and then freed persons under strict racist guidelines and can be read as either extrusion of or exodus by African Americans.[21] One stimulus to MECS cooperation in the establishment of the CME was the success enjoyed by the MEC (the northern church) with the ex-slaves and the even greater and politically more radical advances of the AME and AMEZ.[22] All these population shifts, and not just the emergence of the CME, ought to be seen as important divisions. Also of a divisive quality was the decision by the MEC in 1864 to authorize the creation of separate Black annual conferences, a segregating

19. Luccock and Hutchinson, *Story of Methodism*, 487–88.
20. Goen, *Broken Churches*.
21. Hildebrand, *Times Were Strange and Stirring*. Dvorak, *African-American Exodus*; Melton, *Will to Choose*.
22. Walker, *Rock in a Weary Land*; and Melton, *Will to Choose*.

gesture "perfected" in the north before it was spread across the south. This *de jure* separation of black and white proved as complete as and longer-lived than the division of the MEC and MECS.

Language, Gender, Class

Some internal divisions look benign in hindsight but raised then, as they raise today, questions about the character and unity of the church. I refer to the establishment of distinct language conferences, an issue that has resurfaced recently as highly controversial when requested by Korean-Americans. The year 1864 saw the authorization of German annual conferences by the MEC. German mission conferences had been established in 1844, as also had a mission conference for Native Americans. Swedish, Norwegian, Danish, Spanish, Japanese, and Chinese conferences would emerge later.

Episcopal Methodism granted laity rights in general conference only gradually (in 1866 and 1872 in the MECS and MEC respectively) and had even greater difficulty with overtures to include women as laity or to ordain them. But Methodism did sanction women-run voluntary societies that functioned like conferences, notably the Woman's Christian Temperance Union (1874), interdenominational but always heavily Methodist, the Woman's Foreign Missionary Society (1869), the corresponding entities for the MECS (1878) and MPC (1879), and the Ladies' and Pastors' Union (1872). There was no threat of division along gender lines but the internal structural differentiation deserves notice.

Class differences were not so easily contained. From the 1860s on, the holiness cause increasingly took on aspects of class war. Church leaders who initially embraced their fervent piety increasingly reacted to sustained holiness criticisms and free-lance itineration with a heavy, disciplining hand. Schisms proved inevitable. The Free Methodists had, we noted, already exited in 1860. The National Camp Meeting for the Promotion of Holiness of 1867 led to the formation of a National Camp Meeting Association. Holiness camp meetings and itinerating holiness preachers called Methodism to return to its primitive practices. They recalled a pre-war and pre-1844 Methodism of entrepreneurial circuit-riders, of outdoor quarterly meetings conjoined with camp meetings, of shouting preachers and demonstrative religiosity, of discipline through class meetings, and of sidestreet preaching houses. Many felt ill at ease in the grand, uptown gothic cathedrals, lavishly appointed and funded with pew rents; unnourished by worship centered in the Sunday service rather than the camp; ill equipped to function in the increasingly nationalized and centralized program of the church and in the corporate board and agency structure authorized in 1872; unsatisfied by a view of the Christian life as nurtured by home and in Sunday school and provisioned through John Vincent's uniform lesson plan, teacher institutes, and Chautauquas. The Holiness camp meetings represented one side in a culture war that pitted the anxious bench and class meeting against the Sunday service and the Sunday school. The prophetic spirit became, in places and at times, a come-outer spirit. And so in the 1880s and 1890s, regional and state holiness associations and conventions gradually transformed themselves into new denominations, the Church of God (Anderson), Church of God (Holiness), the Holiness Church, and the Church of the Nazarene. The later separate organizations make it hard to recall and envision the broader war within Methodism in which they had campaigned. The same, with important qualifications, might be said of the Pentecostal movements.

Coda

The twentieth century, of course, represents something of a different story. Its agenda was reunion, the ending of denominational divisions, ecumenism, Christian unity. Methodism experienced several major reunions—the MEC, MECS, and MPC uniting in 1939 to form the Methodist Church; the EA and UB uniting in 1946 to form the Evangelical United Brethren Church; the two new bodies uniting in 1968 to form the United Methodist Church. And the reunions have not yet ended. Recent general conferences have authorized proceeding with COCU/CUIC; with rapprochement with the AMEs, the AMEZs, and the CMEs; with bilaterals with Lutherans and Episcopalians; and with other ecumenical explorations.

Yet unifications, as well, have proved immensely divisive in ways that need to be recalled if one wishes to understand internal and transdenominational coalitions today. For instance, the prospect of unification of the MEC and the MECS caused near division in the south (the MECS), with race as the major concern. And when unification came, it did so with an accommodation to the south that built a radical division into the very fabric of the denomination—namely the segregation of African-Americans nationally into a Central Jurisdiction. And the ending of that scandal coincided with the birth within Methodism of the caucuses and special interest groups.

PART THREE: Case Studies in American Denominationalism

Division and culture wars have been a rather constant feature of Methodist denominational life and, if not an every decade affair for others, at least very common. Conventional wisdom has a short memory.

12

Denominationalism in "Reformed" Perspective

IN A *CHRISTIAN CENTURY* article, Nancy Ammerman counters what seems to be current wisdom—namely that denominations, particularly mainstream Protestant denominations, have been faltering for several decades and that consequently denominationalism as we have known it is doomed.[1] Such a judgment, indeed widely shared, shapes the title of a work that maps American religion, William M. Newman and Peter L. Halvorson's *Atlas of American Religion: the Denominational Era, 1776-1990*.[2] And it recurs in popular discourse.

DENOMINATIONALISM DOOMED?

Has mainstream Protestantism had its day and is the denominationalism that it defined now passé? The evidence for such pessimism abounds—the decline in numbers, vitality and prestige of mainline Protestant denominations; the vigor and vibrancy of competition, including particularly mega-churches and para-church organizations, which flaunts its (apparent) non-denominational character; the internal divisions besetting denominations; marginal loyalty of members; and so forth.[3]

---

1. Ammerman, "New Life."
2. Newman and Halvorson, *Atlas of American Religion*.
3. Coalter, Mulder, and Weeks, *Reforming Tradition*.

PART THREE: Case Studies in American Denominationalism

The decline in "mainstream" Protestant denominations has prompted much comment and worry, a variety of stratagems for renewal, occasional accusations against leadership, and some recognition that the individual denominational experiences belong within a general pattern. And that pattern contrasts with dramatic growth in other sectors of North American religion, with vigorous expansion of mega-churches and the mega-church networks and with continued growth of many communions in the Third World.[4]

Denominational loyalty runs at low ebb. Many congregations, particularly in areas of high mobility, attract new members with limited prior knowledge of the confessional heritage. Some congregations confront confessional minimalism frontally and premise their life on ignoring tradition. They take advantage of their new, post-denominational freedom to chart an independent path programmatically and structurally, borrowing whatever works, attracts adherents, seems in vogue. Other pastors struggle to inculcate confessional sensibilities within congregations lacking in the basics.

Above the congregation, loyalty, unity and identity prove equally vulnerable. Caucuses and struggle groups balkanize denominations, turning presbytery and assembly into contentious and demoralizing rather than unifying and galvanizing experiences. These struggle groups and caucuses align themselves into two broad coalitions, liberal and conservative. Partisans on one hot-button issue or another demand denominational acquiescence, threatening that without it that liberal and conservative[5] or liberal and evangelical[6] concerns and identities will divide, perhaps even destroy, denominations. And these coalitions transcend denominational, indeed religious, boundaries, giving the appearance in North American society of culture wars, various named.[7]

Even beyond the arena of ideological clashes, individuals and congregations distance themselves from denomination and tradition. They protest decisions, priorities, inefficiencies, waste, monetary claims and the overhead of the denominational apparatus. They threaten to or actually withhold apportioned obligations, objecting to the onerous, oppressive

---

4. Coalter, Mulder, and Weeks, eds., *Mainstream*, 29–65.

5. Wuthnow, *Restructuring*; *Struggle*; *Crisis*.

6. Coleman, *Theological Conflict*; Hunter, *American Evangelicalism*; Warner, *New Wine*.

7. Hunter, *Culture Wars*; Roozen, McKinney and Carroll, *Varieties of Religious Presence*.

burden of the bureaucratic board and agency structure which seems to be the cohesive principle in denominations today.[8]

The internal strains reflect and reinforce the slippage of congregations, regional judicatories and denominations from prominence and leadership in civic affairs. Some of the slippage has to do with the paralyzing effect of internal discord. Some slippage with the more genuine pluralism of North American society and the increased prominence in the latter half of the twentieth century of Roman Catholicism, Judaism, Islam, and other world religions. Some slippage with the vigor and political involvement of conservative and evangelical denominations. Some slippage with the decay of, white flight from and radical transformation of what had been Protestantism's citadel the downtowns, leaving dwindling congregations, often largely elderly, to preoccupy themselves with the maintenance of once grand cathedrals, to ponder a new mission with peoples different from themselves, to feel the allure of a move to the suburbs and to face again and again the specter of congregational death.

The diverse decisions and strategies that urban congregations elected were premised upon and produced different public self-conceptions and roles and different degrees of denominational relation, identity and loyalty.[9] But while some few, especially ethnic minority, congregations found ways to reinvent civic roles for themselves, far too many "mainstream" Protestants abandoned the downtowns, literally or figuratively. And judicatory offices often followed the prosperous congregations out to the suburbs or into an airport complex.

For various reasons then, internal and contextual, the once-prominent "establishment" Protestant denominations faded from prominence and leadership in North American society. Interpreters found the term "disestablishment" to be helpful in imaging the seachange which the complex of changes wrought on the religious community and North American society.[10] The term, of course, compares the shifts represented in the displacement of "mainstream" Protestantism from societal hegemony with the transformation of public policy and church-state relations accomplished during and after the Revolutionary area.

---

8. Coalter, Mulder, and Weeks, eds., *Organizational Revolution*; Chaves and Miller, eds., *Financing*.

9. Becker, *Congregations*, and chapters in Richey, Campbell and Lawrence, *Connectionalism*, 267–85; and in Demerath, et al., eds., *Sacred Companies*, 231–55.

10. Hutchison, *Between the Times*.

PART THREE: Case Studies in American Denominationalism

But does this disestablishment and do the range of coping mechanisms, internal divisions, erosion of identity and loyalty within denominations spell, as some would suggest, the end to denominationalism?[11]

A Longer View

The plight of mainstream Protestantism, its disestablishment, and disenchantment with its centralized agency structure figure prominently in judgments about the end of the denomination and of denominationalism. Should the denomination be equated with its current corporate bureaucratic governance structure? And should denominationalism be equated with the Protestant mainstream and establishment versions thereof? The equations must feel right to those within the Protestant denominations anguishing over their revitalization. It doubtless also feels right to those outside those denominations who know megachurches, parachurch organizations or media ministries to be the effective Christian presence for the twenty-first century. The judgment has a motivational value, aiding religious leaders to read the present scene as crisis in such a way as to encourage members to action.

The historian, particularly one conscious of the saga of Presbyterianism in North America, may want to step back to ask whether the sense of crisis over the present status of the denomination and of denominationalism obscures the longer saga of both. She will certainly insist that the church has known itself as a denomination for most, if not all, of its experience in North America. She will recognize that the present corporate structure, though the only denominational form that anyone living has known, is only about a century old. And she may then concede that denominationalism, the larger cultural or organizational field or family within which Presbyterianism operates, has itself differed over time. The historian has some good reasons to define *denomination* and *denominationalism* in such a way as to reject the above equations and to recognize denominationalism prior to its Protestant establishment form and modalities of denominational structure and governance prior to their corporate form.[12] And she may want to argue that the crisis over the present

11. Wuthnow, *Restructuring and Struggle*; Roof and McKinney, *American Mainline Religion*.

12. Mullin and Richey, eds., *Reimagining Denominationalism*; Craig Dykstra and James Hudnut-Beumler in Coalter, Mulder and Weeks, eds., *Organizational Revolution*, 307–31; and chapters in Demerath et al., eds., *Sacred Companies*, especially 7–23; 62–78; 99–115; 154–72; 175–94; 231–55; 256–68; 269–91.

Denominationalism in "Reformed" Perspective

corporate form of the denomination and over mainstream Protestant denominationalism as but the most recent of a series of crises through which denominations have gone. The present denominational crisis may well, like those in the past, be the process by which the denominations reconfigure themselves and so redefine the field or family (denominationalism).

Denominationalism: A Definition

Although the denomination certainly preexists its present corporate form, in the longer saga of religious organization and of the Christian church, it too is a relatively new. It emerged in Western societies as they searched for stratagems and policies, other than coercion and repression, for coping with the religious diversity generated out of the sixteenth century reformations and seventeenth-century religious wars. It can be appropriately defined as a form of the church operative under conditions of toleration. And the collective term *denominationalism* then refers to the larger pattern created by tolerated religious bodies existing in uneasy competition with one another. So a definition:

> Denominationalism presents the denomination as a voluntaristic ecclesial body.[13] The denomination is voluntary and therefore presupposes a condition of legal or de facto toleration and religious freedom, an environment within which it is possible, in fact, willingly to join or not join, and 'space' to exist alongside or outside of any religious establishment. The denomination exists in a situation of religious pluralism, typically a pluralism of denominations.
>
> It is *ecclesial*, a movement or body understanding itself to be a legitimate and self-sufficient, a proper 'church' (or religious movement.) It is *a* voluntary church, a body which concedes the authenticity of other churches even as it claims its own. It need not, however, concede that authenticity indiscriminately, it need not and typically did not regard all other denominations as orthodox.
>
> And it is an ecclesial *body or form*, an organized religious movement, with intentions for and the capacity of self-perpetuation, with a sense of itself as located within time and with awareness of its relation to the longer Christian tradition. It knows itself as denominated, as named, as recognized and recognizable, as having boundaries, as possessing adherents,

13. Winthrop S. Hudson and Sidney E. Mead in Richey, *Denominationalism*.

as having a history. In these several regards, the denomination differentiates itself from reform impulses that may take similar structural form but construe themselves as belonging within; from the church which does not regard itself as voluntary or as sharing societal space with other legitimate religious bodies; from the sect which, though also voluntary, does not locate itself easily in time or recognize boundaries or tolerate other bodies or concede their authenticity.[14]

The denomination, then, is a creature of modernity, a social form emerging with and closely akin to the political party, the free press, and free enterprise. With these other institutions, the denominations and related expressions of voluntary religion produced and have sustained the democratic state.[15] Like these other institutions, the individual denomination fits within, contributes to and borrows from a larger organizational ecology. We term that organizational ecology *denominationalism*. As individual papers and magazines comprise the free press, individual businesses comprise free enterprise, individual parties comprise representative democracy so individual denominations comprise denominationalism. And these four creatures of modernity have tended to evolve together and to influence one another. Indeed, that the denomination has resembled the corporation for the last century should not be surprising. It has resembled the current business form of the day, and also the current form of the political party and of the press.

Ethical Failure? Theological Scandal?

The denominations' and denominationalism's contribution to and borrowing from the social structures and patterns of the day do open the door to the critique and even denunciation which they have so often received. They probably draw more heavily on culture and society than do other ecclesial forms. Unlike sects they define themselves within rather than over against society. Denominations lack the sect's wariness about the world and worldliness and have been more willing to make use of the

---

14. Richey, "Denominations and Denominationalism: An American Morphology," in Robert Bruce Mullin and Russell E. Richey, eds., *Reimagining Denominationalism*, 75–76.

15. The First Amendment lodged several of these together: "Congress shall make no law respecting an establishment of religion, or prohibiting the free exercise thereof; or abridging the freedom of speech, or of the press; or the right of the people peaceably to assemble, and to petition the government for a redress of grievances."

Denominationalism in "Reformed" Perspective

organizational, media and linguistic grammar of the day. Unlike (established) churches, denominations must be chosen, consented to or willed by their members. Their consensual or voluntaristic nature invites them to be continually remaking themselves so as to attract adherents and sustain their loyalty. This remaking and updating typically involves drawing afresh on the societal and cultural resources for organizational self-presentation, promotion, visibility and attractiveness. So North American denominations tend towards Niebuhr's "Christ the Transformer of Culture" or "Christ of Culture" but have moments in which they, particularly those with roots in European Christendom, draw on the insights and strategies of the other relations to culture ("Christ Against Culture," "Christ Above Culture," "Christ and Culture in Paradox").[16]

As voluntary organizations, denominations have emerged out of existing or emergent social groupings, being willed frequently as the group's religious expression. These origins and denominations' difficulty in surmounting them earned the scathing reproach of H. Richard Niebuhr, whose work and views still typify perceptions of denominationalism. He regarded their caste basis as schismatic and evil:

> The evil of denominationalism lies in the conditions which makes the rise of sects desirable and necessary: in the failure of the churches to transcend the social conditions which fashion them into caste-organizations, to sublimate their loyalties to standards and institutions only remotely relevant if not contrary to the Christian ideal, to resist the temptation of making their own self-preservation and extension the primary object of their endeavor.

He went on to assert, "the denominations represent the accommodation of religion to the caste system. They are emblems, therefore, of the victory of the world over the church, of the secularization of Christianity, of the church's sanction of that divisiveness which the church's gospel condemns."[17]

Breaking the unity of the body of Christ and embodying that disunity, denominationalism lacked theological warrant, so thought Niebuhr. However, denominationalism rested on a theology of the church and of its unity, though one that Niebuhr would doubtless have rejected and ecumenists roundly repudiated. Implicit in denominationalism, if not always claimed, is a branch theory of the church. Recognizing differences of

16. Niebuhr, *Christ and Culture*.
17. Niebuhr, *Social Sources*, 21, 25.

PART THREE: Case Studies in American Denominationalism

theological emphases, the diversity of societies and cultures, histories and traditions that separate, and institutional distinctions as givens, a branch theory views the resultant denominational plurality as the many branches of a vine or tree whose integrity derives from the common trunk and shared roots. This was, as indicated, a theology held up for ridicule when the ecumenical agenda was for structural unity. It may be less implausible in an age in which intercommunion rather than organizational merger represents the do-able ecumenical ideal.

The Complexity of the Contemporary Denomination

The denomination, as already noted, has been equated sometimes with its corporate, agency program structure and the unpopularity and vulnerability of the latter taken to apply to denominationalism as a whole. One recent sociological clarification posits that denominations often feature two parallel structures—agency structures and "religious authority structures." The author, Mark Chaves, argues that "these two structures remain essentially parallel structures performing different kinds of tasks, responding to different parts of the environment, coping with different kinds of uncertainty, and containing separate lines of authority..." He continues, "this parallel dual structure should be at the center of any analysis of denominational organization.[18] Chaves goes on then to draw the following contrasts in the two systems:

Dimension	Religious Authority Structure	Agency Structure
relation to congregations & members	"the object of control"	"a resource base" market or constituency
goal orientation	internal/religious control	external/engagement with the world
basis of differentiation	geographic segmentation	functional differentiation
primary role	clergy/bishops	administrators
basis of legitimate authority	traditional/charismatic	rational/legal
primary boundary for scope of authority	member/nonmember	employee/nonemployee

18. Chaves, "Denominations as Dual Structures."

The existence of dual systems within denominations may be a less startling discovery for the historian than for the sociologist but the point is valuable and can even be extended. One might even speak of the denomination as a fourfold or quadrilateral system, with each of the four parts capable of pulling in its own distinct direction:

- the religious authority system, theologically warranted, often biblically based, built into the most constitutionally protected parts of a denomination's minutes, discipline, operations;
- an agency or board system, often mimicked at every level in the denomination, charged with conducting much of the program, publishing, mission, financing for the denomination;
- a representative, delegated or popular assembly system guaranteeing lay consent and providing for lay roles in decision-making, property holding and financial administration;
- a professional-society system, typically under the control of the clergy and other religious professionals and serving the roles played for attorneys by the American Bar Association and for doctors by the American Medical Association.

My own denomination, United Methodism, has borrowed each of these systems. American Methodism's religious authority system welded the emphases of the Wesleyan impulse onto the Anglican tradition (itself shaped by the longer Catholic tradition). From 1784 onward Methodism has conceived of the church as word, order, sacrament (and of late, service). It represents those biblical imperatives in bishops, elders and deacons. And it deploys those ministries through a series of conferences, the latter shaped by the practices of John Wesley. Methodism made its own contribution to the bureaucratization of American society by elaborating within itself, during the early national period, an array of missionary, tract, Sunday-school, and Bible societies. It gave those a corporate structure after the Civil War. Methodism struggled for the better part of two centuries over how to accommodate the democratic impulses of American society, splitting in the nineteenth century several times over just this issue. By the time several branches reunited in 1939, Methodism had provided for lay parity in its several assemblies—general, jurisdictional, and annual conferences. The professional society system evolved gradually in the twentieth century, lodging itself primarily in the middle or regional judicatory: the annual conference. That body absorbed the concerns and principles of professionalism and professionalization, adding them to the ancient procedures for recognizing call, taking those called into probation and eventually ordaining them.

Stages and Shapes of Denominationalism

North American Methodist absorption of these four denominational systems occurred, as indicated, over time. Only in the twentieth century did these four become fully operational and interactive. In earlier decades, Methodism exhibited a different style of denominational life. Elsewhere I have suggested, in fact, that Methodist denominational life could be schematized into seven stages in each of which a certain style of self-promotion and organizational connectivity dominated:

- an oral/aural revivalistic Wesleyan style
- an event-defined camp-meeting and conference popular style
- a voluntary society stage characterized by emphasis on print media
- a program-oriented corporate style
- a professional stage shaped by the various guild protocols
- a federal stage during which democratic governance was fully operative
- a postcorporate stage in which accountability issues were highly salient.[19]

Patterns within other confessional families had their own distinctive stages, the sequencing and character affected by that tradition's particularities. Yet, allowing for that variation by confession, one can observe some overall tendencies, some typifying denominational signatures, some stages to the history of the larger ecology—denominationalism.

In some ways the Presbyterians serve best to illustrate these overall tendencies (1) because Presbyterianism emerged during and gave shape to the very earliest stages of North American denominationalism; (2) because Reformed theology, aspiration and practice oriented Presbyterianism to self-consciousness in thinking about politics and polity; and (3) because Presbyterians took active roles in the formulation and structuring of what would be mainstream Protestantism's establishment agenda.[20]

---

19. Richey, in *Connectionalism*, 1–22.

20. Balmer and Fitzmier, *Presbyterians*; James H. Smylie, *Brief History*; Coalter, Mulder, and Weeks, eds., *Mainstream and Organizational Revolution*.

Denominationalism in "Reformed" Perspective

As the above Methodist schema suggests, one might identify an array of styles or stages, the number affected by the tradition under closest review. I have found at least five stages or models to be necessary to capture the predominant trends in the rich texture of American religious institutional life. Presbyterians exhibit each. The first (ethnic voluntarism or provincial voluntarism) characterized movements in the religiously pluralistic middle colonies of the eighteenth century, the institutional innovations led by New Side Presbyterians. The second (purposive missionary association) emerged in the early national period, the form fabricated by the popular denominations and the theory worked out by the Reformed. The third (churchly) style qualified the second, rather than transforming it fully. It might be seen as inaugurated by the Old School, flourishing during and after the Civil War, drawing some inspiration from romantic currents, deriving impetus from massive immigration and resulting competition and taking expressive form in various confessional movements (high church and primitivist). The late nineteenth and early twentieth centuries, saw a corporate or managerial revolution overtaking the Protestant mainstream. A fifth style, like the third, builds on rather than displacing its immediate predecessor, and emerges in the late twentieth century, the product of the mainstreaming of conservative and evangelical movements and of the coping responses by the once-mainstream Protestants.

The five-stage typology serves useful analytical purposes. It accents the dynamic principles most powerfully operative in denominationalism at a given period and the goals that individual denominations tended to share vis a vis the American social and political orders. Individual denominations would have internalized these goals and principles to different degrees and in somewhat distinct fashion. The typology does not, then, characterize individual denominations for any period perfectly. It "idealizes" the predominant denominational style for a given period. It cannot cover the full range of religious institutions of a period, as do sociological typologies. Beyond its purview lie religious structures shaped by church, sect and cult impulses. Nor does a typology respect denomination's ecclesial self-understanding. Rather, this typology focuses on operative patterns—life and work, not faith and order. It does make the case, I hope clearly, that both denominations and denominationalism change.

PART THREE: Case Studies in American Denominationalism

Ethnic Voluntarism

Denominationalism has a long prehistory, much of which occurred in Reformed contexts. Three moments in this prehistory deserve mention. First, denominationalism presumes the fragmenting of the church. Of particular importance for North American denominationalism were the dramatic splintering of the British churches during the Puritan revolution, the emphasis put by the contesting movements on church order as a divine imperative, the exporting of these fractious, predominantly Reformed, polity-conscious movements to the New World, and the imprinting there of various continental European churches. Second, the eschatological but society-transformative orientation of the Presbyterian and Non-Separatist Congregationalists would be of long-term significance in the agenda-setting of North American denominationalism. Third, out of the turmoil of Puritanism, religious wars, Restoration and Glorious Revolution came several intellectual and policy resources for Protestants and colonial administrators to understand how the church might itself be divided and yet one and how society might be divided and yet one. These included conscience driven aspirations for religious freedom, theological schemes for a "catholic" unity, transcending differences, Pietist gestures beyond confessional lines, and civic or political theories of toleration when differences could not be transcended.

The first stage or style of denominationalism emerged in what has been termed the First Great Awakening, specifically in the ethnic ferment of the middle colonies, under conditions of toleration, and as Presbyterianism, organized (minimally) for only a couple decades underwent one of its periodic crises of identity. Subsequent Presbyterian crises, typically also affecting Protestantism generally, would define later stages of denominationalism.

In the middle colonies peoples of Dutch Reformed, Quaker, Scottish, Scotch-Irish and Irish Presbyterian, English Baptist, Anglican, transplanted New England Congregationalist *and* various (German-speaking) persuasions (Dunker, Lutheran, Reformed, Moravian, Schwenckfelder, Mennonite) jostled up against one another. Needing resources for understanding themselves in this strange new world, provided in quite minimal fashion with resources and leadership from the homeland, and physically quite beyond the European authority systems by and through which their confessions sustained themselves, these communities emerged as they fended for themselves. Drawing on their (often lay) memories of church practice and structure, they put in place processes by which to recognize authority. They founded congregations. They called together leadership from congregations of the same apparent "persuasion" to initiate presbyteries (or their tradition's counterpart). And they used these modest structures to establish proper order. They looked to some home country judicatory for ministerial supply, for print resources and for adjudication of disputes that threatened community.

These congregations and associations, quasi-independent because of the sheer distance to "proper" authority, accomplished through their problem solving two related but distinguishable social transactions. First, they stabilized (indeed, brought into being) that hyphenate new ethnic community that would thereafter be the first stage for a new migration. They created, in effect, German American Moravians or Scottish American Presbyterians even though the civic reality of America lay still decades in the future, a social-political reality itself partially actualized by these religious processes. Second, these processes brought denominations into being: in effect, the religious face and legitimation of that ethnicity.

Though both processes of formation began early, with the beginning of immigration and settlement, the Great Awakening constituted the mature form of the hyphenated community and denomination formation. This claim may seem strange and hollow for Presbyterians because the most immediate impact of the itinerant, revivalistic, and conversionist practices that characterized the Awakening was the division of the small Presbyterian community into *pro-* (New Side) and *anti-* (Old Side) wings. Moreover, such divisiveness replicated itself in other religious communities, as did also very complex play of European background and of appeal to European authority. Notwithstanding the ethnic cacophony and religious division it unleashed, the Awakening established as normative and operative very powerful resources for religious cohesion, identity, and integrity. In particular, the repertoire of revivalism—affective, invitational preaching and itinerant, deployment thereof; authorization for Puritan-Pietist practices of lay testimony; encouragement of prayer, Bible reading, and disciplining small groups; the expectation of conversion for members and leaders; and colonial training and credentialing of leadership—this repertoire proved to be of enduring value in forming (religious) community. Through the communal spiritual struggles which yielded conversion and revival, strangers became brothers and sisters (religious family), moral authority and discipline became shared, and congregational and denominational structures emerged.

PART THREE: Case Studies in American Denominationalism

Revivalism's methods of conversion, testing of one another's religious experience, and commitment to a common discipline produced denominational identity and what can only be termed an elective ethnicity. For Presbyterians, the Awakening and the later negotiations between New and Old Side yielded a kind of Celtic American ethnicity that would authorize ever increasingly local authority and autonomy but keep the community ever conscious of its spiritual anchorage in Scotland.

With conversions authorizing persons to negotiate themselves into this elective ethnicity, and revivals understood to be an outpouring of the Holy Spirit, the denominations defined themselves sociologically in one way and theologically in quite another. They established an affinity group, defined by nationality, language, prior involvement. Elective ethnicity defined actual community. Yet, denominations saw their purpose and their unity in pneumatological and eschatological terms. Conversions and revivals that grew Presbyterianism and drew persons into Presbyterianism came not by human agency but through divine intervention and for God's purposes of redeeming humanity.[21]

Despite such grandiosity, denominations in this first stage, tended to focus inward and to view the divine, redemptive ends as being achieved through the elaboration of Presbyterian structure, discipline, doctrine, and presence. Denominations concerned themselves with the care of their membership and its needs. Evangelization tended to honor ethnic and linguistic boundaries and to make only modest appeal to outsider and then only a proper one. Denominations did not elaborate a public theology, see themselves caring for the whole of colonial society, or seek to transform the social order. They had enough to do with the basic task of achieving the consent and cohesion sufficient to establish discipline within the community and set in order processes by which to sustain themselves over time.

Denominational apparatus beyond the congregation consisted in small, occasional gatherings—associations concerned with problem solving, leadership supply and credentials, hymnals and service books, catechism, and the like. As ethnic, voluntaristic, provincial and provisional, denominations viewed themselves as accountable to European authority. By these small beginnings and by due regard to confessional touchstones, the denominations built their *religious authority systems*. European legal privilege meant little here. These denominations required consent to function and emerged initially as ethnic communities, as ethnic voluntarism.

21. Timothy Smith, "Religion and Ethnicity."

Purposive Missionary Association

The second stage of denominationalism, unfolding in what has been termed the Second Great Awakening, occurred as Presbyterians organized for leadership in the new nation, founded or revivified educational institutions, struck a coalition with the Congregationalists for mission, established voluntary societies and elaborated a civic theology appropriate to this public presence. In mounting these activities, Presbyterians played the key intellectual role in framing an outward (indeed, civic) purposiveness for denominationalism. Their construct rested heavily on the Reformed traditions,[22] on Scottish moral philosophy, and on the rubrics of republicanism. It elaborated denominational purposes in providential and eschatological language; applied covenantal imagery to the nation; tied both civil and religious well-being to a society appropriately ordered; and pointed the several denominations towards the building of a Christian America.

Presbyterians elaborated policy and structures for extending their community but it was the popular, evangelistic movements—Baptists, Methodists and Christians (Restorationists)—who suffused denominationalism with its missionary energy. Diversely shaped by Pietism's expansiveness, the popular denominations shattered ethnic constraints and inward orientation. They sought adherents, requiring only, as the Methodists put it, "a desire to flee the wrath to come." Such expansive, missionary imperatives and self-understanding oriented denominations to the entirety of North American society and all its peoples. Most remarkably the denominations worked across both color and linguistic lines. To be sure, social barriers (class, ethnicity, region, language, and race) were breached rather than transcended. Race-specific (African Methodist and Baptist) and language-specific (German and Scandinavian particularly) communities reemerged. Nevertheless, the missionary impulse established new, expansive, outwardly oriented denominational presumptions. Old boundaries of parish, of ethnicity, of confession, of prior Christianization, of existing loyalty need not be respected. The whole nation, indeed, the whole world needed evangelization. The religion business would thereafter be expansive, aggressive, competitive, entrepreneurial, expressive, boosteristic. Missionary self-understanding elicited new skills of leadership and

---

22. Hood, *Reformed America*; Noll, et al., eds., *Evangelicalism*, and Noll, *Rise of Evangelicalism*.

new patterns of organization characterized by initiative, risk taking, mobility, openness, experimentation, vernacular idioms, popular expression.

Purposive, missionary denominationalism put together the evangelical style of the popular movements with the Reformed institutional and covenantal self-understandings which oriented denominations towards the civic realm and the upbuilding of a Christian America. The combination of mission and covenant unleashed an incredible institution-building effort, much of which went into transforming the denominations from modest associational structures into engines for national ministerial deployment and governance, making them powerful democratizing and creative forces.[23] Some of it found expression in voluntary societies focused on various urgent national causes and drawing supporters and workers from various traditions. The voluntary societies made explicit place for a *representative, delegated assembly system*, typically permitting membership on the basis of subscription and delegating leadership to lay and clergy who could assemble at national meetings. Some denominations also made internal provision for this system, either out of their own theory of church order or under the democratizing impulses of the new nation. Others would defer this to later. Eventually, denominations internalized the voluntary societies but only with some trauma and ecclesiastical soul-searching. Purposive, missionary association established structure and procedures faster than formal theologies and ecclesiastical polities could adjust. The adjustment would yield yet another style of denominationalism.

CHURCHLY DENOMINATIONALISM

A third stage or style of denominationalism, like the first focusing more inward than outward, might be dated to the division of the Presbyterians in 1837, followed by divisions of Baptists and Methodists in the early 1840s. Each of these divisions had something to do with slavery, indeed may have been primarily motivated by the conflicts over slavery.[24] But each involved vital unresolved issues in purposive, missionary organization. Old School theologians saw clearly the problem. Expansive, cooperative endeavors functioned with a quasi-Arminian theology. They conveyed ecclesial power to voluntary, often cooperative organizations that acted in the denomination's name but not under its authority. They encouraged ventures and expressions that lacked or exceeded their theological warrant. They

23. Hatch, *Democratization*.
24. Smith, *In His Image, But*.

Denominationalism in "Reformed" Perspective

raised questions about the appropriate lodging of 'ultimate' authority. They undertook missions lacking proper relation to regular judicatories, indeed in some instances invading other's turf. They presumed the right to speak on the church's behalf on matters of great sensitivity—slavery being a case in point. Counterparts to the Old School among Methodists and Baptists framed issues similarly.

The slavery-induced ecclesiastical crises reoriented attention inward as the divided churches justified themselves by ethical, theological, and ecclesiastical appeals and restated denominational self-understandings in confessional or quasi-confessional terms. In similar fashion, the evangelical norms of purposive denominationalism and of the Protestant establishment elicited strong confessional or quasi-confessional defensiveness from various outsider groups.[25] Especially pressured were those whom a contemporary, Robert Baird, labeled the "non-evangelical bodies," including Catholics, Jews, Unitarians, and Mormons.[26] But the new evangelical norm also threatened churchly bodies, movements which enjoyed "established" status in Europe but found the revivalistic price of full acceptance into the Protestant Establishment unacceptable. At least so thought some leaders from the Reformed, Lutheran and Anglican communities. Intellectual counterparts to the Old School theologians emerged who pressed their denominations in more confessional directions. These included the Mercersburg theologians, Philip Schaff and John W. Nevin, whose parodies of revivalism, the anxious bench, and the whole methodistical scheme exposed the threat of purposive denominationalism to their German Reformed tradition. Similarly, Charles Philip Krauth spoke for confessional Lutheranism and John Henry Hobart and Calvin Colton for proper Anglicanism.[27] Reinforcing these impulses intellectually were various currents of Romanticism, which valued tradition, confessions, sacraments, mystery, catechism, and other hallmarks of ecclesial identity.

The confessional impulse led denominations to restructure themselves so as to bring under ecclesial authority the functions and tasks that had been launched by the interdenominational voluntary societies. Missions, Sunday school, tract, temperance and various other reforms became denominational causes. The effort to put such activities under church control led some Baptists and Restorationists to denounce voluntary societies as unbiblical. And a kind of nonconfessional confessionalism emerged,

---

25. Moore, *Religious Outsiders*.
26. Baird, *Religion in America*.
27. Mullin, *Episcopal Vision*.

typified by Anti-mission and Landmark Baptists, which repudiated much of the Christian heritage, or more properly narrowed it, to warrant ecclesiologies of localism and close communion.

Divisions and debates on confessional issues continued (indeed, intensified) as the sectional crisis worsened, war came, and reconstruction opened the South to imperialistic and missionary incursions by Northern churches. The theological and cultural impulses towards inward-facing denominationalism eventually found expression in the trans-Atlantic denominational fellowships, the Lambeth Conference (1867), the World Presbyterian Alliance (1877), the Methodist Ecumenical Conference (1881), and the International Congregational Council (1891). These too encouraged denominations to focus inward on polity, improved governance, the structures for mission, educational ventures.

Corporate Organization

In the late nineteenth and early twentieth centuries, Presbyterians and most of mainstream Protestantism undertook structural reform, brought the complex of societies—men's and women's—under judicatory control, and thereby established a *corporate, board* and *agency system*. Adopting techniques and structures of the then emerging corporate world and encouraged by the capitalists playing key leadership roles, denominations experienced a "managerial revolution."[28]

The aims of this revolution were to increase the effectiveness of the array of enterprises being undertaken on the denomination's behalf, to achieve some coordination of the several efforts, and to bring the coordinated efforts under denominational authority. For its various missionary, publishing, educational and reform commitments, denominations had allowed a complex of essentially voluntary societies to be created and to wear the denominational name. Multiple missionary societies, for instance, ran with separate boards, distinct collections and appeals for funds, their own programs, target populations, their own staff, separate publishing endeavors, and a network of auxiliary societies from regions down to congregations—all under an executive secretary. Counterpart executive secretaries ran publications, education, Freedman's aid, Sunday schools and Sunday school literature, church extension, home missions, temperance, and the

---

28. James H. Moorhead, in Mullin and Richey, eds., *Reimagining Denominationalism*, 264–87; and Coalter, Mulder, and Weeks, eds., *Organizational Revolution*.

like. Free enterprise—uncooperative, unchecked, competitive—reigned in denominational programming.

The managerial revolution occurred gradually, important steps coming in northern denominations as a result of organizational lessons learned during the Civil War. Key initiatives included appointing denominational boards to govern the agencies, elaborating procedures and structures for coordination and collaboration among the agencies and between agencies and local churches, and prescribing an organizational grammar so that every level of the church from congregation to state to regional to national structured itself with the same bodies, with the same names. The changes created national power centers, essentially bureaucratic in nature. Gradually the churches began staffing agencies with professionals, increasing their numbers dramatically, requiring higher degrees of specialization and expertise, and exploring new schemes of systematic finance.

As denominations gave their program a corporate structure and professional leadership they welcomed professionalism in at other levels as well. In particular, they established *professional systems for clergy* within the traditional authority system. The changes proved subtle because the traditional systems had always functioned to credential clergy. However, increasingly the systems behaved for clergy like the bar associations did for attorneys and medical associations for doctors. They established standards, admitted to practice, assessed credentials, controlled access and numbers, safeguarded prerogative, politicked for compensation, oversaw pension programs, sought insurance and health care, and elaborated professional ethics. Other workers in the churches sought professional status as well, finding accommodating niches within the apparatus to greater and lesser extents. These several campaigns for professional recognition interplayed with lay (democratic), gender and racial aspirations in very complex fashion. The professionalization efforts of Christian educators, women's efforts to control their missionary societies, and the slow recognition of women's call to ministry require more attention than can be given here. Suffice it to say, clergy professionalization, provisions for greater lay participation, (partial) desegregation, and admission of women into governing and clergy roles interplayed in very complex fashion.

Complexity indeed characterized mainstream Protestant denominations. By the mid twentieth century they functioned with a fourfold system. The traditional religious authority system remained a denomination's norm, its face to the religious world, its medium of belief and ethic. That system had become sufficiently representative and lay-friendly to govern.

And it had oversight of and made financial provision for programming through an elaborate corporate board and agency system. By mid century, denominations and their professional society subsystems were beginning to accommodate women and minorities in the ministry. Mainstream Protestantism had weathered theological crises early in the century and seemed to be poised for continued societal leadership. Instead, for reasons already cited, mainstream Protestantism found itself upstaged by conservative and evangelical movements, badly divided itself, facing a much more pluralistic society and effectively disestablished.

Postdenominational Confessionalism: A Conclusion

A fifth stage of denominationalism, if such there be, is more difficult to characterize than prior styles because we stand within it. The name *postdenominational confessionalism* may be something of a placeholder for a more apt characterization. *Postdenominational* recognizes the disestablishment of mainstream Protestantism, the incredible loss of purpose those denominations suffered in yielding their goal of a Christian America and the traumatizing of the fourfold denominational system—indeed, all the turmoil outlined early in this essay. *Confessionalism* recognizes the inwardness and self-preoccupation stimulated by culture wars, division, and ideological skirmishes. The phrase as a whole suggests some comparison of a fifth stage with the first and third styles of denominationalism. And the comparisons imply that a fifth stage, when more fully evident, may like prior stages be a fabrication that draws as much on the conservative and evangelical movements as on the internally divided mainstream denominations.

This fifth style then finds expression among the conservative and evangelical networks, both outside and within mainstream Protestantism, in the denominations emerging out of the megachurches, and in coping mechanisms in congregations and within the board and agency structures of the old mainstream. It features a number of contemporary cultural forms. These forms may be found among Presbyterians though they are more fully exhibited elsewhere. Especially noteworthy are the ways in which this new denominationalism experiments with technique and technology, with

- using electronic media aggresively
- packaging program into franchises

- credentialing through modular training events
- demanding accountability drawn from the regulatory agency and hermeneutics of suspicion
- structuring along caucus and ideological lines
- inhabiting new church architecture that resembles the mall in overall size and permitting both boutique (special purpose) and anchor (sanctuary) space
- using extensively grant making and consultancy to focus financial and human resources
- forming new networks of connection, publication, information, and influence
- employing elaborate strategies for recruitment and church formation among specific age cohorts

To the repertoire of borrowed technique and technology, leaders and judicatories in the old mainline counterpoise highly confessional and traditional expectations, particularly for new clergy. The latter function to some extent as an antidote to the former. When denominationalism seem to be eroding in the program system and among laity and the popular assemblies traumatized by explosive issues, leaders put intense confessional/denominational pressures within the professional society system. In places, church life behaves in nondenominational fashion. In other places, a hyper denominationalism reigns. Both belong to an institutional ferment that suggests that both denominations and denominationalism would, in transformed shape, prosper in the new post-Protestant pluralism of North American society.

PART FOUR

Denominationalism as Enacted Ecclesiology

13

Denominationalism

A Theological Problem?

WHEN WAS THE LAST time you heard something positive uttered about denominations and denominationalism?[1] A long time ago? Never? Neither religious nor theological studies has thought the topic really worth attention. In religious studies, to which I will return below, denominations, particularly mainstream or old-line denominations, represent a tyranny over the mind from which academe has thankfully escaped. Denominations? Sectarian! Controlling! Denominationalism? The church-owned and controlled college! Required chapel! A Protestantized curriculum! Clergy presidents and restrictive moral codes! A topic for serious scholarship? Hardly. I recall with some continuing exasperation proposing years ago to the American Society of Church History (ASCH) that it devote a spring meeting to scholarly treatment of Methodism, in acknowledgment of the church's bicentennial. Dismissed without serious discussion, such attention to a mainline denomination the scholarly guild knew impulsively to be beneath it. However, in a year or so, ASCH devoted a session to the Shakers, finding that decision an easy one. A dead sect demanded study but not a large denomination.

A similar disdain about denominationalism persists within the movements themselves and among interpreters of those churches. Indeed, a recent multidenominational study addressing the question, "Does your

1. An early version of this was delivered as a Matriculation Address in Craig Chapel, Drew University.

PART FOUR: Denominationalism as Enacted Ecclesiology

church understand itself as a denomination?" found reticence all around.² In mainstream Protestantism—the world of the *Christian Century*, the major theological schools, and "enlightened" religious leadership—denominationalism remains a taboo. A topic best shunned. If comment is required, denunciation shows good taste and theological sophistication. It was not uncommon, especially in the heyday of neo-orthodoxy and twentieth-century ecumenism, to find denominations and the fact of denominational divisions scathingly treated and blamed for the various ills in Protestantism. Ronald E. Osborn, writing in that epoch and out of that ethos, sought to liberate Christians "from the extremes of the denominational system" so that "the church may be delivered from its self-centeredness." He wrote:

> Largely because the denominational crazy-quilt reveals so inadequately the wholeness of the church, local congregations in America are weak in their understanding of what it means to belong to the universal Christian fellowship. They tend to become self-satisfied clubs of like-minded people in competition with people in other clubs like their own. So the institutional form of the American church exaggerates the introversion brought on by its spiritual deafness to the gospel... Only by ending the folly and sin of meaningless division will the church in America find strength equal to her task.³

He deemed the denominations 'antiques,' interesting but scarcely serviceable. More scathingly, H. Richard Niebuhr affirmed:

> For the denominations, churches, sects, are sociological groups whose principle of differentiation is to be sought in their conformity to the order of social classes and castes. It would not be true to affirm that the denominations are not religious groups with religious purposes, but it is true that they represent the accommodation of religion to the caste system. They are emblems, therefore, of the victory of the world over the church, of the secularization of Christianity, of the church's sanction of that divisiveness which the church's gospel condemns.

Denominationalism for Niebuhr represented "the moral failure of Christianity."⁴ Harvey Cox, in characteristic understatement, termed denominational divisions "idiotic" and employed the classification

2. Collins and Ensign-George, *Denomination*.
3. Osborn, *Church*, 17, 60.
4. Niebuhr, *Social Sources*, 25.

"Paleolithic" to locate denominations in time.⁵ Another interpreter levied the following charge:

> DENOMINATIONALISM. We believe that denominationalism is obsolete, both theologically and in terms of the capacity of denominations to organize the Church in the most effective and obedient manner. We believe that participants in a renewal movement must openly express their willingness to forsake denominational loyalty at every point that such loyalty impedes the ecumenical witness of the Church, particularly at the local and metropolitan level. Denominationalism is theologically obsolete because it denies to all church members the total theological resources of all the denominations, forcing upon individual church members an intolerable choice of modes of worship and an equally intolerable allegiance to a fragment of the total Church. The denominations are structurally obsolete because they have turned into national bureaucracies, removed from local situations, which, by their very nature, impede the development of the Church's mission at the local level.⁶

Were it still fashionable to ascribe evils to the antichrist, surely the denominations, their bureaucracies, executives, programs, pronouncements, and literature would be portrayed as tools and minions of Satan. Some few do make the functionally similar charge of "communist." Many more would, as Ronald Osborn noted, affirm that "Denominationalism is divisive, and division is sin." Or acknowledge that Scripture recognizes no such creature as the denomination and explicitly condemns the factionalism, ill will, and alienation produced by denominationalism.⁷ Among other charges levied against denominationalism is that it seriously hampers the witness to the world;⁸ that its parallel organizations are wasteful and impractical; that the organizations themselves are coercive, tyrannical, and cumbersome; that denominationalism insures the irrelevance of the churches' work by accenting sectarian peculiarities at the expense of the central and shared emphases of the gospel; that "denominationalism by its 'churchism' derogates from the proper dignity of the church as the whole body of Christ."⁹

---

5. Cox, "Introduction," in Rose, *Grass Roots Church*, xiii, x.
6. Rose, *Grass Roots Church*, 167–68.
7. Osborn, "The Role of the Denomination," 162–63.
8. Outler, *That the World May Believe*, 11.
9. Osborn, "Role of the Denomination," 163–65.

PART FOUR: Denominationalism as Enacted Ecclesiology

Further criticisms doubtless occur to you. They are the staple of our reflection about denominations. Denunciation rather than serious theological analysis is the denominations' due. As one commentator notes, "we have never really explored the denomination in ecclesiological terms."[10] The basic structuring of the church in modern democratic societies has somehow escaped most theologians' serious attention. There are some notable exceptions to the general trend. I would mention in particular Paul Collins and Barry Ensign-George's *Denomination: Assessing an Ecclesiological Category*; David Roozen and James R. Nieman's *Church, Identity, and Change: Theology and Denominational Structures in Unsettled Times*; Keith Harper's *American Denominational History: Perspectives on the Past, Prospects for the Future*; various works by Nancy Ammerman, including her *Pillars of Faith: American Congregations and Their Partners*; and such older works as Ronald Osborn's *A Church for These Times*, James Gustafson's *Treasure in Earthen Vessels* and *The Church as Moral Decision-Maker*; and of course H. Richard Niebuhr's *The Social Sources of Denominationalism*. But given the importance, pervasiveness, and persistence of denominations and denominationalism, the subject is neglected. To some degree the theologians have left the subject to other disciplines. The latter contributions we will mention later. Yet it remains a matter of gravity that denominationalism has received so little theological analysis. If you doubt me, search for a recent theology of denominationalism. I think your finds will be modest. And theology's lack of concern suggests the larger curricular or systemic avoidance of denominationalism in theological education.

Reasons for Neglect of Denominationalism

Ecumenism

Reasons for the neglect are not difficult to discover. First, the twentieth century was an ecumenical age, in ethos if not accomplishment. Ecumenists took as sinful the divisions within the Christian fold and therefore the mere existence of separate denominations—each claiming its vision of the gospel to be the most valid, some unchurching others, all vying for adherents—their agendas seemingly frustrating rather than promoting the unity of believers for whom Jesus Christ prayed. Such unity "in Christ" the missionary enterprise which birthed the

---

10. Ibid., 160.

ecumenical movement had also eventually sought, finding itself embarrassed in non-Western settings by the many separations in Christianity, precious perhaps in the Western world but less so abroad. For the work of the kingdom of God, in outreach and in unity, denominations were regretted or taken to be a stage of ecclesiastical formation that was being superseded. Brief attacks rather than sustained reflection sufficed. And attacks there were, many of the salient points already mentioned in the prior section and not needing rehearsal here.

Religious Free Enterprise

There have been countervailing currents to ecumenism, groups and individuals proud of their own denomination and therefore of the free-for-all of denominationalism. Some Southern Baptists could hail denominationalism as though it were "God's providential arrangement for giving the Christian faithful a suitable range of choice—in liturgy, theology, polity, and also in congenial social, racial and business contacts as well." For them competition stimulates growth and strength. So division and diversity function as guarantors of liberty, tests of viability, ways of providing individuals with opportunities for selecting their churches, and of course, opportunities for the like-minded to congregate.[11] The ecumenically minded can be smug about such a posture. One of my graduate students of some years back, a Baptist, used to quip (when overwhelmed with his own dissertation ordeal), "What is/was the shortest PhD thesis ever submitted?" His answer? "Baptist contributions to the ecumenical movement." In fact, Baptist celebration of religious free enterprise sustain a very American attitude, a latter-day echo of the views of the warriors for religious liberty and disestablishment. Tom Paine in *Common Sense* recognized the social utility of a plurality of denominations!

> For myself, I fully and conscientiously believe, that it is the will of the Almighty that there should be a diversity of religious opinions among us. It affords a larger field for our Christian kindness; were we all of any one way of thinking our religious dispositions would want matter for probation; and on this liberal principle I look on the various denominations among us, to be like children of the same family, differing only in what is called their Christian names.[12]

11. Outler, *That the World May Believe*, 3–4.
12. Stokes, *Church and State*, 1:319.

PART FOUR: Denominationalism as Enacted Ecclesiology

Thomas Jefferson also pointed to a social or political value in *Notes on Virginia*: "Difference of opinion is advantageous in religion. The several sects perform of the office of a *censor morum* over each other."[13] Edmund Rudolph on June 10, 1788, debating in the Virginia convention, shared Jefferson's view: "I am a friend to a variety of sects, because they keep one another in order."[14] Madison two days later put the same point in a letter but more positively:

> Happily for the states, they enjoy the utmost freedom of religion. This freedom arises from that multiplicity of sects, which pervades America, and which is the best and only security for religious liberty in any society. For where there is such a variety of sects, there cannot be a majority of any one sect to oppress and persecute the rest.[15]

The sentiments of these architects of American religious freedom were repeated and refined by church leaders as well as politicians during the nineteenth century. To such perceptions of political utility were added positive evaluations of denominationalism and other expressions of religious diversity for religion itself. Americans were proud of religious liberty, of the vigor of their voluntary churches, of the unities that overrode denominational competition, of the denominations themselves. They celebrated what they termed the voluntary principle.[16]

That celebration became rarer in the twentieth century, though perhaps again prospering in the twenty-first. At any rate, valuing of religious liberty and voluntarism does not, in and of itself, focus upon and explain denominationalism. Rather, such valuations prize diversity of various sorts—the conscience or soul liberty (Baptists) of individuals, congregational independence (to which we return), diversity of denominations, even for some the varieties of living world religions. So though voluntarism and religious freedom constitute preconditions for denominationalism—as we noted in earlier chapters—they by no means explain fully the nature of the denomination and the collectivity, denominationalism.

13. Ibid., 1:335.
14. Ibid., 1:533.
15. Ibid.
16. Baird, *Religion in America*; Powell, *Voluntary Church*.

Decline of Liberalism

This suggests a third reason for the neglect of denominations. The eclipse of religious liberalism. Liberalism and liberal theology valued diversity, freedom, choice, debate, pluralism and frequently saw denominations as positively related to such values. Decline in liberal theology, decline in attachment to liberal values, and decline in estimation of denominationalism have occurred together. The state of theology at present is not easy to read. As far as the denominations are concerned the antiliberal judgments of neo-orthodoxy seem to prevail even though we have been through several subsequent theological movements. To put it mildly, denominations were withered by neo-orthodox theologians. My theological generation and those before it viewed the denomination through H. Richard Niebuhr's eyes. The blistering attacks in *The Social Sources of Denominationalism* and in *The Kingdom of God in America* reverberated in our ears. What little respect for denominations remained has been eroded by the succession of theologies—worldly theology, Black theology, Women's theology, Liberation theology generally—which dismiss denominations as suburban, bourgeois, racist, male chauvinist, and capitalist. And what had been one of the institutional homes of classic liberal thought and progressive politics—the boards and agencies of mainline Protestantism—have shrunk and their leaders hunkered down as those denominations have imploded.

Social Factors

Fourth, theologians and theological students have been affected, to various degrees of course, with the views of institutions popularized by the Left during the 1960s and 1970s and by conservatives thereafter. Both movements feature strongly anti-institutional agendas. The Left at times flailed at all institutions. At other times it would affirm popular and spontaneous institutions. Denominations might be useful for those seeking to evade the draft and service in Vietnam and therefore willing to pursue ordination. Or as funders for civil rights and antipoverty efforts. Otherwise, student radicals deemed denominations part of the problem rather than its solution. Religious conservatives and evangelicals favored small, local, and state institutions. They tended and do tend with conservatives traditionally to accord business organization its license. But they have a passion for dismantling other national institutions (religion and government

PART FOUR: Denominationalism as Enacted Ecclesiology

included).[17] Both Left and Right attack elitism and bureaucracy. And not surprisingly denominations were assailed.

As fate would have it, denominational efforts on the concerns of the '60s,—race, poverty, social justice and the like—both dissatisfied the prophets of the '60s and enraged (perhaps even fueled) the conservative reactions. Denominations lost support vital to their well-being. And the support was not simply the public goodwill and constituency approval necessary for effective action. Real setbacks in the sacraments of institutions—money and members—were experienced by mainline denominations. Slowed growth or actual decline in membership, change in giving patterns, and growth of conservative and evangelical denominations have occasioned soul searching and retrenchment.[18] The experience of adversity and the climate of anti-institutionalism have not fostered sympathetic study of denominations.

Academic Trends

Fifth, trends in academia have distanced scholars from denominations and discouraged attention to them. The study of religion has for some time been gravitating out of theological schools and into universities. This development has materially affected scholars' relations with and understanding of denominations in a variety of ways. A few discernable features can be noted. The academic and scientific study of religion now establishes the arena, concepts and tools, methodologies of research. Conversation and interchange among scholars now takes place through academic membership organizations like the American Academy of Religion (AAR) and kindred academic societies. Denominational research offices have long been closed and interdenominational bureaus downsized.

Some of the slack in attention to matters denominational has been picked up by local, regional, and national church digital and Internet efforts and by kindred efforts on the part of theological schools, their libraries and librarians, and by denominational colleges. However, a good portion of such effort focuses on resource recovery and on scholarship guided more by guild passions than denominational needs. My own involvements as a student of Methodist history illustrate such investments

17. Tipton, *Public Pulpits*.
18. Wuthnow, *America*; Wuthnow, *Restructuring*; Wuthnow, *Struggle*; Hoge, *Division*; Coalter et al., *Reforming Tradition*; Hunter, *Culture Wars*; Roozen et al., *Varieties*; Roof and McKinney, *American Mainline Religion*.

in "pure research." I am an officer in the publication of a scholarly edition of John Wesley's *Works*; a board member of the American Methodism Project, a collaboration among theological libraries to digitize important resources; a research fellow of Duke Divinity School's Center for Studies in the Wesleyan Tradition, which hosts a summer seminar for academics and has invested heavily in retrieval of both Wesleys' works; and one of the editors of the *Methodist Review*, a scholarly and peer-reviewed journal for the field. Each of these projects, we who are involved believe, should help in our understanding better the religious movements birthed by the Wesleys. However, each of these gets attention from precious few denominational leaders, despite our efforts to stimulate interest. Other centers and initiatives focus on leadership or spirituality or congregational studies—efforts more aligned with denominational well-being—but also not dedicated to understanding national denominational structures and the nature of denominationalism.

Within denominational theological schools, scholars whose predecessors might have specialized in confessional studies increasingly orient their scholarly interests along lines now represented by AAR. With university doctorates, some without a master of divinity degree, others lacking any theological degree, still others representing different confessions than the school's, the theological professoriate does not come equipped to understand the denomination for which it supposedly trains persons. Even church history and church historians cannot be counted upon to have research and teaching interests in the school's own denominations (on this topic, see below). And in some schools, both the faculty and student body have become so denominationally diverse as to worry the sponsoring church. Church leaders demand accountability, want statistics about numbers of their own on faculty and staff and in the student body. In my own denomination, United Methodism, such accounting determines the amount of money from central coffers (the Ministerial Education Fund). Deans and presidents struggle to find faculty members who belong to the sponsoring denomination, by accrediting standards expecting a doctorate and no longer able to pop clergy into teaching church history, Bible, or theology.

In the stronger schools, promotion and tenure and other reward systems function with university standards and prize scholarly publication and effective teaching over service to denominations. Faculty who get involved in denominations beyond the congregation on any significant level—research, consulting, dialogue, office holding—do so at some peril

PART FOUR: Denominationalism as Enacted Ecclesiology

if they have not paid their scholarly dues as well. (Similar patterns beset the students. The strong mainline denominational and interdenominational student organizations that formerly introduced students to denominational life have died or been sidelined by parachurch and conservative-evangelical movements less invested in the denominations.) DMin and leadership programs have rectified the involvement side to some extent but tend to orient themselves less to the denomination, its nature and needs and more to individual clergy and their professional advancement.

That relates to another preoccupation or trend, one sustained among students and faculty as well as clergy: the presumption that individuals do and should determine what prepares them for ministry and their ministry is indeed *just their own* ministry, theirs to define, theirs to pursue. Here clergy and clergy to be differ little from other professionals. American culture and religious life suffer from nostrums of self-improvement, personal advancement, dieting, coaching, and other stimuli to egocentrism. Individuals should think of themselves as their own creators and pursue such a vision! Underpinning this egocentrism are several persistent and resilient habits of mind—the long tradition of American individualism, the myth of the self-made man, liberalism's quaint notion that ministerial freedom is the essence of Protestantism, a pedagogy of bastardized progressivism, a century-long fascination with psychology, which legitimizes the anthropocentric focus, and a recent vogue of careerism and professionalism that reinforces the conception of ministry as an individual affair. So, not the church's ministry! My ministry! By thinking of ministry in personal terms and permitting students to psychologize and professionalize even that understanding, schools graduate "ministers" who have little sense of the larger contexts of their ministry, the denomination and the world. With little appreciation of and less comprehension for denominations, they are ill equipped to cope with them. They do cope by making ministry a career and climbing the ladder, by capitulating to the system, by accepting the bureaucracy, by rat-racing for the petty inducements and subtle penalties that officialdom offers, by a variety of ways of dropping out, or by rebelling. Students with little sense of what might be done with and to denominations have little alternative but to accept them as permanent, unchanging, bureaucratic employment or coordinating structures that confine ministry. That capitulation is unnecessary and based on little or poor information about denominations.

Theological education, then, is not consistently structured or pursued as though students were going to assume ministry within denominations.

The intellectual concerns and professional language of faculties of theological schools are being less and less shaped by denominations. To be sure field education, polity courses, and judicatory oversight during seminary play important corrective roles. Still our faculties, our curriculum, our way of thinking and doing, our structuring of theological education do not reckon with sponsoring denominations as much as they might. And the collectivity, denominationalism—its reality, nature and evolution—also is slighted. Some with eyes on past conflicts within the Lutheran and Southern Baptist folds and the earlier experience of many American denominations would doubtless reply, "consider the alternatives—education under confessional constraints, dogmatic inhibitions on the pursuit of truth, purges, heresy trials." There is wisdom in such counsel. But cannot one find intermediate positions between education as the exact repetition of the truth once delivered to the saints and theological education which derives its direction mainly from the university, from guild interests, from student ego-centrism. Since faculties do assume the prerogative of establishing the program for ministerial training, they should be professionally sensitized to the world of the denominations as well as to that of the universities.

Congregational Ecclesiologies

A sixth reason why denominations are ignored affects theologians, seminarians, ministers, and laity alike. A congregational theory of the church pervades American religion.[19] The theory derives from the ecclesiologies of Puritanism and Anabaptism. Championed by folk preachers of the popular churches—especially Baptists, Christians, and Congregationalists—it was accorded legal status in the nineteenth century by state and federal courts. Where congregationalism lacked a proper theological underpinning, it developed quite adequate social bases. From the early days of Anglican Virginia, the American laity has understood, intuitively it would seem, that preaching was more satisfying, the sacraments more gracious, the cure of souls more efficacious, discipline more just, if each local church ran its own affairs and the laity had significant authority. This congregationalism, then, is a curious mixture of theology and localism. It can also reflect stinginess, distrust of authority, individualism, and racism. But it is quite real. Deep down, Americans believe that the church is a local

19. Wind and Lewis, *American Congregations*.

body of believers. Insofar as there is a universal or catholic church, it is only the assemblage of local churches.

Strong denominations have been built with such a view, e.g., the variety of Baptists, the Disciples, the United Church of Christ. But self-conscious congregationalism is antidenominational. The history of the Disciples and the Churches of Christ and the superb analysis of the American Baptist Convention by Paul Harrison illustrate the dilemmas lived out by bodies (denominational in nature) united by commitment to positions that make corporate, self-understanding, structural unity and national decision-making problematic.[20] The agonies of committed "Congregationalists" are shared in less acute forms by other American denominations. American theologians, ministers, and laity tend to think of the church as a local body. Denominations and denominationalism are not then theological or theoretical problems, nuisances perhaps, *adiaphora*, matters indifferent but not topics for serious inquiry.

Pragmatism

Buttressing the congregationalism and seventh, Americans are pragmatists, given to doing. Denominationalism has been accorded some theological attention in the past. But even when theologians were predisposed to discuss denominations, the predominant approach has been practical. Denominations were serviceable instruments. Best just to use them and not worry about them. What was important was the work of salvation they carried on. Denominations were there for the Lord's purpose, not to be discussed or examined.

Theological Antidenominationalism

Several other reasons for neglect of denominations function as excuses by theologians for ignoring denominations. Their importance lies in the way they permit reflection about the church—ecclesiology—to ignore the reality of denominations. First among these is the confessionalism that takes one's own group as the whole or true church. Roman Catholics, the Orthodox, even Southern Baptists in the past and sectarian groups up to the present have sometimes so equated their body with the whole or true church. More widespread is a habit of mind that might termed covert

---

20. Harrison, *Authority and Power*.

confessionalism—formal acknowledgment that the church exceeds one's own denomination followed by acting and speaking as though the church were one's own denomination. In either its proper or covert form, confessionalism allows one to ignore other denominations and the phenomenon of denominationalism.

Second, inattention to denominationalism can come from too-easy collectivizing or unifying Christianity so as to finesse confessional and denominational disunity. By treating the church abstractly or generically or spiritually, theological attention focuses on supposed reality which in some way transcends the observable disunity. Reflexively moving from the local congregations to "the Church" achieves something of the same effect. Here too the conceit ignores observable realities of national and international confessional structures.

A third evasion begins with the reality of denominations but then may short-circuit the challenges of analysis by conceiving of the denominations as "different branches of the same tree." Like its sister notions, this "branch theory" of the church, potentially useful for ecclesiological purposes, does not necessarily face the nature of the denomination and denominationalism.[21] (Furthermore, for reasons not entirely clear, ecumenists decided that it did not serve their purposes, perhaps because it justified the continuation of difference, and undercut plans for organizational union. However, much of the late twentieth- and early twenty-first-century ecumenical efforts have moved away from structural unity to bilateral dialogues and full communion of ministry and sacraments. On such agendas, a branch theory might be worth revisiting.)

At any rate, such patterns of thought that move readily from local church or denomination to "the Church" without facing the reality of denominationalism do not serve theology or theological education very well. By finessing denominations and denominationalism as theological issues, they confer a false aura of legitimacy on the individual denomination a student must enter. They permit students to enter ministry within denominations complacent in identifying denomination with "the Church." They inhibit the criticism and ferment that would make denominations more effective structures for Christian action. They foster habits of sloppy thinking. Theology and theological education need to come to grips with the reality of denominationalism as a theological challenge.

---

21. Miller, *Nature and Mission of the Church*, 122–25. Osborn, "The Role of the Denomination," 166.

PART FOUR: Denominationalism as Enacted Ecclesiology

RESOURCES

Denominational History

Denominationalism has not been totally forgotten. Several approaches to the study of the denomination are represented in theological schools. Individually and collectively, however, they do not redress the theological and overall inattention. They can and do introduce students to the institutional world they are destined to enter. First, denominational history and polity provide access to denominationalism by examination of individual denominations. It is, I would argue, only a partial corrective. One major problem is that the analysis does not get the collectivity of denominations into view and is not comparative.[22] Often interpretations, concepts, and emphases drawn from that denomination's own inner life guide presentation and interpretation. Often highly idiosyncratic, it fails to place the individual denomination within the larger denominational picture (within denominationalism) and its place in societal development. Potentially this approach mires the student conceptually in the denominational status quo just as denominational bureaucracy could imprison him or her actually. Put crudely, denominational history may instill an awe for, a sense of the permanence of, denominational patterns. It does not necessarily recognize denominations as human structures, institutions that have changed dramatically and should certainly be changed. One might expect that the more generic church-history courses, typically degree requirements, would compensate with comparative analyses and attention to the collectivity: denominationalism. However, since the mid-twentieth century, historians have found other, more general patterns of greater interest. Among such concerns and topics. These include consensus history; attention to a Christian America and civil or public religion; social history; inclusion of women and minorities; attention to evangelicalism and Pentecostalism; conflict and boundaries; gay and lesbian issues; culture wars. Church historians teaching in seminaries found themselves pulled by trends in the academic study of religion and pushed by Black, female, gay and evangelical students to get their story into the grand narrative. Denominationalism proved less urgent than other topics. To be sure, we saw something of a corrective as the Lilly Endowment invested in several large research projects on individual denominations and denominationalism. I profited personally from the foundation's largesse, represented by *Reimagining Denominationalism* and the five volumes of the United Methodism

---

22. But see Frank, *Polity*.

and American Culture series. The latter we developed benefiting from the experience and counsel of the trilogy who led the Presbyterian Presence: The Twentieth Century Experience and published its seven volumes.[23] During this same period, American Methodism, long neglected except by insiders, enjoyed considerable attention by non-Methodist scholars. However, these mainly social histories focused on early American Methodism as a popular movement and took little interest in its denominational nature. So, despite these countertrends, church history tended to deemphasize the study of particular bodies as denominations and the phenomenon of denominationalism.

Ideal Typology

The dominant resource for understanding denominationalism has been sociology. Of several possible approaches within sociology, one long favored is that of ideal typology, which treats religious groups as authority systems. Beginning with the labors of Max Weber and Ernst Troeltsch and for the American scene, Niebuhr, the familiar typology (Niebuhr's) of Church, Sect, and Denominationalism has been frequently revised and refined.[24] The yields for the sociologists through ideal types are immense. However, others tend to misuse the typology in employing it (historians in particular), and I am not the first to observe that it has never seemed to work as well for the analysis of American religion as it has for the societies with some form of national establishment. Furthermore, the typology has seemed to be most useful in exploring sectarianism. With several exceptions (H. Richard Niebuhr, Liston Pope, J. Milton Yinger, David Martin), scholars seem too intrigued either with abstract theoretical considerations or with sectarianism. Denominationalism receives attention only as these other topics necessitate it. Finally, for my pedestrian historical mind the typological approach, despite its theoretical universality, is more useful in explaining individual denominations (or sects) than the historical reality of denominationalism. It does not tell us why we have denominationalism. It tells us rather, for instance, at what point an individual sect becomes a denomination. For me, the really important issues raised by the emergence of what Andrew Greely has called "The Denominational Society"—the

---

23. Coalter et al., *Reforming Tradition*.
24. Glock and Hammond, *Beyond the Classics?*, 355–408.

PART FOUR: Denominationalism as Enacted Ecclesiology

causes, the consequences, the implications for both religion and society, the theological meaning of denominationalism—are not in view.[25]

Voluntary Associations

Three other approaches to denominationalism, widely used outside the field of religion, ought to be more seriously employed in theological education. The first is the study of voluntary associations, now a subspecialty within the social sciences, political science especially. Denominations are understood as voluntary associations, compared with voluntary groups generally and understood both individually and in their inter-action in terms of theories of voluntary association. Some theologians now object to thinking of the church in those terms;[26] and so also do some social scientists. However there is a long tradition of thinking about denominations as voluntary associations. From Robert Baird's *Religion in America* (1844; 1856) and Alexis de Tocqueville's *Democracy in America* (tr. 1835, 1840) in the nineteenth century down to the twentieth century labors of James Gustafson and James Luther Adams,[27] denominations have been successfully analyzed as voluntary associations.

Organization Research

A second approach classes the denomination with an even broader range of social groups. This is the field of organizational research. It assumes, as Lyle Schaller once put it, "that religious organizations tend to behave like other institutions and organizations rather than to display a distinctive *religious* emphasis in making decisions."[28] The denomination is treated along with General Motors and TVA as one organization among the many in what Robert Presthus called "the organization society." Not surprisingly this approach has not been widely appreciated in the theological field. It tends to highlight the bafflingly crude, self-serving, power-oriented character of denominational bureaucracy. However, scholars like

---

25. Greeley, *Denominational Society*.
26. Outler, *That the World May Believe*, 2; Welch, *Reality of the Church*, 31.
27. Robertson, *Voluntary Associations*, 359–73.
28. Schaller, *Decision-Makers*, 12–13.

David Moberg, James Gustafson, Gibson Winter, and Lyle Schaller have shown the approach to be most helpful in understanding denominational behavior.[29]

Ethnic Studies

A third approach perceives the denomination as an ethnic group. Probably the least utilized of the three, it might have greater utility if more widely used. Andrew Greeley in *The Denominational Society* has most baldly stated the relationship. He argued that

> American religion is vigorous precisely because it is denominational—that it is able to be pluraform precisely because it is pluralistic. American religion, in short, is successful because American religious denominations are ethnic groups. The secret of the survival of the organized churches in the United States, we are contending, is their ability to play an ethnic, or at least quasi-ethnic role in American society.[30]

Greeley moved us beyond the long-standing recognition of immigrant or ethnic churches—Lutheran, Reformed, Mennonite, Moravian, Eastern Orthodox, etc.—to perception of ethnic characteristics functioning in many if not all denominations and of course in other dimensions of American religion than the structural. Another illustration of the approach was Martin Marty's *Righteous Empire*, self-consciously an effort to portray the WASP character of what has often passed for the American experience.

Conclusion

These approaches do not, either individually or collectively, redress the neglect. The denomination and denominationalism are not taken seriously in theological education as the institutional framework of ministry nor reflected upon theologically. Seriousness would be evidenced by attention to the fact of denominationalism across the spectrum of the theological disciplines and explicit attention within systematic theology in particular. We should not, it seems to me, do ecclesiology, or for that

---

29. Moberg, *Church*; Gustafson, *Treasure*; Winter, *Religious Identity*; Schaller, *Decision-Makers*; Demerath, *Sacred Companies*.

30. Greeley, *Denominational Society*, 108.

PART FOUR: Denominationalism as Enacted Ecclesiology

matter theology at all, ignoring the actualities of religious structures. Nor undertake theological education. Nor strategize for ministry. Nor attempt social ethics. Nor teach leadership. Nor engage in programs in ministerial self-understanding.

Redress, attention to the denomination by the theological disciplines, will necessitate changes in the way we attempt education for ministry. The various theological disciplines need to dialogue with those already engaged in examination of the denomination. Out of such engagement should come integration of the several approaches into a more holistic understanding. And new perspectives on and interpretations of denominationalism should emerge. The appreciative endeavor need not mean acquiescence in the status quo or abandonment of ecumenism. It would imply beginning with institutional realities in efforts at change and unity. Institutionalization, politics, bureaucracy, inertia are inevitabilities. We need strategies for coping with, changing, surmounting these inevitabilities. Clearly entailed is more serious examination of freedom, pluralism and diversity. Those concerns of liberalism should find new purchase, even if we do not cannot, should not, return to liberalism.

Pedagogy will be altered as well. The theological disciplines must be willing to set agendas with denominations in mind. Internal disciplinary developments and the purely academic study of religion cannot supply the only norms. Nor can students and faculty operate as though individual predilections were all that mattered in education. We must break with the radically individualized, excessively psychologized, and over-professionalized notions of ministry. Theological education should not be conducted as though disciplines were little empires and the student was simply getting herself together.

Ministry will continue to be within institutions, whether they look like the denominations of the past or not (as other chapters suggest they will not). We now appreciate the parish and community context of ministry. We need also to think of the denomination—its boards and agencies, officialdom, functions, line authority, levels of ministerial organization. Theologians, ministers and laity will have to face their covert "Baptist" notions that the congregation is the church. The dodges and mystifications will have to end. Abstract or spiritualize invocations of "the Church" or profusions of Biblical labels do not alter American realities. They simply obscure them. For students at least in the short run, denominations lie ahead in ministry. The real question is whether they will facilitate or frustrate ministry, whether they will follow their bureaucratic tendencies or rise to service of God and the world.

Above all, the bonds between theological schools and the denominations need to be reknit. Whether denominational or interdenominational, education for ministry must be conducted with denominations in mind.

Bibliography

Addison, W. G. *Religious Equality in Modern England, 1714-1914.* London: SPCK, 1944.
Allen, Richard. *The Life Experience and Gospel Labors of the Rt. Rev. Richard Allen.* 2nd ed. New York: Abingdon, 1960.
The American Preacher or A Collection of Sermons from Some of the Most Eminent Preachers, Now Living, in the United States, of Different Denominations. 3 vols. Elizabethtown, NJ, 1791.
Ammerman, Nancy Tatom. "New Life for Denominationalism." *Christian Century* 117/9 (March 15, 2000) 302–7.
———. *Pillars of Faith: American Congregations and Their Partners* (Berkeley: University of California Press, 2005.
Andrews, Dee. *The Methodists and Revolutionary America: The Rise of the Methodists in the Greater Middle Atlantic, 1760-1800.* Princeton: Princeton University Press, 1999.
Armstrong, Maurice W. "The English Dissenting Deputies and the American Colonies." *Journal of Presbyterian History* 40 (1962) 24–37, 75–91, 144–59.
Asbury, Francis. *Journals and Letters of Francis Asbury.* Edited by J. M. Potts et al. 3 vols. Nashville: Abingdon, 1958
Bailyn, Bernard. *The Ideological Origins of the American Revolution.* Cambridge: Belknap, 1992.
———, editor. *Pamphlets of the American Revolution 1750-1776.* The John Harvard Library. Cambridge: Belknap, 1965.
Baird, Robert. *Religion in America.* Harper Torchbooks. New York: Harper & Row, 1970.
Baker, Frank, *John Wesley and the Church of England.* Nashville Abingdon, 1970.
Balmer, Randall, and John R. Fitzmier. *The Presbyterians.* Denominations in America 5. Westport, CT: Greenwood, 1993.
Bangs, Nathan. *History of the Methodist Episcopal Church.* 4 vols. New York: T. Mason and G. Lane for the Methodist Episcopal Church, 1838–41.
Barlow, R. B. *Citizenship and Conscience: A Study in the Theory and Practice of Religious Toleration in England during the Eighteenth Century.* Philadelphia: University of Pennsylvania Press, 1962.
Baxter, Richard. *The Saint's Everlasting Rest.* London 1677, Preface to Part II.
Bebb, B. D. *Nonconformity and Social and Economic Life, 1660–1800.* London: Epworth, 1935.
Bebbington, D. W. *The Dominance of Evangelicalism: The Age of Spurgeon and Moody.* A History of Evangelicalism 3. Downers Grove, IL: InterVarsity, 2005.

Bibliography

———. *Evangelicalism in Modern Britain: A History from the 1730s to the 1980s.* London: Unwin Hyman, 1989.
———, editor. *Protestant Nonconformist Texts.* 4 vols. Aldershot, UK: Ashgate, 2005–6.
Becker, Howard Paul. *Through Values to Social Interpretation: Essays on Social Contexts, Actions, Types, and Prospects.* Duke University Press. Sociological Series. Durham, NC: Duke University Press, 1950.
Becker, Penny Edgell. *Congregations in Conflict: Cultural Models of Local Religious Life.* Cambridge: Cambridge University Press, 1999.
Beckford, James A. "Religious Organizations: A Trend Report and Bibliography." *Current Sociology* 21 (June 1973) 7–104.
Belsham, Thomas. *The Importance of Truth, and the Duty of Making an Open Profession of It.* London: Johnson, 1790.
Bercovitch, Sacvan. *The American Jeremiad.* Madison: University of Wisconsin Press, 1978.
Bogue, David, and James Bennett. *History of Dissenters, from the Revolution to the Year 1808.* 4 vols. London: Printed for the authors, 1808–12.
Blau, Joseph. *Judaism in America: From Curiosity to Third Faith.* Chicago History of American Religion. Chicago: University of Chicago Press, 1976.
Bolam, C. G. et al. *The English Presbyterians: From Elizabethan Puritanism to Modern Unitarianism.* London: Allen & Unwin, 1968.
Bourn, Samuel. *A Vindication of the Principles and Practice of Protestant Dissenters.* London, 1747.
Bretland, Joseph. *Sermons by the The Rev. Joseph Bretland to which are Prefixed Memoirs of His Life.* 2 vols. Exeter: Hedgeland, 1820.
Bridenbaugh, Carl. *Mitre and Sceptre: Transatlantic Faiths, Ideas, Personalities, and Politics, 1689–1775.* New York: Oxford University Press, 1962.
Brown, Peter. *The Chathamites.* London: Macmillan, 1967.
Buckley, James M. *A History of Methodists in the United States.* 4th ed. New York: Scribner, 1900.
Butler, Jon. *Awash in a Sea of Faith: Christianizing the American People.* Studies in Cultural History. Cambridge: Harvard University Press, 1990.
Calamy, Edmund. *An Abridgement of Mr. Baxter's History of His Life and Times.* 1702; 2nd ed., in 2 vols. 1713; Samuel Palmer edited and republished Calamy's Abridgement as *The Nonconformist's Memorial.* London, 1775.
———. *A Defence of Moderate Nonconformity.* 3 vols. London, 1703–5.
———. *An Historical Account of My Own Life.* 2 vols. London, 1829.
———. *Thirteen Sermons Concerning . . . the Trinity.* London, 1722.
Campbell, Dennis M. et al. *Doctrines and Discipline.* United Methodism and American Culture 3. Nashville: Abingdon, 1999.
Caplan, N. "The Lean Years of Sussex Nonconformity." *Congregational Historical Society Transactions* 19 No. 4. 1963.
Chandler, Alfred D., Jr. *The Visible Hand: The Mangerial Revolution in American Business.* Cambridge: Belknap, 1977.
Chaplin, Lloyd W., Jr. "The Theology of Joseph Priestley: A Study in Eighteenth-Century Apologetics." ThD diss., Union Theological Seminary, 1967.
Chaves, Mark. "Denominations as Dual Structures: An Organizational Analysis." *Sociology of Religion* 54 (1993) 147–69.

Chaves, Mark, and Sharon L. Miller, editors. *Financing American Religion.* Walnut Creek, CA: AltaMira, 1999.
Chillingworth, William. *The Works of W. Chillingworth, M.A.* 12th ed., complete in one vol., with life by Birch. London: Printed for B. Blake, 1836.
Christie, I. R. *Wilkes, Wyvill and Reform.* London: Macmillan, 1962.
Clark, Henry W. *History of English Nonconformity.* 2 vols. New York: Bussell & Bussell, 1965.
Clebsch, William A. "American Churches as Traducers of Tradition." In *New Theology No. 9,* edited by Martin E. Marty and Dean G. Peerman 73-90. New York: Macmillan, 1972.
Coalter, Milton J. et al., editors. *The Mainstream Protestant "Decline": The Presbyterian Pattern.* The Presbyterian Presence: The Twentieth-Century Experience. Louisville: Westminster John Knox, 1990.
———, editors. *The Organizational Revolution: Presbyterians and American Denominationalism.* The Presbyterian Presence: The Twentieth-Century Experience. Louisville: Westminster John Knox, 1992.
———, editors. *The Reforming Tradition: Presbyterians and Mainstream Protestantism.* The Presbyterian Presence: The Twentieth-Century Experience. Louisville: Westminster John Knox, 1992.
Cookman, George G. *Speeches Delivered on Various Occasions.* New York: George Lane, 1840.
Coleman, Richard J. *Issues of Theological Conflict: Evangelicals and Liberals.* Grand Rapids: Eerdmans, 1972.
Collins, Paul, and Barry Ensign-George, editors. *Denomination: Assessing an Ecclesiological Category.* Ecclesiological Investigations 11. T. & T. Clark Theology. London: T. & T. Clark, 2011.
Cone, Carl. *The English Jacobins: Reformers in Late 18th Century England.* New York: Scribner, 1968.
Conner, R. Dwayne. "Early English Baptist Associations." *Foundations* 20/2 (1972) 163-85.
Cornish, Joseph. *A Serious and Earnest Address to Protestant Dissenters of All Denominations.* London, 1772.
Crooks, George R. *The Life of Bishop Matthew Simpson.* New York: Harper & Brothers, 1891.
Dana, James. "Christian Union." In *The American Preacher, Or A collection of sermons from some of the most eminent preachers now living in the United States of different denominations in the Christian Church,* 3:57-80. 4 vols. Elizabeth-Town, NJ: Printed by S. Kollock for the editors, 1791-1793.
Davies, Horton. *The Worship of the English Puritans.* Westminster: Dacre, 1948.
———. *Worship and Theology in England.* Vol. 3, *From Watts and Wesley to Maurice, 1690-1850.* Princeton: Princeton University Press, 1961.
Davies, Rupert, and Gordon Rupp, editors. *A History of the Methodist Church in Great Britain,* 4 vols. London: Epworth, 1975.
Demerath, N. J. III et al., editors. *Sacred Companies: Organizational Aspects of Religion and Religious Aspects of Organizations.* Religion in America Series. New York: Oxford University Press, 1998.

Bibliography

Dexter, Henry M. *The Congregationalism of the Last Three Hundred Years as Seen in its Literature . . . with a Bibliographical Appendix*. New York: Harper & Brothers, 1880.
Dieter, Melvin E. *The Holiness Revival of the Nineteenth Century*. Studies in Evangelicalism 1. Metuchen, NJ: Scarecrow, 1980.
Disney, John. *A Friendly Dialogue between a Common Unitarian Christian, and an Athanasian . . . To which is now added, a Second Dialogue*. London, 1787.
Doddridge, Philip. *The Works of the Rev. P. Doddridge*. 10 vols. Leeds, 1802–10.
Dvorak, Katharine L. *An African-American Exodus: The Segregation of the Southern Churches*. Chicago Studies in the History of Religion 4. Brooklyn: Carlson, 1991.
Drysdale, A. H. *History of the Presbyterians in England*. London: Publication Committee of the Presbyterian Church of England, 1889.
Enfield, William. *The Principles and Duty of Protestant Dissenters Considered, in a Sermon . . . at the Ordination of . . . John Prior Estlin*. London, 1778.
Estlin, John Prior. *Sermons, Designed Chiefly, as a Preservative from Infidelity, and Religious Indifference*. Bristol, 1802.
Frank, Thomas Edward. *Polity, Practice, and the Mission of the United Methodist Church*. Nashville: Abingdon, 2006.
Fuller, Andrew *The Calvinistic and Socinian Systems Examined and Compared in The Principal Works and Remains of the Rev. Andrew Fuller, with a New Memoir of His Life, by His Son, the Rev. A. G. Fuller*. London, 1852.
Galambos, Louis. "The Emerging Organizational Synthesis in American History. *Business History Review* 44 (1970) 279–90.
George, Carol V. R. *Segregated Sabbaths: Richard Allen and the Rise of Independent Black Churches, 1760–1840*. New York: Oxford University Press, 1973.
George, Charles H., and Katherine George. *The Protestant Mind of the English Reformation, 1570–1640*. Princeton: Princeton University Press, 1961.
Gleason, Philip. *Keeping the Faith: American Catholicism, Past and Present*. Notre Dame: University of Notre Dame Press, 1987.
———. *Speaking of Diversity: Language and Ethnicity in Twentieth-Century America*. Baltimore: Johns Hopkins University Press, 1992.
Glock, Charles Y., and Phillip E. Hammond, editors. *Beyond the Classics?: Essays in the Scientific Study of Religion*. New York: Harper & Row, 1973.
Goen, C. C. *Broken Churches, Broken Nation. Denominational Schisms and the Coming of the American Civil War*. Macon, GA: Mercer University Press, 1985.
Goold, William H., editor. *The Works of John Owen*. 16 vols. London, 1850–53.
Gordon, Alexander. *Philip Doddridge and the Catholicity of the Old Dissent*. London: Lindsey, 1951.
Goss, C. C. *Statistical History of the First Century of American Methodism*. New York: Carlton & Porter, 1866.
Gough, Strickland. *Enquiry into the State of the Dissenting Interest*. London, 1730.
Graves, J. R. *The Great Iron Wheel: or, Republicanism Backwards and Christianity Reversed*. 12th ed. Nashville: Graves, Marks and Rutland, 1856.
Greeley, Andrew. *The Denominational Society: A Sociological Approach to Religion in America*. Glenview, IL: Scott, Foresman, 1972.
Griffiths, Olive M. *Religion and Learning, A Study in English Presbyterian Thought from the Bartholomew Ejections (1662) to the Foundation of the Unitarian Movement*. Cambridge: Cambridge University Press, 1935.

Grove, Henry. *The Works of the Reverend and Learned Mr. Henry Grove.* 4 vols. London 1747.
Gustafson, James M. *Treasure in Earthen Vessels: The Church as a Human Community.* New York: Harper & Row, 1961.
Halévy, Elie. *The Growth of Philosophical Radicalism.* Translated by Mary Morris. London: Faber & Faber, 1949.
Halley, Robert, *Lancashire, Its Puritanism and Nonconformity.* 2 vols. Manchester: Tubbs & Brook, 1869.
Handy, Robert T. *A Christian America: Protestant Hopes and Historical Realities.* 2nd. ed. Oxford: Oxford University Press, 1984.
Handy, Robert. "The American Religious Depression, 1925–35." *Church History* 29 (1960) 3–16.
Harmon, Nolan B. et al., editors *The Encyclopedia of World Methodism.* 2 vols. Sponsored by the World Methodist Council and the Commission on Archives and History, UMC. Nashville: United Methodist Publishing House, 1974.
Harper, Keith, editor. *American Denominational History: Perspectives on the Past, Prospects for the Future.* Religion and American Culture. Tuscaloosa: University of Alabama Press, 2008.
Harrison, Paul M. *Authority and Power in the Free Church Tradition.* Princeton: Princeton University Press, 1959.
Hatch, Nathan O. *The Democratization of American Christianity.* New Haven: Yale University Press, 1989.
Haykin, Michael A. G., and Kenneth J. Stewart, editors. *The Advent of Evangelicalism: Exploring Historical Continuities.* Nashville: B. & H. Academic, 2008.
Heitzenrater, Richard P. *Wesley and the People Called Methodists.* Nashville: Abingdon, 1995.
Henriques, Ursula. *Religious Toleration in England, 1787–1833.* Studies in Social History. Toronto: University of Toronto Press, 1961.
Hermann, Richard E. "Nathan Bangs: Apologist for American Methodism." PhD diss., Emory University, 1973.
Heyman, Christine Leigh. *Southern Cross: The Beginnings of the Bible Belt.* New York: Knopf, 1997.
Hildebrand, Reginald F. *The Times Were Strange and Stirring: Methodist Preachers and the Crisis of Emancipation.* Durham: Duke University Press, 1995.
Hill, Christopher. *Antichrist in Seventeenth-Century England.* Rev. ed. Riddell Lectures 41st ser. London: Verso, 1990.
Hoge, Dean R. *Division in the Protestant House: The Basic Reasons behind Intra-church Conflict.* Philadelphia: Westminster, 1976.
Holt, Raymond V. *The Unitarian Contribution to Social Progress in England.* London: Allen & Unwin, 1938.
Hood, Fred J. *Reformed America: The Middle and Southern States, 1783–1837.* University: University of Alabama Press, 1980.
Humphreys, J. D., editor. *The Correspondence and Diary of Philip Doddridge.* 5 vols.; London, 1829–1831.
Hudson, Winthrop S., "Denominationalism as a Basis for Ecumenicity: A Seventeenth-Century Conception." *Church History* 24 (1955) 37–47.
Hudson, Winthrop S. "The Methodist Age in America." *Methodist History* 12 (April 1974) 3–15.

Bibliography

Hunt, N. C. *Two Early Political Associations: The Quakers and the Dissenting Deputies in the Age of Sir Robert Walpole*. Oxford: Clarendon, 1961.

Hunter, James Davison. *American Evangelicalism: Conservative Religion and the Quandary of Modernity*. New Brunswick, NJ: Rutgers University Press, 1983.

———. *Culture Wars*. New York: Basic Books, 1991.

Hutchison, William R. *Between the Times: The Travail of the Protestant Establishment in America, 1900–1960*. Cambridge: Cambridge University Press, 1989.

Ivimey, Joseph. *A History of the English Baptists*. 4 vols. London: Printed for the author, 1811–1820.

James, T. S. *The History of the Litigation and Legislation Regarding Presbyterian Chapels and Charities in England and Ireland Between 1816 and 1849*. London: Hamilton Adas & Co., 1867.

John, Richard R. "Elaborations, Revisions, Dissents: Alfred D. Chandler, Jr.'s, 'The Visible Hand' after Twenty Years." *Business History Review* 71 (1997) 151–200.

Jones, R. Tudor. *Congregationalism in England, 1662–1962*. London: Independent Press, 1962.

Jordan, W. K., *The Development of Religious Toleration in England*. 4 vols. Cambridge: Harvard University Press, 1932–1940.

Kammen, Michael. *People of Paradox*. New York: Vintage, 1973.

Kewley, John. *An Enquiry into the Validity of Methodist Episcopacy*. Wilmington: Joseph Jones, 1807.

Kippis, Andrew. *The Life of Nathaniel Lardner*. London: Johnson, 1788.

———. *A Vindication of the Protestant Dissenting Ministers, with Regard to Their Late Application to Parliament*. London, 1772.

Kirby, James E. et al. *The Methodists*. Denominations in America. 8. Westport, CT: Greenwood, 1996.

Lamont, William M. *Godly Rule: Politics and Religion 1603–1650*. London: Macmillan, 1969.

Lardner, Nathaniel. *The Works of Nathaniel Lardner*. Edited by Andrew Kippis. 11 vols. London, 1788.

Lawrence, William B. et al., editors. *The People(s) Called Methodist*. United Methodism and American Culture 2. Nashville: Abingdon, 1998.

Lee, Jesse. *A Short History of the Methodists*. Baltimore: Magill &Clime, 1810; facsimile edition, Rutland, VT: Academy Books, 1974.

Lee, Leroy M. *The Life and Times of The Rev. Jesse Lee*. Charleston: John Early, 1848.

Lincoln, Anthony. *Some Political and Social Ideas of English Dissent, 1763–1800*. Cambridge: Cambridge University Press, 1938.

Lindsay, A. D. *The Modern Democratic State*. Oxford: Oxford University Press, 1943.

Lindsey, Theophilus. *Apology on Resigning the Vicarage of Catterick*. London, 1774.

Lloyd, Walter. *The Story of Protestant Dissent and English Unitarianism*. London: Philip Green, 1899.

Locke, John, *The Works of John Locke, Esq*. 3 vols. London, 1714.

Luccock, Halford E., and Paul Hutchinson, *The Story of Methodism*. New York: Methodist Book Concern, 1926.

Lyerly, Cynthia Lynn. *Methodism and the Southern Mind, 1770–1810*. New York: Oxford University Press, 1998.

Lynd, Staughton. *Intellectual Origins of American Radicalism*. New York: Pantheon, 1968.

Bibliography

Maccoby, Simon. *English Radicalism*. Vol. 1, *1762-1785: The Origins*. London: Allen & Unwin, 1955.
M'Crie, Thomas. *Annals of English Presbytery*. London: James Nisbet, 1872.
McLachlan, Herbert. *English Education under the Test Acts: Being the History of the Nonconformist Academies, 1662-1828*. Manchester: Manchester University Press, 1931.
McLoughlin, William G. *New England Dissent, 1630-1833*. 2 vols. Cambridge: Harvard University Press, 1971.
McNeill, John T., and James Hasting Nichols. *Ecumenical Testimony*. The Historical Series of the Reformed Church in America 21. Philadelphia: Westminster, 1974.
McNeill, John T. *Unitive Protestantism: The Ecumenical Spirit and Its Persistent Expression*. Rev. ed. Richmond: John Knox, 1964.
Martin, David A. "The Denomination." *British Journal of Sociology* 13 (March 1962) 1-14.
Marty, Martin E. "Ethnicity: The Skeleton of Religion in America." *Church History* 41 (March 1972) 5-21.
―――. *A Nation of Behavers*. Chicago: University of Chicago Press, 1976.
―――. *Righteous Empire: The Protestant Experience in America*. Two Centuries of American Life: A Bicentennial Series. New York: Dial, 1970.
Mather, Cotton. *Manuductio ad Ministerium*. Reproduced from the Original Edition, Boston, 1726, with a Bibliographical Note by Thomas J. Holmes and Kenneth B. Murdock. Published for The Facsimile Text Society by Columbia University Press, New York, 1938.
Mathews, Donald G. "The Second Great Awakening as an Organizing Process, 1780-1830." *American Quarterly* 21 (1969) 23-43.
Mead, Sidney E. *The Lively Experiment*. New York: Harper & Row, 1963.
Melton, J. Gordon, editor. *The Encyclopedia of American Religions*. 7th ed. Detroit: Gale Research, 2003.
―――. *A Will to Choose: The Origins of African American Methodism*. Lanham, MD: Rowman & Littlefield, 2007.
Melton, J. Gordon, and James V. Geisendorfer. *Religious Bodies in the United States: A Directory*. 3rd ed. New York: Gale Research, 1952.
Middlekauff, Robert. *The Mathers: Three Generations of Puritan Intellectuals*. New York: Oxford University Press, 1971.
Miller, Donald. *The Nature and Mission of the Church*. Richmond: John Knox, 1957.
"Minutes of Conference from the year 1774 to the year 1779." *Western Christian Advocate* 4/5 (May 26, 1837).
Minutes of the Methodist Conferences, Annually Held in America; From 1773 to 1813, Inclusive. New York: Published by Daniel Hitt & Thomas Ware for the Methodist Connexion in The United States, 1813) = *Minutes*/MEC/1784. 1813.
Moberg, David. *The Church as a Social Institution*. Englewood Cliffs, NJ: Prentice-Hall, 1962.
Moore, R. Laurence. *Religious Outsiders and the Making of Americans*. New York: Oxford University Press, 1986.
Mullin, Robert Bruce. *Episcopal Vision / American Reality: High Church Theology and Social Thought in Evangelical America*. New Haven: Yale University Press, 1986.
―――, and Russell E. Richey, editors. *Reimagining Denominationalism*. New York: Oxford University Press, 1994.

Bibliography

Murray, James A. H., editor. *A New English Dictionary on Historical Principles.* Oxford: Clarendon, 1893.

Neal, Daniel. *The History of New England.* London, 1747.

———. *The History of the Puritans, or Protestant Nonconformists.* 4 vols. London, 1732–38, republished in 1754 in 2 vols.

Newman, William M., and Peter L. Halvorson. *Atlas of American Religion: The Denominational Era, 1776–1990.* Walnut Creek, CA: AltaMira, 2000.

Niebuhr, H. Richard. *Christ and Culture.* New York: Harper & Brothers, 1951.

———. *The Kingdom of God in America.* New York: Harper & Brothers, 1937.

———. *The Social Sources of Denominationalism.* New York: Meridan, 1957.

Niebuhr, H. Richard et al., editors. *The Church against the World.* Chicago: Willett, Clark, 1935.

Nightingale, Benjamin. *Lancashire Nonconformity.* 3 vols. Manchester: Heywood, 1890–1893.

Noll, Mark et al., editors. *Evangelicalism: Comparative Studies of Popular Protestantism in North America, the British Isles, and Beyond 1700–1900.* Religion in America Series. New York: Oxford University Press, 1994.

Noll, Mark. *The Rise of Evangelicalism: The Age of Edwards, Whitefield, and the Wesleys.* A History of Evangelicalism 1. Downers Grove, IL: InterVarsity, 2003.

Norwood, Frederick A. *The Story of American Methodism: A History of the United Methodists and Their Relations.* Nashville: Abingdon, 1974.

Nuttall, Geoffrey F. "Northamptonshire and 'the Modern Question': A Turning-Point in Eighteenth-Century Dissent." *Journal of Theological Studies* n.s. 16/1 (1965) 101–23.

———, editor. *Philip Doddridge, 1702–1751: His Contribution to English Religion.* London: Independent Press, 1951.

———. "Philip Doddridge and 'the Care of all the Churches': A Study in Oversight." *Congregational Historical Society Transactions* 20/4 (1966) 126–38.

———. *The Puritan Spirit: Essays and Addresses.* London: Epworth, 1967.

———. *Richard Baxter and Philip Doddridge: A Study in a Tradition.* Friends of Dr. Williams's Library, Fifth Lecture. London: Oxford University Press, 1951.

———. *Visible Saints. The Congregational Way 1640–1660.* Oxford: Blackwell, 1957.

Nuttall, Geoffrey F., and Owen Chadwick, editors. *From Uniformity to Unity 1662–1962.* London, SPCK, 1962.

The Occasional Papers. 3 vols. London, 1716–19.

O'Dea, Thomas F. *Sociology and the Study of Religion.* New York: Basic Books, 1970.

Orr, Robert R. *Reason and Authority: The Thought of William Chillingworth.* Oxford: Clarendon, 1967.

Osborn, Ronald E. *A Church for These Times.* New York: Abingdon, 1965.

———. "The Role of the Denomination: An Essay in Ecclesiology." *Encounter* 22 (1961) 160–74.

Outler, Albert C., editor. *John Wesley.* Library of Protestant Thought. New York: Oxford University Press, 1964.

———. *That the World May Believe. A Study of Christian Unity.* New York: Joint Commission on Education and Cultivation, The Methodist Church, 1966.

Palmer, Samuel. *The Nonconformist's Memorial.* 2 vols. 2nd ed. London, 1778. A republishing of Calamy's *Abridgement* as *The Nonconformist's Memorial.*

Patterson, Frank Allen, editor. *The Works of John Milton*. 18 vols. New York: Columbia University Press 1931–1938.

Patterson, L. Dale. "The Ministerial Mind of American Methodism: The Course of Study for the Ministry of the Methodist Episcopal Church, the Methodist Episcopal Church, South and the Methodist Protestant Church, 1876–1920." PhD diss., Drew University, 1984.

Peaston, A. Elliott. *The Prayer Book Reform Movement in the XVIIIth Century*. Oxford: Blackwell, 1940.

———. *The Prayer Book Tradition in the Free Churches*. London: Clarke, 1965.

Peck, Jesse T. *The History of The Great Republic, Considered from a Christian Standpoint*. New York: Broughton and Wyman, 1869.

The Pew Forum on Religion & Public Life. *U.S. Religious Landscape Survey*. Washington DC: Pew Research Center, 2008.

Piepkorn, Arthur C. *Profiles in Belief: The Religious Bodies of the United States and Canada*. 4 vols. in 3. New York: Harper & Row, 1977–79.

Pilkington, James Penn, and Walter N. Vernon, *The Methodist Publishing House: A History*. 2 vols. Nashville: Abingdon, 1968–89.

Powell, Milton, editor. *The Voluntary Church*. New York: Macmillan, 1967.

Price, Richard. *Observations on the Importance of the American Revolution*. London, 1785.

Putnam, Robert D. *Bowling Alone: The Collapse and Revival of American Community*. New York: Simon & Schuster, 2000.

Priestley, Joseph. *The Theological and Miscellaneous Works of Joseph Priestley*. Edited by J. T. Rutt. 26 vols. London G. Smallfield, 1817–32.

Richey, Russell E., editor. *Denominationalism*. 1977. Reprinted, Eugene, OR: Wipf & Stock, 2010.

———. *Doctrine in Experience: A Methodist Theology of Church and Ministry*. Nashville: Kingswood, 2009.

———. *Early American Methodism*. Religion in North America. Bloomington: Indiana University Press, 1991.

———, editor. *Ecumenical & Interreligious Perspectives: Globalization in Theological Education*. Nashville: QR Books, 1992.

———. "Effects of Toleration on Eighteenth-Century Dissent." *Journal of Religious History* 8 (1975) 350–63.

———. *Extension Ministers: Mr. Wesley's True Heirs*. Nashville: United Methodist Church General Board of Higher Education and Ministry, 2008.

———. "Institutional Forms of Religion." In *Encyclopedia of the American Religious Experience*, edited by Charles H. Lippy and Peter W. Williams, 1:31–50. 3 vols. New York: Scribner, 1988.

——— et al. *Marks of Methodism: Theology in Ecclesial Practice*. United Methodism and American Culture 5. Nashville: Abingdon, 2005.

———. *Methodist Connectionalism: Historical Perspectives*. Nashville: United Methodist Church, General Board of Higher Education and Ministry, 2010.

———. *The Methodist Conference in America: A History*. Nashville: Kingswood, 1996.

——— et al. *The Methodist Experience in America*. 2 vols. Nashville: Abingdon, 2010.

———. "The Origins of English Unitarianism." PhD diss., Princeton University, 1970.

——— et al., editors. *Perspectives on American Methodism: Interpretive Essays*. Nashville: Kingswood, 1993.

Bibliography

———et al., editors. *Questions for the Twenty-First-Century Church*. United Methodism and American Culture 4. Nashville: Abingdon, 1999.

———. "United Methodism: Its Identity as Denomination." In *Denomination: Assessing An Ecclesiological Category*, edited by Paul Collins and Barry Ensign-George, 67–85. Ecclesiological Invesitgations 11. T. & T. Clark Theology. London: T. & T. Clark, 2011.

Richey, Russell E., Dennis M. Campbell, and William B. Lawrence, editors. *Connectionalism: Ecclesiology, Mission, and Identity*. United Methodism and American Culture 1. Nashville: Abingdon, 1997.

Richey, Russell E., and Thomas Edward Frank. *Episcopacy in the Methodist Tradition: Perspectives and Proposals*. Nashville: Abingdon, 2004.

Richey, Russell E., and Donald G. Jones, editors. *American Civil Religion*. New York: Harper & Row, 1974.

———, editors. *American Civil Religion*. San Francisco: Mellen Research University Press, 1990.

Richey, Russell E., and Kenneth E. Rowe, editors. *Rethinking Methodist History*. Nashville: Kingswood, 1985.

Robbins, Caroline. *The Eighteenth-Century Commonwealthman*. Cambridge: Harvard University Press, 1961.

Robinson, Robert, *Miscellaneous Works of Robert Robinson*. 4 vols. Harlow, 1807.

Robertson, D. B., editor. *Voluntary Associations: A Study of Groups in Free Societies*. Richmond: John Knox, 1966.

Roof, Wade Clark, and William McKinney. *American Mainline Religion: Its Changing Shape and Future*. New Brunswick, NJ: Rutgers University Press, 1987.

Rose, Stephen C. *The Grass Roots Church: Manifesto for Protestant Renewal*. New York: Holt, Rinehart and Winston, 1966.

Roozen, David A., and James R. Nieman. *Church, Identity, and Change: Theology and Denominational Structures in Unsettled Times*. Grand Rapids: Eerdmans, 2005.

Roozen, David A. et al. *Varieties of Religious Presence: Mission in Public Life*. New York: Pilgrim, 1984.

Rouse, Ruth, and Stephen C. Neill, editors. *A History of the Ecumenical Movement*. 2 vols. London: SPCK, 1954–1970.

Routley, Erik. *English Religious Dissent*. English Institutions. Cambridge: Cambridge University Press, 1960.

Rowe, Kenneth E. *Methodist Union Catalog: Pre-1976 Imprints*. Metuchen, NJ: Scarecrow, 1975–.

Schaff, Philip. *America, A Sketch of Its Political, Social, and Religious Character*. 1855. Edited by Perry Miller. Cambridge: Belknap, 1961.

Schaller, Lyle. *The Decision-Makers: How to Improve the Quality of Decision Making in the Churches*. Nashville: Abingdon, 1974.

Schneider, A. Gregory. *The Way of the Cross Leads Home: The Domestication of American Methodism*. Religion in North America. Bloomington: Indiana University Press, 1993.

Scudder, M. L. *American Methodism*. Hartford: Scranton, 1868.

Semple, Neil, *The Lord's Dominion: The History of Canadian Methodism*. McGill-Queen's Studies in the History of Religion 21. Montreal: McGill-Queen's University Press, 1996.

Simpson, Matthew. *A Hundred Years of Methodism*. New York: Nelson & Phillips, 1876.

Singleton, Gregory H. *Religion in the City of Angels: American Protestant Culture and Urbanization. Los Angles, 1850–1930*. Ann Arbor: UMI Research Press, 1979.

Smith, H. Shelton. *In His Image, But . . . : Racism in Southern Religion, 1780–1910*. Durham: Duke University Press, 1972.

Smith, J. W. Ashley. *The Birth of Modern Education: The Contribution of the Dissenting Academies, 1600–1808*. London: Independent Press, 1954.

Smith, Timothy L. "Congregation, State, and Denomination: The Forming of the American Religious Structure." *William and Mary Quarterly* 3rd ser. 25 (1968) 155–76.

———. "Religion and Ethnicity in America." *American Historical Review* 83 (1978) 1155–85.

———. "'Religious Denominations' as Ethnic Communities," *Church History* 35 (June, 1966) 207–26.

Smylie, James H. *A Brief History of the Presbyterians*. Louisville: Geneva, 1996.

Spalding, J. C., "The Demise of English Presbyterians, 1660–1760." *Church History*, 23 (1959) 63–83.

Stevens, Abel. *A Compendious History of American Methodism*. New York: Eaton & Mains, 1868.

———. *History of the Methodist Episcopal Church in the United States*. 4 vols. New York: Carlton & Porter, 1864–67.

———. *History of the Religious Movement of the Eighteenth Century Called Methodism*. New York: Philips & Hunt, 1858–61.

———, *Supplementary History of American Methodism*. New York: Eaton & Mains, 1899.

Stokes, Anson Phelps. *Church and State in the United States*. 3 vols. New York: Harper & Brothers, 1950.

Swatos, William H., Jr. "Beyond Denominationalism: Community and Culture in American Religion." *Journal for the Scientific Study of Religion* 20 (1981) 217–27.

———, editor. *Encyclopedia of Religion and Society*. Walnut Creek, CA: AltaMira, 1998.

———. *Into Denominationalism: The Anglican Metamorphosis*. Society for the Scientific Study of Religion Monograph Series 2. Storrs, CT: Society for the Scientific Study of Religion, 1979.

———, and Lutz Kaelber, editors. *The Protestant Ethic Turns 100 Essays on the Centenary of the Weber Thesis*. Boulder, CO: Paradigm, 2005.

Sweet, Leonard I., editor. *Communication and Change in American Religious History*. Grand Rapids: Eerdmans, 1993.

Sweet, William Warren. *The Story of Religion in America*. Rev. ed. New York: Harper & Brothers, 1939.

———. *Methodism in American History*. Nashville: Abingdon, 1954.

———. *Religion in the Development of American Culture, 1765–1840*. New York: Scribner, 1952.

Sykes, Norman. "Ecumenical Movements in Great Britain in the Seventeenth and Eighteenth Centuries." In *A History of the Ecumenical Movement*, edited by Ruth Rouse and Stephen C. Neill, 121–67. London: SPCK, 1954.

Telford, John, editor. *The Letters of the Rev. John Wesley, A.M.* 8 vols. London: Epworth, 1931.

Thernstrom, Stephan, and Abigail Thernstrom. *America in Black and White: One Nation, Indivisible*. New York: Simon & Schuster, 1997.

Bibliography

Thernstrom, Stephan, editor. *Harvard Encyclopedia of American Ethnic Groups*. Cambridge: Belknap, 1980.
Thrift, Minton. *Memoir of Jesse Lee: With Extracts from His Journals*. N. Bangs 7 T. Mason for the Methodist Episcopal Church, 1823.
Tibbutt, H. G. "Pattern of Change." *Congregational Historical Society Transactions* 20 (May 1967) 166–73.
Tigert, Jno. J. *A Constitutional History of American Episcopal Methodism*. 3rd ed., rev. Nashville: Publishing House of the Methodist Episcopal Church South, 1908.
Tipton, Steven M. *Public Pulpits: Methodists and Mainline Churches in the Moral Argument of American Life*. Chicago: University of Chicago Press, 2007.
Tocqueville, Alexis de. *Democracy in America*. Edited by Phillips Bradley. 2 vols. New York: Vintage, 1945.
Toon, Peter. *The Emergence of Hyper-Calvinism in English Non-conformity 1689–1765*. London: The Olive Tree, 1967.
Toulmin, Joshua. *The Present and Future State of the Human Frame*. Taunton, 1781.
———. *An Historical View of the State of the Protestant Dissenters in England*. Bath, 1814.
Towgood, Micaiah. *Dissent from the Church of England Fully Justified*. Boston, 1768.
Trinterud, Leonard J., editor. *Elizabethan Puritanism*. New York: Oxford University Press, 1971.
Underwood, A. C. *A History of the English Baptists*. London: Baptist Union Publication Department, 1947.
Walker, Clarence E. *A Rock in a Weary Land: The African Methodist Episcopal Church during the Civil War and Reconstruction*. Baton Rouge: Louisiana State University Press, 1982.
Walker, Williston. *The Creeds and Platforms of Congregationalism*. New York: Scribner, 1893.
Walzer, Michael. *The Revolution of the Saints*. Cambridge: Harvard University Press, 1965.
Warner, R. Stephen. *New Wine in Old Wineskins: Evangelicals and Liberals in a Small-Town Church*. Berkeley: University of California Press, 1988.
Watson, Richard. *A Collection of Theological Tracts, in Six Volumes*. Cambridge, 1785.
Watts, Isaac. *The Works of . . . Isaac Watts . . . selected . . . by Dr. Jennings and Dr. Doddridge*, 6 vols,. London, 1810–11.
Watts, Michael R. *The Dissenters*. Vol. 1, *From the Reformation to the French Revolution*. Oxford: Clarendon, 1978.
———. *The Dissenters*. Vol. 2, *The Expansion of Evangelical Nonconformity*. Oxford: Clarendon, 1995.
Wiese, Leopold von. *Systematic Sociology, on the Basis of the Beziehungslehre and Gebildelehre of Leopold von Wiese*. Adapted and amplified by Howard Becker. New York: Wiley & Sons, 1932.
Wesley, John. *The Letters of the Rev. John Wesley, A.M.* Edited by John Telford. 8 vols. London: Epworth, 1931.
Welch, Claude. *The Reality of the Church*. New York: Scribner, 1958.
Wesley, John. *The Works of John Wesley*. Edited by Thomas Jackson. 14 vols. 1872. Reprinted, Grand Rapids: Zondervan, 1958.

———. *The Works of John Wesley*; begun as *The Oxford Edition of The Works of John Wesley*. Oxford: Clarendon, 1975-1983; continued as *The Bicentennial Edition of The Works of John Wesley*. 35 vols. Nashville: Abingdon, 1984-.

Wheeler, Henry. *One Thousand Questions and Answers concerning the Methodist Episcopal Church*. New York: Eaton & Mains, 1898.

Whitley, W. T. *A History of British Baptists*. 2nd ed. London: Kingsgate, 1932.

———, editor. *Minutes of the General Assembly of the General Baptist Churches in England, with Kindred Records, 1654-1728 and 1731-1811*. 2 vols. London: Kingsgate, 1909-10.

Wiebe, Robert H. *The Search for Order, 1877-1920. The Making of America*. New York: Hill & Wang, 1967.

———. *The Segmented Society: An Introduction to the Meaning of America*. New York: Oxford University Press, 1975.

Wigger, John H. *Taking Heaven by Storm: Methodism and the Rise of Popular Christianity in America*. Religion in America Series. New York: Oxford University Press, 1998.

Wilbur, Earl Morse. *A History of Unitarianism in Transylvania, England, and America*. Cambridge: Harvard University Press, 1952.

Williams, Colin W. *John Wesley's Theology Today*. New York: Abingdon, 1960.

Wilson, Bryan R. *Religion in Sociological Perspective*. New York: Oxford University Press, 1982.

———. *Religious Sects: A Sociological Study*. World University Library. London: Weidenfeld & Nicolson, 1970.

———. *The Social Dimensions of Sectarianism: Sects and New Religious Movements in Contemporary Society*. Oxford: Clarendon, 1990.

Wilson, John F. *Pulpit in Parliament: Puritanism during the English Civil Wars, 1640-1648*. Princeton: Princeton University Press, 1969.

Wilson, Walter. *The History and Antiquities of Dissenting Churches and Meeting Houses in London, Westminster, and Southward*. 4 vols. London, 1808-1814.

Wind, James P., and James W. Lewis. editors. *American Congregations*. 2 vols. Chicago: University of Chicago Press. 1994.

Winter, Gibson. *Religious Identity*. Studies in Religion and Soceity Series. New York: Macmillan, 1968.

Wolfe, John, editor. *Evangelical Faith and Public Zeal: Evangelicals and Society in Britain 1780-1980*. London: SPCK. 1995.

———. *The Expansion of Evangelicalism: The Age of Wilberforce, More, Chalmers and Finney*. Downers Grove, IL: InterVarsity, 2007.

Wood, Gordon S. *The Creation of the American Republic, 1776-1787*. Chapel Hill: University of North Carolina Press, 1969.

———. *Empire of Liberty: A History of the Early Republic, 1789-1815*. The Oxford History of the United States. Oxford: Oxford University Press, 2009.

Woodhouse, A. S. P. *Puritanism and Liberty*. 2nd ed. Chicago: University of Chicago Press, 1951.

Wright, Conrad. *The Beginnings of Unitarianism in America*. Boston: Beacon, 1966.

———. *The Liberal Christians: Essays on American Unitarian History*. Boston: Beacon, 1970.

Wuthnow, Robert. *America and the Challenges of Religious Diversity*. Princeton: Princeton University Press, 2005.

Bibliography

———. *Christianity in the Twenty-First Century: Reflections on the Challenges Ahead.* New York: Oxford University Press, 1993.

———. *The Crisis in the Churches: Spiritual Malaise, Fiscal Woe.* New York: Oxford University Press, 1997.

———. *The Restructuring of American Religion: Society and Faith since World War II.* Princeton: Princeton University Press, 1988.

———. *The Struggle for America's Soul: Evangelicals, Liberals, and Secularism.* Grand Rapids: Eerdmans, 1989.

Yinger, J. Milton. *The Scientific Study of Religion.* New York: Macmillan, 1970.

www.ingramcontent.com/pod-product-compliance
Lightning Source LLC
Chambersburg PA
CBHW032051220426
43664CB00008B/951